AND THERE WE WERE.

I0646520

LINDA S. CONE

LAURUS BOOKS

And THERE WE WERE.

By LINDA S. CONE

Paperback Book: ISBN 978-1-943523-05-4
Kindle: ISBN 978-1-943523-06-1
ePub (iBooks, Nook): ISBN 978-1-943523-16-0

Front cover photograph by Rodney Campbell

Special photography by Brenda J. Barnes

Foreword by Ralph P. Brown (Tawennihake)

Published by LAURUS BOOKS

Printed in the United States of America

LAURUS BOOKS
www.TheLaurusCompany.com

Laurus Books is an imprint of The Laurus Company, Inc. This book may be ordered in paperback from TheLaurusCompany.com, Amazon.com, Barnes and Noble, Spring Arbor, and other retailers around the world. Also available in formats for electronic readers from their respective stores.

DEDICATION

This book is dedicated to those
contributing to the stories in my life...

—Linda S. Cone

Bad Decisions Make Good Stories

"To err is human, but when the eraser wears out
ahead of the pencil, you're overdoing it."

—Josh Jenkins

FOREWORD

One Thread in the Tapestry of Life

The "tapestry of life" is a fitting metaphor for the whole of our existence because it speaks to the relationships of one thing to another and how they relate to the whole. As with any tapestry, each strand is connected to another, which is connected to another, which is connected to everything else. Connections are vital to our physical, spiritual, mental, and emotional well-being. Connected people are happy people. These connections begin even before we are born. How happy we are as an adult depends on how connected we are throughout our lifetime.

At birth, we come into the world attached to the umbilical cord that connects us to our mother. We are born connected. In addition to the physical connectedness, the brain is hard-wired to connect with the things and people in our environment. Humans are herd animals, and, quite simply, we function better as part of the group.

Our relationships with others occur through a process called "attachment." Children who fail to attach in the early stages of life develop problems that severely affect their quality of life. Children who are raised in abusive homes where their physical needs are met but who are deprived of the emotional, mental, and spiritual needs necessary to form the bonds of attachment are prime examples of just how important this is. These children have difficulties recognizing social cues, learning to set appropriate boundaries, regulating emotions, acquiring coping skills, and have many other social, psychological, and emotional problems.

Attachment is largely acquired through learning. Indian people knew and understood this. After the birth of a baby, he or she was wrapped tightly in the softest deer skin and placed in a cradleboard padded with clumps of moss, providing a warm, soft, secure, and comfortable environment in which the baby could accompany the mother as she went about daily life. From this cradleboard, the baby was a part of all aspects of tribal life as he or she learned what it was to be Indian.

This is important on many levels, but, most importantly, it maintains a connection between the baby and caregivers, which includes all members of the "tribe." A well-loved child is never set aside or placed in a crib and left to entertain and fend for himself or herself. A baby has no concept of time. The baby does not know if you are leaving for a minute or an eternity, only that you are leaving. What the child learns is that people leave. With that can come mistrust, fear, and anxiety that can affect relationships well into the future.

Trust is essential in the process of attachment. Connections are maintained until a child gains the confidence necessary to reinforce this understanding and knows that we are connected to and are part of all things. To further this understanding, Indian women made a child's first pair of moccasins with a hole in the sole. This was so the child could maintain the connection with the Mother (Mother Earth).

People who are connected enjoy more fulfilling relationships and are more likely to be empathetic. They trust; they share more of themselves and are capable of receiving more from others. All of this enhances a relationship. Those who are disconnected are more likely to be reserved, selfish, and/or even apathetic, preventing the bonds of relationships from occurring.

It is not too late for anyone to learn and work to establish the connections that were lost, or perhaps never learned, as a child. The rewards are certainly worth the effort.

Are you happy? Are your relationships fulfilling? Are you connected?

In Spirit,

Ralph P. Brown (Tawennihake)

Table of Contents

AND THERE WE WERE.

In my life, I have lived, I have loved, I have lost,
I have missed, I have hurt, I have trusted,
I have made mistakes, but most of all, I have learned.
The following is a sampling of those stories.

CHAPTER ONE:
Traditions and Trademarks

Family Motto

We the unwilling led by the unqualified have been doing the unbelievable for so long with so little that we now attempt the impossible with nothing.

House Rules

"A sibling is a friend given by nature." —Jean Baptiste Legouve

As my children, each and every one, are exceptionally smart, totally talented, engaging conversationalists, accomplished storytellers, and good-looking (they are obviously their mother's children), there is no need to repeat a rant or preach the process. To streamline and downsize, they will just number the nags. To acknowledge they "get the message," they will call out "Sermon #537," or whatever number pops into their heads. I always suspect they change these labels willy-nilly. I will admit this practice saves a lot of time.

Rule #9:   Efficiency is everything.

Rule #47:   Always listen with an open mind and a closed mouth.

Rule #33:   Do not offer advice unless asked. Sometimes all that is needed is a sounding board.

Rule #19:   If you confide a problem, offer possible solutions. These may seem like the same basic rule, with the same applications. There are subtle differences.

Rule #69:   Always knock before entering, unless you want to see white, and then red.

Rule #21:   Always be specific when you lie. That is how liver and onions become "beefsteak" (not to be confused with beef steak!).

Rule #67:   Be ready for responsibility.

Rule #71:   No gasoline on the bonfires. The neighbors will rush over thinking the furnace exploded. They then will complain that it woke up their mother from her afternoon nap.

Rule #27:   Do not poke the bear. Or, wake it, either.

Rule #4:   Clean up your own messes. My friend always told me the house I lived in looked ready for a party of forty people. She claimed her house differed in one respect. Her house looked like she just had a party for forty people.

Rule #4 corollaries: Leave the world a better place than you found it. Take care of things, especially the earth and the water. Recycle, reuse, regift.

Rule #1:   Always respect others, especially your mother. No whining. It will not change the outcome in a good way.

Rule #18:   It is easier to do something right the first time than to explain why you did not.

Rule #101: Do not reflexively say "no" without listening to and hearing the options, opinions, and attitudes of others. New ideas offer opportunities and adventures.

Rule #201: Never use a chainsaw unless someone else is there to call 911. You may slide down a steep clay bank in the middle of the night, catch yourself on a tree instead of plunging into the raging fire in the ravine, all while the blade is rotating, and live to tell about it. You may not!

Rule #76:   It is easier to ask for forgiveness than permission.

Rule #311: There is never, ever to be any flammable work done in the garage without a working fire extinguisher nearby. If you come running into the house, looking for one, it may be too late to save the garage or the vehicles in it. Also the neighbors will come running, thinking the worst, call the fire department, and otherwise impede progress. This has been documented in Nebraska and in Washington.

Rule #37:   Never be unreachable. Never fly to California for a week without telling someone in the family you will be gone. Not communicating is not being independent; it is a form of irresponsibility. It is never nice to needlessly worry people, especially your loved ones.

Rule #39:   There is no such thing as coincidence.

Rule #14:   When everything seems to be going right, it means we are probably overlooking something. Be vigilant.

Rule #1:   Never screw over your partners. They know how to get even. Some may even know how to get ahead. In the words of Rambo, "Paybacks are a bitch."

Rule #15:   Always work as a team. (Just make sure you are in charge of that team.)

Rule #85:   If you walk with confidence, others will follow.

Rule #36:   If you feel like you are being played, you probably are. Trust your instincts.

Rule #3:   Do not believe what you are told; double check. Do not believe everything you see, and very little of what you hear from others.

Rule #8:   Never take anything or anyone for granted.

Rule #23:   The best thing you can do for your child is take him or her along with you; even while driving a tractor for hours at a time.

Rule #17:   Never put your "suspects" together in the same room. Interview them separately. Never punish just the one who *seems* guilty. The guilty one may be excellent at faking innocence. Watch out for ducks. If it quacks like a duck…

Rule #87:   If you kill it or catch it, you skin it or scale it.

Rule #10:   Never get personally involved in a situation. Do not let anger dictate outcomes. Just express disappointment. Do not say: "I am done with all of you." Keep your heart open. Practice Rule #1: Always make time for family.

Rule #5:   Do not waste goods. Two or three paper towels are usually adequate.

Rule #22:   Never ever bother someone who is working. Do not interrupt genius.

Rule #12:   Never date a co-worker, the hired hand, or someone who does not "get" you.

Rule #13:   Never involve lawyers.

Rule #42:   Never accept an apology from someone who just sucker-punched you, cheated on you, betrayed you, or stole from you. This just encourages them to do it again.

Rule #44:   Stand up for yourself. Be proud of who you are. If you have it, flaunt it.

Rule #63:   At family gatherings, always sit at the head of the table or near the head of the table on the left side. That is where the food is first passed. My youngest brother was twelve years old before he realized chicken was anything more than gravy.

Rule #16:   Always keep one foot on the floor when dining, especially when company or extended family is present.

Rule #99:   Always be prepared. Bring a jacket, even when you are certain you will not need it.

Rule #77:   Always carry a screwdriver in the trunk of your car, even if it matches or fits nothing in the vehicle. The one time Daughter forgot to carry one, she needed it to get the gas cap off, because she lost her fuel key. One time, I accidently left my key ring with the fuel key on it in my purse. I left the purse in my hotel room in Montana. I made this discovery after traveling nearly five hours on snowy, icy roads to Casper, Wyoming. Since I needed fuel to continue home, or to return to Montana, I had to find someone with special pliers and a screwdriver to remove the gas cap. Thank goodness I had my "Mad Money" in the "hooch hole" to pay for the fuel and a new gas cap.

Rule #78:   Make a plan and stick to it.

Rule #83:   Always keep a pair of sunglasses in your vehicle, even if they are sparkly purple ones like Rambo wears.

Rule #88:   Do whatever it takes to get the job done. You can sort out the details later.

Rule #30:   Our wealth is the gold others see shining in our word, our reputations, and our hearts. Be a beacon.

Rule #41:   Never apply logic to an illogical act. Time and faith may reveal a better solution.

Rule #20:   Always take a towrope when kayaking. In the event you get swept away, there is a way to be rescued.

Rule #75:   If there is a fifty-fifty chance of it being a bad decision, like driving through a big snowdrift, there is a seventy-five percent chance that we will try it and only a twenty-five percent chance that we will make it. Go figure.

Rule #25:   Accept the responsibility of choice.

Rule #6:   Do not try to teach a pig to sing or dance. It is a waste of time and annoys the pig.

Rule #97: Whatever we are, as we grow older, we become even more so.

Rule #61: Always carry three-quarters of a gallon of water with you (to allow for freezing).

Rule #80: Always carry a spare pair of underwear and one day's worth of essential meds. The family outdoorsman also suggests carrying three handkerchiefs—for cooling, filtering, and/or personal hygiene.

Rule #28: Carry a covered roll of TP and a roll of paper towels in your vehicle. Do not carry them in the trunk. In California, a squirrel got in the trunk and absolutely shredded them.

Rule #14: Never throw out good food, even if the "use by" dates have passed. This also applies to beef tongue and kidneys, heart or liver, parsnips, beets, or anything else taking up freezer space.

Rule #49: A place for everything, and everything in its place.

Rule #89: Follow through. Promises are not like piecrust, make to be broken.

Rule #29: Be courteous, especially to those who do not appear to deserve it.

Rule #57: Never do business with neighbors or family and expect to come out ahead.

Rule #59: Never loan something to someone if you think you will miss it if it does not come back. Do not loan anyone money and expect to get it back. Be appreciative if and when it is returned.

Rule #2: Living with integrity keeps you humble and honest.

Rule #50: Learn to recognize the hard, thankless work parents put into raising children. A parent makes rules to help but cannot force anyone to follow them, no matter how hard they try. Others have to make their own choices.

Rule #73: How we perceive the world is a reflection of our inner world (thoughts, beliefs, principles).

Rule #51: Sometimes … we are wrong. It is okay to admit it. Really, it is okay.

Rule #29: Always be authentic. You will be loved for being yourself. There is no need to try to impress others.

Rule #95: Rules are meant to prevent or mitigate messes and mistakes. When problems happen, and they will, the rules serve to protect.

Rule #43: To insure equity and fairness, the one dividing the cookie lets the other one choose first.

Rule #55: The highways of life are full of flat squirrels that could not make up their mind. Be decisive; make a change if needed.

Rule #999: Ignorance can be overcome through experience and education. Stupidity cannot be fixed. Intolerance is learned and can be changed through enlightenment and effort. Be understanding of the ignorant and uneducated. Be a shining beacon of compassionate love and an example of acceptance, so the intolerant may become enlightened.

Rule #45: There will be someone in your life to fall back on, someone who will give you a second chance. Exercise that opportunity. Extend the same opportunity to others.

Rule #1: Always make time for family.

Rule #11: Rules are made to be broken. Differentiate. You may have noticed there is more than one Rule #1. Learn to think for yourself.

We know the rules. We just do not always play by them. We like long walks, especially when they are taken by people who annoy us.

Communication may not be our strong suit. We may not always see eye to eye. The rules (and the deliberate breaking of them), our ensuing arguments, the certain consequences, every moment together means something. The first to apologize is the bravest. The first to forgive is the strongest. The first to forget is the happiest. To quote Henry Ford: "Coming together is a beginning. Keeping together is progress. Working together is success."

I believe my job is to comfort the disturbed and disturb the comfortable. When we dance, our purpose is not to get to a certain place on the floor. It is to enjoy each step along the way. Before I say goodbye, I will say thank you, for everything. Have a Merry Christmas. I love you. 12-13-14

"It's all about quality of life and finding a balance between work and friends and family." – Philip Nelson

The Rule of Five

The rule of five helps in perspective and reactions by maintaining the big picture. You simply ask yourself:

1. Will this matter in five minutes?
2. Will this matter in five hours?
3. Will this matter in five days?

If not, you need to graciously let it go and move forward productively. Otherwise, you continue asking yourself:

20

1. Will this matter in five weeks?
2. Will this matter in five months?
3. Will this matter in five years?

Any of these results means that a proper, dignified conversation needs to exist. It needs to be a conversation that involves "I" statements and active listening. The most important thing when asking yourself these questions is that you must be honest. The whole point is that nearly everything people get angry or frustrated about does not actually matter in the scheme of things, and this helps you regain perspective in a moment when you are struggling for it.

I recommend that you use this. It works wonders for me.

Survival Kit for Life

- **Balloon** – To remind you not to blow up
- **Band-Aid** – To help heal hurt feelings in yourself and others
- **Chewing Gum** – To remind you that if you stick with it, you can accomplish anything
- **Compass** – So you will know where you are and where you are going
- **Eraser** – To remind you that you can always start again
- **Glove** – For when you need an extra hand
- **Happy Face Sticker** – To remind you to have fun
- **Jolly Rancher Crunch 'n' Chew** – To remind you to appreciate the differences in others
- **Kiss** – Because Walmart was out of hugs, but some people are not. Ask if you need one!
- **Lifesaver** – To remind you of the many times others will need your help and you will need theirs
- **Lollipop** – To remind you that you can lick any obstacles that come your way
- **Magnifying Glass** – To help you see the bigger picture
- **Paper Clip** – To remind you that you have all the tools to hold it together
- **Penny** – For your thoughts. Flip it to determine if you should step up or step back
- **Rubber Band** – To help you stay flexible; to remind you to bend, not snap
- **Safety Pin** – To remind you to stay sharp
- **Smarties** – To help you make good decisions
- **Snickers Bar** – To remind you to take time to laugh
- **Soap** – To help you wash away your troubles
- **Sponge** – To help you soak it all in

- **Star** – To remind you to shine brightly
- **Starburst** – For that burst of energy when you do not have any
- **String** – To keep you going a bit longer when you reach the end of your rope
- **Tissue** – To help you clean up those little messes
- **Toothpick** – To help you pick out the good in everything
- **Tootsie Roll** – To remind you to let the small things roll off your shoulders

Things My Mother Taught Me

Teresa (while jaywalking in Seattle): My mother taught me to look both ways before crossing the street, in case there are cars.

Rick: My mother taught me to stare them down.

Teresa: Yeah, she probably did.

Daughter's Rules to Life

1. Never throw up on the first date.
2. Never seduce a man while dressed like your grandmother.
3. Never thwart the time god.
4. The god of ivory always laughs last.
5. The world revolves around the sun, not you. Or does it?

To him who watches, everything is revealed. – Italian proverb

Uncle Fred's Toast

Here's to you, as good as you are; and here's to me, as bad as I am. As bad as I am and as good as you are, I am as good as you are as bad as I am!

CHAPTER TWO:
Summers Come and Go

- *Trust Steadily in God*
  - *Hope Unswervingly*
    - *Love Extravagantly*

In the Summer of ...

And there we were, sitting in the shade, talking about this summer, and summers of the past. The days of summer can be long, lazy days. They can bring times of tribulation, trauma, and triumph. Some of the most important events in life occur during the summer.

During the summer of 1947, a very young-looking, brash, and brazen fellow met a quiet city girl who was completely out of her element. She was spending the summer picking strawberries and other fruits and vegetables on a farm near Prairie Island, east of Grand Island, Nebraska. He often went to Prairie Island to hang out with his best friend or pick him up to go hunting or fishing. By the end of the summer, this country guy and this city gal decided to get married, but that had to wait until he turned twenty-one. He wanted to be "of age" so he did not need to ask his parents' permission. The very next week after his twenty-first birthday, they were man and wife.

The summer of 1948 found them expecting me, their firstborn. I turned out not to be the boy Dad had hoped for. Reportedly, I was not only walking, I was running at nine months, a real bundle of energy.

The summer of 1958, my father bought a ranch four miles east of Ravenna. While the legal work was getting hashed out and the papers signed, Dad and I traveled back and forth from our current home, living in a very small trailer, taking care of the cattle, and putting up the hay. We still had farming to do back home. We did not get everything moved until after the corn was harvested, but that was the summer I officially became the "hired man."

The summer of 1966 cemented that "top hired hand" status. I watched my classmates drift off to summer jobs or prepare to attend college or begin their careers. I had to *earn* my college money by running the ranch for the next year and two more summers.

The summer of 1969, I invited my college friends to a hayrack ride, wiener roast, and campout to celebrate my twenty-first birthday. Days later, I loaded my belongings into the old '56 Chevy and headed out to my first teaching job at a one-room school on the fringe of the Nebraska Sandhills.

The summer of 1970, I married the man who became the father of my three children. We honeymooned in Estes Park, Colorado. I brought my herd of cows and my favorite mare and colt to our rented cottage. My mother-in-law taught me how to cook, freeze and can vegetables, and to quilt. I missed my five sisters and three brothers but gained five brothers and a sister.

The summer of 1972, when I went to my family reunion, everyone was

24

ecstatic. I was expecting the first grandchild of that generation. They told me I never looked better or seemed so happy. I *was* happy. Several months later, my son was born, with ten fingers, ten toes, and lots of hair.

The summer of 1975, my grandparents asked us to drive them to Minnesota and stay with them at their fishing cabin for a week or so. We left Son with my parents and had our first vacation since he joined our little family. We also forgot to bring along my birth control and were later *surprised* by another addition to the family, our second son who joined us the next spring. We still laugh about our vacation that left a legacy.

The summer of 1978 was a busy time. I spent the entire summer in the 4230 John Deere tractor doing the farming and putting up the hay. I was thankful it had an air-conditioned cab and a radio. I climbed out of the tractor about a week before I delivered my daughter. The neighbors were shocked to read about the birth in the newspaper because they had seen me (in the tractor) every day that summer and had no idea we were adding to our family.

The summer of 1989 brought many changes. I was no longer teaching school. I was too sick to work on the ranch and spent most of the summer with relatives, trying to relax and rethink my priorities. That summer, I turned the big 4-0. I drafted our divorce papers. The judge approved them.

The summer of 1990, I was a new divorcée, living in town, finding new friends, and learning to enjoy life again. I started playing coed volleyball, coed softball, and attending a coed card club. I felt reborn.

The summer of 1991, I gave my "icebreaker" speech at Loup Valley Toastmasters. I began writing. I started taking dance lessons. I started dating. I hosted the reception for Son #1's high school graduation at my house in town. Family and friends, even the ex's family and friends, came. It was a huge milestone, watching Son leave for college at UNL.

The summer of 1995, I was living in my "house on the hill." My ex and I co-hosted the reception at the church we attended, so no one would feel uncomfortable. FFA Star Chapter Farmer Son #2 barbequed the meat himself. That summer he left the ranch and attended SECC at Beatrice. It was not easy to watch him leave and begin his own life.

The summer of 1997, Daughter hosted her high school graduation reception at the town house. Per her wishes, we first had to paint the interior walls and completely redecorate. Since it was looking so spiffy, I hosted Son #2's college graduation party that same month.

The summer of 1998, I spent planning the wedding of my dreams, while serving as Toastmasters International District 24 Governor. My future husband wrote a special song, dedicated it to me, and performed it at dances. I moved from Ord to Kearney, Nebraska, after our wedding.

The summer of 1999, that same husband performed "my special song" publicly at the Toastmasters Talent Show, yet privately, dismantled our marriage. I returned to my house on the hill in Ord and divorced him that fall.

The summer of 2003, my first grandson was born, four days after my "33rd" birthday. (I had been "33" for a number of years.) He was named Chance because the doctors told Son there was no chance he could have a child. Thankfully, they were very wrong.

This brings me to the summer of 2006. I was still "33 years old," now a twin to Son who was also 33 years old. I had recently attended my forty-year class reunion. There were no other "33-year-olds" there, but I had a great time anyway with all those gray-haired grannies and grandpas.

The summer of 2008 found me weary from ranch work, seeking renewal on the dance floor. There, I met my "latest," but time revealed he was not the "greatest." I moved on.

The summer of 2011, I left Son #2 in charge of the ranch and relocated to Scottsbluff, Nebraska, just a twenty-minute drive from the Wyoming state line. My friends told me I could not be much farther west and still be in Nebraska. I went to be with Daughter. She attended college at WNCC and tended the big horned sheep in the Wildcat Hills. I spent a lot of time in the thermal pool at the YMCA. Also, I went dancing. This is where I met Rambo, my current dancing partner and playmate. (We use code names to better elude the "fun police.")

The summer of 2013, I welcomed freshly retired Chief Petty Officer Son #1 and his wife to our new digs in North Carolina. Rambo and I had been sent in by the relocating family as the advance guard, to reconnoiter, to clear and repair the premises, to establish fence lines and stables for the livestock, and to make sure everything was habitable. This turned out to be a nine-month prelude to our retirement on Easy Street. We liked it so well in the foothills of the Appalachians that we decided to stay. We call our five acres of fresh air the Shack Ranch East Headquarters. We have two houses, two garages or shops, two horses, two goats, two dogs, Daughter's two cats, plus two more. Rambo and I go dancing a couple times a week.

The summer of 2014, we hosted our first annual block party. Most forgot to bring their block, according to our "punny" guest, Santa Claus. Grandkids, friends of the family, and friends of ours came to picnic and play Polish horseshoes.

The summer of 2015 brought exciting new plans for our next cookout at the ranch. Our neighbor and his band provided live music; we got the real horseshoe pits dug. We invited more new friends and had extended family here. The menu was upgraded from grilled hot dogs and hamburgers.

I ask, "What will the coming summers bring?"

Today is Kelsey's Birth Day

Kelsey Lynn is an alter ego of the author. KL says and does things LC would not dare to do. This section is an exercise in creative writing and may not be strictly autobiographical.

"Remembrance of things past
is not necessarily
the remembrance of things as they were."

- Marcel Proust

Mom: Say, have I ever told you about the day you were born?

KL: No, I don't believe so…

Mom: That summer found us expecting our firstborn. I woke up about 6:30 AM with a minor pain that I attributed to the watermelon I had eaten the night before. It was not the watermelon. Dad was out milking the cows, and by the time he came in with the milk, I had decided it was time to go to the hospital, which was in an old gray converted house about four miles away. Dad left the milk pails just sitting there, unseparated, and we jumped into the old 1932 Chevy.

It was about 8:00 AM when we arrived at the hospital. The doctor was just telling Dad that he might as well go back home for a while, since this was a first baby. It might be some time before anything happened. Right then the nurse hollered for the doctor to come "NOW." Inside of thirty minutes, you were born, fairly tiny, and rather short. "Hmmm," Dad quipped, "It looks like we are missing a few parts." Nope. I counted. You had ten fingers, ten toes, and lots of hair. We were very happy with our new little bundle. Your name had already been agreed upon, taken from the title of a song popular that year. All the nurses kept raving about how short you were, and about all your dark hair. Such a precious baby! One of three born in that hospital that special day!

I made a baby quilt for you, with the words, "Now I lay me down to sleep…" embroidered in the center. Using outing flannel and the old Singer treadle sewing

27

machine, I made all of your diapers. Grandma helped me make some "tummy bands," which were used to hold in your navel. As the very first grandchild of that generation in our family, you were showered with gifts and visits, especially from Auntie. Much better than a watermelon!

Today is Kelsey's Birthday

Mom: Do you remember your second birthday and the party we had for you?

KL: No, I do not believe so ...

Mom: It was a special day, with the three girls born on that same day in the same hospital as honorees. Of course, Daughter #2 had joined our family by that time. Three other neighbor girls were invited, making a party of seven. Seven was always a lucky number for you.

Each of the seven girls wore handmade party dresses, with white anklets and white sandals. You sported a barrette with a ribbon in your hair, which had been pin-curled earlier that morning. You looked so sweet that day, enjoying the attention.

Today is Kelsey's Fifth Birthday

Mom: Do you remember your fifth birthday?

KL: How could I forget it?

My life changed that day in a big way. You and I walked together down the road a block or two to the one-room schoolhouse on the corner. I was scared to death. There were about twenty-five kids there, some as big as my dad. It was a K-through-8 school with a first-year teacher who had no teaching experience and very little self-confidence. You left me there in my brand new dress, my brand new shoes, with my "violin" pencil case, and my fancy hairdo. I had ribbons on both sides that day. We had already taken the "first day of school" photos. I was ready for school.

Whoops, remember that "scared to death" part. Despite assurances that I had met the children in my class (at previous birthday parties) and that I would be just fine, I was not so sure. I could see my house from the schoolyard and desperately wanted to return there and hang out with Dad, as usual. Instead, I was asked to stand up and recite "The Pledge of Allegiance." I refused. I stayed in my desk. Resisting all urges, pleas, encouragements, I clung to my seat. This was not a good start to my education, but it was my first opportunity to participate in public speaking.

As the week progressed, I regressed. My obstinate behavior was reported to my parents. I was severely punished. No improvement. At the suggestion of my parents, I was locked in the storage room during the pledge. It had windows and was quiet. I rather enjoyed the seclusion. The following day, I was shut inside the coat closet, a small smelly place with no light and no room to maneuver. The next week, I surrendered to the inevitable and stood beside my desk during the pledge. I did not speak. The teacher decided that was good enough. I knew better. I thought I had won that battle. We had a difficult and contentious year.

I was not so sweet in those days, except during the Christmas program. I got to sing, dance, and recite. I shyly did my part. I felt a part of something special. That was the key to my happiness.

Today is Kelsey's Twelfth Birthday

Dad: Do you recall what we were doing on your twelfth birthday?

KL: That was a long time ago. Please remind me.

Dad: That was the summer we started relocating from my parent's rental farm to our very own ranch along the river. You were my right-hand "man" and spent the summer alongside me. We spent more time at the ranch "baching" in the trailer house than we did at the farm. You were chief dishwasher and keeper of the castle. I managed to get us fed, with the help of supplies sent with us by your mother. Our specialty was fried egg sandwiches. Between caring for the cattle, harvesting and planting the wheat, putting up acres and acres of hay, and stacking those small square bales, we did not have much time for rest or play.

That day we were hurrying to finish the haying on the ranch so we could return to the farm in time for the opening day of school. Mom had your birthday cake waiting, but the other kids were already in bed. The widening gulf between you and your sisters really grew. This perception of "specialness" reflected the increasing independence, the growing responsibilities, and your developing talent for problem-solving. We were a team, at least in your eyes.

Those days, you wore your hair in braids, fixed once a week. Mom had five girls now and did not have time to fuss with curls. You were still walking to the one-room school on the corner. It did not seem so far to walk anymore. You continued down the pathway of a contentious student making the teacher earn her salary.

Today is Kelsey's Seventeenth Birthday

Mom: Seventeen is an awkward age. You were no longer a child but not yet an adult. It was a rebellious time of testing boundaries and flaunting authority. What do you remember the most about this birthday?

KL: Practically nothing comes to mind. Was there anything special about it?

My birthday just seemed like another day of unrelenting work and endless chores. No special guests. There were seven siblings around the table and a new baby in the crib. Never a quiet moment. Never a time to just sit and read my favorite books. Getting ready for school seemed like an imposition. No matter how early the alarm rang, how soon I got dressed and started the day, I was inevitably late for my first class. Today was no different.

Dad stayed in bed or inside the house in his favorite easy chair until the children left for school. Mom was busy with the new baby, getting everyone's breakfast ready and lunches packed. This left the responsibilities for doing chores resting upon my young shoulders. Resentments began to build, a harbinger of things to come.

Today is Kelsey's Twenty-First Birthday

Dad: Today, my baby girl turned twenty-one and left home.
KL: Why didn't you wish me well and tell me goodbye?
Dad: This was a tortuous summer. I was so torn. One moment, I could not wait for you to be gone. The next, I wanted to keep you here. One part of me knew you had to leave. It was time. I just could not say goodbye. Dads do not cry.

At least we had a real party for your birthday this year. Some of your college friends made the trip to the ranch and reportedly had "once-in-a-lifetime" experiences. Introducing them to the family of nine "littles" and two "bigs" was the easy part. Digging the fire pit, roasting the hotdogs and marshmallows while keeping the flies out of the food was a bit more challenging. The best part came later, after the baseball game.

We hitched up the team of sorrels to the flatbed hayrack, lined the sides with bales of hay to sit on, loaded up everyone, including Mom and the baby, and started around the square. The trip "around the block" went west two miles, north across the river bridge, three miles east on a winding river road, back south across another river bridge, and another mile and a half home. By this time the stars were out, the moon appeared, the locusts were singing, and we had exhausted our supply of songs everyone knew. So we tried improvisation. We had a whole hayrack full of wisecrackers. Everyone was grateful to get back to the ranch house.

The very next morning you loaded the '56 Chevy with personal belongings and supplies for your job teaching school in the Sandhills. It was a big step to an independent life away from home. I did wish you the best. I just was not ready to say goodbye. I let Mom do it for me.

Today is Kelsey's Thirty-Third Birthday

Chorus from the kids: Happy Birthday, Mom!
KL: Aren't birthdays fun?

This birthday is so much fun that we make it into a birthday week. As a special birthday treat, my family takes me to the local three-day celebration. It features rides, turtle races, horseshoe tournaments, team penning, open class vegetable/art show, a lengthy parade, a talent show, free entertainment on the outdoor stage, a raffle, the free dance, and all the popcorn and watermelon we can eat. It is an opportunity to see neighbors, friends, and meet new people.

Later in the week, we invite personal friends and family to the ranch for an outdoor picnic. Kids run rampant. When evening falls, we move inside. The adults play progressive pitch. The kids run rampant. We bring out the ice cream, cake, and punch. The kids run rampant. Aren't birthdays fun? Sometimes they are unforgettable.

Today is Kelsey's Thirty-Third Birthday?

Friends and family of KL: Once again we celebrate your 33rd birthday…
KL: Why, yes, that's right, for the 11th time!

And here we are, celebrating. The afternoon begins with a boisterous and rugged tussle on the sand volleyball court in the park. It is a perfect day with ideal weather for this activity. Only the adventurous participate. The rest watch the action, keeping an eye on the youngsters, or simply visiting, exchanging stories.

The party transforms, moves to the house on the hill, and catches the birthday girl unaware on several fronts. Two bolder fellows capture her and administer birthday wishes on her derriere with a fly swatter. She shrieks in feigned terror, nothing injured except her pride. Who dares to do such a thing? Only her best friends…

One of her sisters brings a fancy decorated sheet cake to the party. All admire it but (gasp) it has the wrong age written on it. It says, "Happy 44th Birthday!" Surely a monumental mistake… on someone's part, anyway.

The friends are astonished. One proclaims, "My mom is younger than that, and she is old. She would never even think of playing volleyball. How do you do

31

it?" After that day, they never expect me to dive for the balls. Blessings come in many guises, sometimes as complete surprises.

Once again, the party transforms. The die-hard card players set up tournaments. The casual card players choose easier games and do not even keep score. No one watches the time. No one even notices until the little ones get cranky and need their pajamas and their own beds.

Those without little ones play on into the wee hours. Pretty soon someone mentions staying until dawn. Except that everyone is starting to yawn. Soon everyone helps clean the tables, and they leave.

Today is Kelsey's Thirty-Third Birthday, Again!

Friend of the Family: Are you up for a game of river volleyball?
KL: Yes, but I was instructed to keep my new perm dry for the next three days if I want it to last. Will I be safe?
Friends and Family: (as a smirking chorus) Sure!

As an annual observance of August birthdays—not just mine—family members and friends come to the special "cream can" party and play volleyball. It is an honor to be invited; sacrifices are made just to attend. Setting the volleyball net up either in the riverbed or on the wet sand beside it adds a touch of coolness. An occasional quick dip adds to the fun.

Not usually tame crews any day, the players on this day were wild, with long serves, strong spikes, and errant passes into the river. Scrambling after one, I dashed into the water, intent on getting the ball before it caught the current and floated away. I did not hear the thundering feet behind me, or even glimpse the diving tackler that playfully pinned me to the river bottom. The impact knocked the wind out of me. Instantly sucking sand, I tried to hoist the big bruiser so I could breathe. I could not do it. Desperately, I squirmed around, trying to roll out from underneath. I could not. Seeing my life scrolling past in a slow-motion sequence, I thought it was my time to die. He was afraid if he let me up, after deliberately getting my hair wet, that it would be his time to die. He nearly hesitated too long before getting up and running some distance away.

Everyone had stopped. They feared fireworks from me. As I stepped ashore, red-faced and panting heavily, they were certain trouble was coming. They just waited for the explosion. After quickly catching my breath, I gave a slow smile, looked at everyone, and informed them I was lucky to be alive. I added that I was thankful He let me live. The wet hair was no longer an issue. I could hear the

32

round of relieved sighs.

My calm forgiving response astounded every person there, including me. It just seemed like the right thing to say. I felt the most peaceful calm overtake me. I felt like I became one of them in that moment. A small miracle!

If you want to hear a roomful of people laugh, just have someone ask if I am up for a game of river volleyball.

Today is Kelsey's Fiftieth Birthday

KL: A half century of stories, wow! A week to celebrate.

Daughter: Yes, and celebrate we did! First, I made certain your life insurance was quadrupled. Next, I checked that I was listed as one of the beneficiaries. Then I planned your birthday surprise. All you were asked to do was meet me at my place, on a day you were free to have a spontaneous day of adventure.

Spontaneity is not your favorite modus operati. No fear. We hopped into the car, and traveled east. We went somewhere you had never been before. We did something you had never done before. It was not as simple as I had hoped.

The day turned out to be overcast, and more so the farther we traveled east. We stopped at a small airport where the surprise was revealed. It required taking lessons, watching a video, and signing your life away with numerous waivers. The plane was grounded until the cloud cover lifted. No guarantee that it would happen any time soon. It even started to rain.

After being advised not to hang around, but to wait for a phone call, we drove back to the big city, found our favorite fancy restaurant, and ordered entreés, complete with an expensive bottle of wine. When the telephone call came, we were over an hour away from the airport, and a bit tipsy.

Rushing back, battling sundown, the adrenalin pumping, we ran inside. There was time for only one of us to go up before nightfall. We had to make a decision. It was supposed to be a joint adventure, with both of us taking turns jumping out of a fairly decent airplane.

We decided it was a very special day for you, so you were strapped into the gear, and up you went. You were recorded on videotape muttering to yourself, "I can do this, I can do this? I can do this!" while climbing up to eleven hundred feet. Then it was time to climb out on the wing struts, where the wind tried to tear you away. Your tandem-jumping partner had to uncurl your fingers to get you to let go and start the jump.

After a quick flip, you began to freefall, saying it was like riding a really fast motorcycle with no windshield. After the chute opened, things seemed to slow down. Drifting in wide spirals over the fields, watching the sun set in the red-tinged sky, you began to fully appreciate what was happening. The ground came up to meet you. The jump was over too soon. The photos and video preserved the moments forever. You were elated and checked skydiving off your bucket list.

Our biggest regret was that I would have to reschedule my jump to another day, and you would not be there to watch. It still went down as the neatest birthday present I ever gave my mom. You agreed.

Today is Kelsey's Sixty-First Birthday Party

KL: Wasn't that a fab party?

BBF: Mmmm.

KL: The guests really enjoyed the house tour. You got a lot of compliments.

BBF: (Silent stare.)

KL: Aren't you glad we cleaned out the garage and ate out there? Clean-up was so easy.

BBF: MmmHmm.

KL: Your idea of serving finger foods was wonderful. Any leftovers will make fixing meals easier. You really enjoy snacking anyway.

BBF: MmmHmm.

KL: Did you enjoy meeting my friends?

BBF: MmmHmm.

KL: We are joining some of them at the dance tomorrow night. Are you looking forward to going dancing?

BBF: (Groan.)

KL: Are you still hurting?

BBF: MmmHmm.

KL: Will we be able to go dancing?

BBF: MmmHmm.

KL: How long will we stay?

BBF: Ummm ...

KL: I HOPE YOU DANCE!

BBF: I intend to.

KL: How come you still love dancing if it hurts so much?

BBF: How come I still love you?

Kelsey's Best Birthday Ever

And there we were, once again celebrating my 33rd birthday, for the twenty-fifth time. Birthdays come only once in a year, and last year I celebrated my birthday the way I wanted to—doing volunteer work at the Nebraska State Fair. There were so many new faces, so many interesting stories, and so much laughter. I dipped ice cream, I ran the till, I drummed up business, I closed up the joint. At the end of the evening, after the money was counted and placed into the bank deposit bag, I was escorted by the State Patrol to my vehicle for safety's sake. I went to bed with the satisfaction of having enjoyed the best birthday of my life. No thoughts of self, but of serving others.

Birthdays do not usually cause me to reflect on years past, but this year had got me thinking! Honestly, I really do not remember many before age five. That year, my mother invited all the neighbor children, dressed me in a frilly dress, and baked a fabulous birthday cake. It was an excruciatingly painful experience for me, as I really did not "know" any of the guests. Shyness kept me from enjoying that day.

How far I have come on my journey of life… I now celebrate each birthday, sometimes for a day, a week, or a month. Always, I am thirty-three once again! It keeps me feeling young. Thirty-three, plus shipping and handling…

CHAPTER THREE:
Sunbeams and Shadows

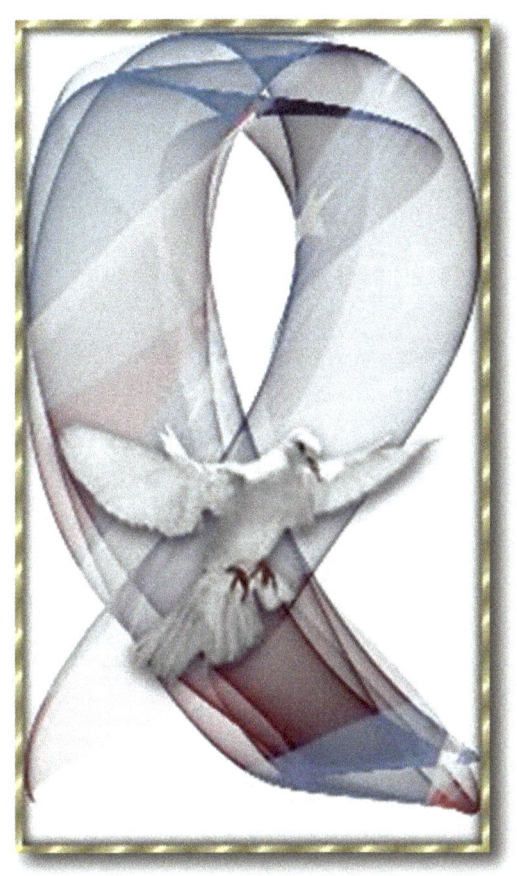

I have heard
the crying of your heart.
I have seen
the searching of your soul.

The Loving Link

Children desire to please;
  Failing that, needing love,
They nag, they pester, they plead.

Truths become distorted;
  Exaggerations abound.
Their selfishness leads to greed.

Children who are trusted,
  Nurtured, valued, and respected
Develop a knack for life.

They learn to listen with love,
  Accept help from Above,
Don't need surrounded by strife.

Give these gifts to your children:
  Teach them the value of hope;
Let them know you "believe."

Tell them they do well;
  Let their spirits run free.
The desire to please won't leave.

For that special connection,
  To forge that lasting bond,
It takes a loving link.

There is no greater tribute,
  Nor any better reward,
Than parent and child in sync.

By Linda S. Cone   5-2-1995

A Children's Christmas Story

And there we were, creating Christmas magic for the little ones. I told them: I believe in Santa, the magic of Christmas, the innocence of children, and the importance of make-believe.

Do you believe in Santa? Well, I do!

I remember when I was twelve. I had just moved to a different school. The children and the teacher tried to explain that there was no Santa. They were upset because I believed in Santa. I was twelve. Old enough to know!

No Santa Claus? I knew better. I "unheard" what I had just been told, "willed" myself back to innocence, and returned to the "magic" of Christmas. I reclaimed Santa Claus and never let go again.

Others just do not get it. Childhood "must" be magical. For children, fantasy is the natural medium, magic the birthright. It is okay to believe in magic.

As a child, I experienced my magic in the very heart of rural America. No miracle on 34th Street, but quite a few on the ranch.

I will never forget lying in bed, too awake, one Christmas Eve, too excited to sleep, and hearing something hit the roof. I just knew it was Santa … so I scurried out to the living room … and caught my mom and dad putting together a tricycle.

Mom merely looked sheepish. Dad calmly explained that Santa had just that moment left all these presents. He was right outside feeding his reindeer the hay we left for them, but if he heard me stirring around, he would come back and gather up all the gifts.

I vanished instantly, back to bed, eyes shut tightly, snuggled in the covers securely. I still smile gently in memory and feel the "magic." Even now, drifting off to sleep on Christmas Eve, I listen for a thump against the roof … I believe in Santa Claus.

Living in a Man's World

And there she was, growing up too fast. Her first ten years were spent at Central City, living on a farm owned by her grandparents. As the firstborn of five daughters born to her parents during those ten years, she set precedence and created traditions.

As one of five siblings living in a man's world, she was given no opportunity to be a "girl." Each child did chores from early on, helping with field work and tending livestock at an obscenely young age.

Her favorite memories center on haying the east quarter of prairie hay, a natural grass meadow. The extended family, consisting of grandparents, uncles and aunts, her dad, and his two older girls, typically spent nearly a week mowing, raking, and stacking.

The family used her dad's team of sorrel horses to pull the dump rake and her grandpa's black team to raise the stacker. Her grandma told the stacker team when to go forward and back, raising the hay and dumping it. Her dad and uncle used pitchforks to layer it evenly, a hot, dirty job.

Those young girls wore halter tops and matching shorts made by their mother. They got a wonderful tan (and a head start on cancer) that way. Four o'clock was always "lunch" time.

Mom would bring out jugs of water, sweet iced tea, sandwiches, and cake. Everyone there would gather 'round and chat a bit while resting. She felt so big, just being a part of that "man's world."

Dads Do Cry Sometimes

And there we were, scattered in loose lines, walking the west pasture, digging out the musk thistles on the sandhills around the swamp. It was a tedious task, and no one wanted to be there. That was when I made one of the most regrettable choices in my twenty-year life.

This happened "that" summer after I had attended college for two years. My father insisted I give up my cushy "college" job and return to work on the ranch as the "ramrod." I did not know how to refuse his orders. I supervised my eight brothers and sisters on work crews and directed chores.

That day in late May we were a mile from home, walking the pasture around the "swamp," cutting musk thistles with shovels or machetes. Second-in-Command Sis decided she was hot, tired, and had enough. She told me she was quitting. She started walking toward the house. I regarded it as my responsibility to keep the crew together and working. If she quit, I reasoned, why would the rest keep working?

I tried to stop her, ran her down, confronted her, and even threatened her with my machete. Nothing worked. She kept walking. I got ahead of her, sobbing with frustration and defeat. I was not used to losing, at anything. I ran to my father, and stopped him in the field. He was planting corn.

At that point, I admit I was out of control. He listened to my sob story, then told me to leave Sis alone, go get the other kids, and quit for the day. He gave me something to do, by myself, for the rest of that day, and every day the rest of that long, incredibly lonely summer.

"Words are like arrows.

Once released, they're forever out of reach.

And where they strike and wound,

Though you may pull them out and mend their entry

with the finest healing potions,

There will always be a scar."

—By Rae Turnbull

A couple days later, when I asked him what I should have done in a situation like that, he just started crying and told me he did not know what to do with me. That was shocking because I had never seen my father cry. He was placing the responsibility right back on me. How dare he make me responsible for my own choices! I felt betrayed.

Then he told me he felt I was too dangerous to be left alone with the other children. My parents segregated me, ostracized me from the family, and taught my siblings to fear and hate me. Some of these feelings persist today. I instantly regretted what happened.

I found it difficult to forgive myself. Yes, I believed I was leading just as I had been taught. I should have let her walk away. I lost a lot that day—my positive sense of self, even my self-respect, and any rapport I had with my siblings. While working by myself, with only my thoughts to keep me company, I regained my sense of right and wrong. It was a difficult and lasting lesson.

"Was That Love?"

My parents never told me why
    they had nine kids, brats, rug rats.
        Who told them love was physical?
Why did they work all those hours
    to feed them, educate them,
        and then beat them
With branches cut from trees,
    with straps quickly snatched,
        with ropes still coiled?
Why didn't they talk about real life,
    relationships,
        feelings?
My parents never mentioned why
    they were too busy, too tired,
        too scared
To share some of their love.
    It always felt like
        hate to me.
The day I cry into their coffins
    I will still ask,
        "Did you love me?"
And wonder why they couldn't
    just once have told me,
        "YES!"

The First Seven Days

In the beginning, the spirit moved them. It was said, "Let there be dancing," and there was dancing. And it was good. They began to see the light.

On the second day, it was said, "Let there be dating." There was dating, and it was good. They caught a glimpse of heaven.

Then it was said, "Let there be sharing." Each began sharing gifts and thoughts, revealing talents and vulnerabilities, hopes and fears. And it was good. On this third day, they began laying a firm foundation, upon the earth.

On the fourth day, it was said, "Let there be faith—signs, and seasons, and stars in the sky." They watched for signs of trust, respect, and love. They experienced seasons of doubt, of searching, and of hope. They felt the guidance from above, and it was good. The stars were smiling.

On day five, it was said, "Let there be love." Each met friends and family of the other. These loving creatures breathed life into the relationship with their acceptance and good wishes. Love grew. And it was good.

On the sixth day, it was said, "Let there be commitment." Covenants were created, promises made and kept, intentions and expectations shared. This man and woman became a team, a couple, and partners in life. And it was very good.

Then it was said, "Let this seventh day be a day of rest." This time of reflection, of calmness, of peace is dedicated to worshiping God, to counting blessings, to appreciating one another. And their life was good.

Written with input from "Genesis."   June 7, 1970

A Time to Build

And here we are, two devoted people working together, facing life's choices, responsibilities, and opportunities. We can become truly free by standing side by side, pulling in the same direction. When we are coupled together, we may initially feel it to be limiting and burdensome to be so closely yoked to another human being. It seems scary to limit intimacies to that one special person. It seems diminishing to be asked to account for one's movements, plans, and activities. It is a building process.

In a true union, both realize that what may first have been viewed as a limitation or burden becomes true freedom, great joy. We become free from the little games, the intricate dance steps of evasion, and the masks we must wear before others. Since fidelity is promised forever, no matter what, we are free to commit ourselves fully, to passionately share our entire being.

43

We find the promise of completeness in the freedom to be ourselves fully, without restriction, without apology. We wear the yoke of love with pride, knowing it brings us peace, contentment, fulfillment and freedom to "fly." Our souls soar in triumph. Color life beautiful.

"Coming Home"

He entered.
She noticed.
He waited.
She wondered.
He looked.
She smiled.
He asked.
She answered.
He led.
She followed.

He kissed.
She quivered.
He rose.
She reached.
He poised.
She placed.
He pressed.
She parted.
He sank.
She surrounded.

They shuddered.
They dissolved.
They were home.

Home was the
    essence of love,
One heart residing
    within another.

"A wedding anniversary is the celebration of love, trust, partnership, tolerance and tenacity. The order varies for any given year."

– Paul Sweeny

"Dedicated to You"

And there we were, face to face…
    He laughed self-consciously,
The way people do
    Who have no humor in their soul.

No really spontaneous chuckle
    Ever came from his lips.
When he did laugh, it was only on cue,
    And seldom because he just wanted to.

And it often seemed to be
    At somebody else's expense.
For he was too full of FEAR
    To ever laugh at himself.

So often, he told me,
    He had been an object of ridicule.
It saddened me that he seemed to find
    No real joy in his life, not even in his wife.

I told him so once,
    And he laughed out loud.
But a cloud of pain darkened his face,
    And what my heart heard was a cry.

Big Girls Don't Cry (Son #1's Tale)

So there I was, about eleven years of age or so, in a tree-climbing phase, as many eleven year olds happen to be. This was a unique summer because the cherry trees in our orchard were putting out like nothing you have ever seen. Every free moment involved us kids up in a tree, picking bucket after bucket of cherries. Then pitting bucket after bucket of cherries. Then cooking up bucket after bucket of cherries into pies, or cherry crisps, or cherry cobblers, or many other cherry-related desserts. Then foisting off said desserts onto various relatives, or taking them to church potlucks, or picnics, or wherever they could be foisted.

Cherry pies are not my favorite.

One afternoon, we were picking cherries, as usual, along with two of my aunts who had been bamboozled into picking their own quota of cherries. This was deep into cherry picking season, and suffice it to say, my interest in cherry picking had waned. I took advantage of the fact that the presence of my aunts limited my mother's options for discipline and snuck off to climb a cottonwood in the middle of the nearest pasture.

Now, a cottonwood is a softwood tree. Softwoods tend to do better in Nebraska than hardwoods because they are much more tolerant of wind. Cottonwoods are especially challenging to climb because they don't grow straight up, but, instead, go kind of all over. A good limb can peter out to nothing, leaving you hanging, sometimes literally. This one was the biggest on the place, with the added mystery of being alone in a pasture next to an old dried-up farm pond. What could one see from up there? Why was it all by itself? These are irresistible questions to an eleven-year-old tree climber.

So I trekked off to conquer the mysterious tall tree. I had to circle around the trunk a couple of times to climb higher. I was way up in the top, into the branches one should not really be climbing. Then the branch started uncoiling onto my arm! It was a bull snake, and it must have been twenty feet long and six inches thick! Or, perhaps it was normal sized, and I was freaking out because it was uncoiling onto my arm. Anyway, I was clearly left with only one possible option and that was to bail. I let go and took the express route down.

Unfortunately, I had circled around to the side of the tree above the pond. After the twenty feet of tree, hitting every branch on the way down, I had to fall ten more feet to the muddy bank of the pond. Luckily, I landed in the muddy bank of the pond, relatively unscathed.

Relatively unscathed, that is. No broken bones. However, there may not have been any skin left on my back. I was hurting. Now the double-edged sword of my aunts' presence came into play once again. There was no way to admit I was hurt in front of the general populace. It was simply not done. I carefully walked up to my mother and carefully whispered, "I fell out of the tree and got hurt." Mother, who had reached the limit of her tolerance of bratty sisters, disobedient children, and picking cherries, snapped, "Great, now grab a bucket and get to picking." I glanced at my aunts and quietly replied, "I can't; I'm hurt." Mother carefully looked at her sisters and then whispered, "Fine, then go sit in the pickup until we are done." Then she gave me the look. I climbed into the pickup and contemplated my eventual demise.

A short time later, Mother's pail was full, and she came over to the pickup to dump it into one of the five-gallon buckets in the pickup bed. She looked at me with eyes narrowed, and told me to show her where I had hurt myself. I turned around and attempted to lift my white t-shirt, which was now stuck to my back. Unbeknownst to me (but known to Mother at this point), there was a lot of blood. It looked quite vivid against the white t-shirt. At this point, Mother was yelling at me for not telling her I was badly hurt. Like I was going to violate Rule #247—*never air family business in public!* I mean, there are rules, and there are RULES.

Anyway, cherry picking was over for the day. Mother had a reason to get rid of her sisters. She exacted her revenge by liberally dousing my back with an entire bottle of methylate ointment. I think at that point I would rather have faced the snake again.

Surprise

And there we were (same day, Mom's side of story), busily picking cherries in the orchard. Two of my sisters came that morning to help harvest and take their share home with them. We brought ladders and step stools, ice cream buckets to pick them in, and milk pails to dump the cherries in to take home. It was a perfect day to be outdoors. The children were asked to pick the lower branches. The rest of us picked the upper branches.

After a couple hours of this, Son #1 had his fill of cherries and wandered off. He climbed an ash tree situated along a pasture dam about a football field's length away from us. I did not notice. The rest of us were busy picking cherries off three huge trees. We were in work mode on the ladders.

Daughter noticed his return. They had a hushed conversation. They understood the family rule: nothing personal was to be revealed to those outside the immediate family. She then quietly informed me, "Mom, he fell out of the tree." I glanced over, saw no limbs hanging crookedly, nothing looking damaged, and told him to get busy picking cherries. A bit later, Daughter insistently whispered, "Mom, he is hurt. He cannot pick cherries." I disgustedly replied, "We are almost finished. Son, you go sit in the pickup until we are done."

After loading up the ladders and step stools, the pails of cherries, and making sure the sisters had everything picked up as well, I went to get into the pickup. Daughter quite forcefully insisted that I look at Son's back. I went to the passenger side of the pickup. Lifting up his shirt, I saw nothing but red. Scrapes, gouges, and an overall rash were gently oozing red fluids. Suddenly, cherry picking was over. I rushed Son home and took care of the situation. Then I asked how and why he fell out of that tree. He was an experienced tree climber, and the tree was not even that tall.

Son explained that as he was gaining some altitude, he unexpectedly came face to face with a huge bull snake that was sunning itself on a larger branch. He surprised it. It raised its head and surprised him mightily. In his panicky attempt to escape, he just let go and plunged downward. He was in the part of the tree that hung out over the dam. Instead of a ten foot fall through the tree branches, it was more of a ten foot fall through gouging tree branches and a twenty foot slide down the face of the dam.

I could not believe he did not tell me the story right away. He was raised to be tough. He refused to cry. But he was one hurting unit. I learned empathy that day. I also learned to put the welfare of my children more to the forefront of my priorities. It took many more years of training to be able to put them first.

Use Caution (Daughter's Tale)

Caution labels are stuck to everything. They are everywhere you look. Safety and fear have become the primary motivators for many people and determine how they approach life. We definitely grew up understanding that it was important to not get hurt and to think things through. It was never quite enough to overcome the tiny thread of "don't give a damn" that flows through all our veins. Despite my parents' best efforts, my brothers and I found plenty of opportunities to throw caution to the wind. We never really saw it as that, however. It was simply a challenge to overcome, an adventure to undertake, or a problem to solve.

I am truly surprised that we did not experience more broken bones in our youth. By age five, I was climbing a three-story cottonwood tree to plant a self-made flag at the top. We would climb to the top of our one-and-a-half story Quonset hut to slide down the side of it into the snow. Sure, there were items lined along the bottom, such as disks and boards with bolts sticking out, but snow is a soft cushion, right? We jumped out of the barn's two-story haymow into hard square hay bales or wagons of corn. Falling correctly is a valuable skill to develop. This came in handy when we built snow jumps that would fling us over ten feet into the air while sledding. The unspoken rule was no one said anything about this stuff later to the parents. All in all, we managed to have a great time without internet, television, or gaming systems.

Lawn darts were a huge part of our childhood. It is crazy to think of how many hours we spent flinging five-pound, lead-tipped, flying apparatuses at each other. This is where I learned what Russian roulette is and that I was not the wussiest of the siblings. We had a different bent on "Olly olly oxen free." One person on each side of the house would fling a lawn dart over the roof toward the other side. We had only a couple seconds to locate the incoming missile and get out of its path. I would like to say that age and wisdom has changed how much fun this game would be, but I would be lying. I would play it today.

One day, we were tired of trudging up the long, steep, snow-covered hills and wanted to find a better way to sled. Our amazing innovative process led us to tie a large inflated tractor inner tube behind the '56 Chevy and pull it down the road. Ross and I sat in the inner tube behind the car eating snow while Rick took the wheel. We deemed this idea a huge success until gravity came into play. While going around a sharp turn, we were reminded that while the car may take the proper route directly, the tube must swing all the way around the corner—something we knew but failed to properly assess the consequences.

After the rope wrapped around a small tree in the ditch, I ended up flung cartoon-form into a snow bank. When I crawled out, you could see the exact pattern in the snow of my landing, which was hilarious and actually pretty cool. Ross ended up getting his head knocked into a small sapling. I am not sure he found the experience as amusing, if he remembers it at all. What is a mild concussion in the scheme of things compared to a fun-filled adventure? We may have used a little more caution, at least for the rest of that day.

Caught Up (Daughter's Tale)

We did not spend much time on planned adventures during our childhood. There was way too much work to be done in such a short period of time. I got pretty good at taking advantage of moments, which has been a useful skillset throughout my life. Utilizing brief interludes was also how I learned to fish.

The first thing of consequence that I remember snaring was by far the largest. My two brothers and I were out at a little cow pond with muddy, murky water. The only things swimming in there were bullheads. Growing up with these as your primary exposure to fish is something that can take years to overcome, and it did. Rick was trying to teach me to cast successfully and gain some distance. I had not quite learned the perfect moment to push the release button down while throwing the line. During one cast, I could not see where the line ended up. I turned around to ask and discovered that I had caught over a hundred pounds of sibling. He did not stand near me after that.

The second fishing journey that stands out to me was with Ross in Kansas. We took a couple of fishing poles to a little pond full of downed trees. Fighting my line out of yet another snag led to the loss of my hook. We had been out there for over an hour without much luck beyond tree fish. Still young to the sport, I needed my brother to put another hook on my line and used his pole in the interim. One cast out and I snagged a ten-pound bass. It was a phenomenal moment for me. This was the first real catch of my life, beyond mud trawlers. Ross pulled the fish off the hook, and I threw out one more cast while he finished up with my pole. Almost immediately, I reeled in a five-pound bass. This day had become much more exciting!

Ross gave me back my fixed pole but was a little disgruntled to have yet to catch anything, especially considering his little sister had just pulled in two large ones without much effort. We stayed another two hours that went just like the first hour. Stick fish after tree snag after stick fish. I was still on cloud nine, though. I do not think that he forgave me for pulling in the big catch with his pole until the end of the night.

We were playing the card game, Pitch, as a team and losing badly. Caught up in the competition of the moment and desperate to win, we "shot the moon." Ross had only the ace and two of hearts, definitely not a great start to winning the entire hand. My luck that day held, however, and we conquered in a burst of greatness that I have yet to match at the card table.

The Seven Salad Summer

And there we were, facing our weekly meal of "beefsteak," again. Smothering it in onions did not help. No amount of mustard or ketchup could disguise its true identity—liver. How had it come to this?

Agriculture prospered in the early 1980s. Prices were good. Real estate values were rising. People had money to spend on new machinery and expansion. Hubby used to brag that he would never buy land unless it joined his. That philosophy cost him dearly when the next-door neighbors decided to sell. First, he added a big block of pastureland to the north side. Then he added farmland to the south and east sides. That real estate was not cheap.

Within the year, runaway inflation sent interest rates soaring to unheard of levels, as high as 18%. To say we were over-extended was an understatement. The next spring, we obtained an operating loan to stock the north pasture with feeder calves (yearlings) and to plant the crops. The plan was to retire the debt as we sold the cattle and harvested and sold the crops.

Less than a month after we signed that sizeable operating note, our bank failed. That is when we learned the FDIC has two faces: the faithful protector of assets and the relentless persecutor of those holding outstanding loans. To our astonishment, those notes we signed as due in one year became payable on demand the instant the bank's assets were seized by the FDIC.

Anything we sold, any revenue that came in, had FDIC's name on it and went to pay off the outstanding, now overdue, note. We were left with nothing to buy groceries, pay utility bills, or for local merchants' bills. Making repairs was not an option. It was a tough time to be in agriculture for us.

To compound the problem, our fat steer we had saved to butcher and eat became lonely, went off feed, then foundered. We found him feet upward just days before he was scheduled to be slaughtered. That left us scrounging in the bottom of the deep freeze for old packages of meat. Only stale fish, neck bones, soup bones, oxtail and organ meats were left. No beef steak. No ground beef.

I decided we could not continue to live like this and enrolled in college classes. I needed my degree to get a good-paying teaching position. The required physical exam for enrollment revealed my severely anemic condition. Ironically, the medical doctor advised eating organ meats to rebuild my hemoglobin.

As the children were quite young, we told them we were having "beefsteak" every time we had liver. Eventually they caught on. It was old, freezer-burned and unappetizing. One day, I faced open rebellion. They refused to let me even cook a package of "beefsteak." I succumbed to the pressure, opened the package, and carried it outside to feed to the farm cats. They came running. Treat time! When they reached the raw liver they stopped, sniffed it, turned around and walked away. "See," the kids chorused, "even the cats refuse to eat it!" And refuse it they did, at least initially. It eventually disappeared.

We lived out of the garden after that. It became known as "the summer of seven salads," per meal.

A Time to Plant

And there we were, the summer of 1985, slaving away in our 4-H garden. We remember Who planted the first garden, on the third day. Gardening is good for the soul. It is a reciprocal relationship. We do our part. He does the rest.

We can learn so much about life by planting and nurturing. Gardening develops character, teaches the fragility of life, and demonstrates the beauty of aging. Some of our best family-bonding times came while gardening. 4-H projects required careful planning, exact plotting, and partnership. As project leaders, parents reviewed, reminded, and reaped the harvest.

Our particular plan required the "junior" partners to plant, cultivate, weed, and water. They learned to select specimens for exhibits, display produce for profit, and deliver orders promptly. "Senior" partners were responsible for canning, freezing, or preserving any leftover produce. Not to mention pie-baking. No one we knew went hungry during those years.

Special unforgettable moments like "listening to the corn grow," comparing "before, during, and after" photos, and taking trips to the Nebraska State Fair to demonstrate judging skills does build family unity. Putting the garden to bed for the winter completes the cycle and emphasizes the tenacity of life.

If we want something good, we have to look UP for it, instead of down. Many times, a beautiful and bountiful harvest depends upon a harmony of timing versus aging. It can be a treasured time or a time of unrealized expectations. Sometimes our "harvests" are completely unexpected. Gardening is good for the soul.

Three Sides

And there we were, starting out small. It started with a small triangle, an irregular patch of ground formed by the irrigation head, the cornrows, and the access road. It was a nice spot to run in some early garden, beans, and tomatoes.

The ground was rich, the water easy to get flowing, the garden easy to get growing. The next year, we added a couple rows of potatoes to the long side of the triangle and planted two rows of sweet corn, instead of field corn. It was starting to look like a real garden.

The third year, we had to add another four rows for melons, and rearranged the plot. We added carrots, beets, kohlrabi, cucumbers, and whatever else looked good. The area to be weeded had grown exponentially.

By that time, my children were old enough to be in 4-H and logically chose gardening as a project. They were already helping with the weeding, watering, and harvesting. They started planning the plot and keeping records. When it came time to select fair exhibits, my fun started. In the search for the "perfect" produce, they brought tons of veggies to the house. I had to can, freeze, or refrigerate the "rejects." It was a tough job to be doing all that during Valley County Fair week.

The children did so well with their gardening exhibits that they were selected for State Fair. What a major disappointment to discover that veggies in their prime in late July were pretty much done in September, offering limited choices for State Fair exhibits.

The following year, they decided to plan for State Fair exhibits. This meant a "July" garden and a "September" garden—two plantings of most things. It was double the work for Mom, who was trying to put up the produce and was running out of room to store it. We got a second refrigerator, bought more canning jars, and built fancy shelves in the basement to store the canned goods. All of those purple ribbons and State Fair premiums kept the children focused and motivated.

When they added their marketing and management plan, "Gardening for Profit," the situation mushroomed. They started taking orders from people, picking produce, and delivering. Their own private "farmer's market" flourished. They started planting the sweet corn in the field. That meant going out in the dewy, dripping cornfield and picking bushels of sweet corn early in the morning, making deliveries before noon, and taking care of our own share in the afternoons. They ended up selling pickup loads, packed in special boxes with accurate "ear" counts, to Cetak's Market. Besides those sold as retail, employees there ordered bushels for themselves. That initial little "triangle" transformed into a thriving business that carried my children through high school.

The Day the Dream Died

And here I am, emptying out my files, busily filling my car with my teaching materials. This is the year, 1989, that I must leave this learning place. When the children ask me why, I merely say, "It's time." They have no way of knowing how hard it is to not be here to see the wonder of knowledge, newly clear, as it lights their eyes. To see that special shine and feel that new-found accompanying pride makes this decision painful.

But leave I must, to answer the call of other claims. I empty my room of books and boxes. I will wrap them up with memories and whisper a sad goodbye to the part of my heart I leave behind. I will miss them.

My memory moves in slow motion today. Like a camera that slowly pans across the scene, it lingers on the moments that marked changes in my life, changes that seemed bearable when they came, yet became turning points for my life. Little we know when a moment occurs how it may alter the course of our days. The time moves so fast that the moment has passed before we realize just what it might mean. We only learn later, when we play it again in our memory. It becomes a shallow ribbon of sadness.

Judging (Son #1's Tale)

And there I was, in Boelus, Nebraska, participating in a livestock judging contest. A senior in high school later that summer, I had my own wheels and, as a budding young man, made my own decisions. Since we finished the judging competition early in the day, I decided to surprise my grandparents with a visit. We lived an hour away. I was unfamiliar with the backroads in the area. It was before the era of cellphones, MapQuest, and GPS. I asked around to find the best route to get there. Boelus was in the Middle Loup River valley. My grandparents lived on the South Loup River.

One bystander suggested taking a dirt road out of town, following it until I reached the power line road, turning left and continuing south until I crossed the South Loup River, then turning right toward Ravenna. As we visualized the route, he asked, "Just who are your grandparents?" I told him and asked if he knew them. "Oh, yes," he drawled and chuckled knowingly, "my boys used to chase those girls. Never could catch them though. Which one of the girls is your mother?" Then he laughed and told me how he knew my family:

"One year, hay was short, and your Grandpa leased my field of alfalfa. He baled it into small square bales weighing seventy-five to eighty pounds. He sent the "Hot Chicks Hay Crew" over with a tractor pulling two hayracks. My boys, initially uninterested in helping pick up bales, became instantly adamant about helping those sun-tanned, attractive girls dressed in halter tops, jeans, and boots.

The girls graciously offered to let the guys stack the bales on the hayrack while they picked them up and threw them onto the rack. The guys insisted on picking up the bales, and letting the girls stack them on the hayrack. Yep, they were fresh and frisky. They started out throwing the bales onto the hayrack. Wearily, they began just setting them on the corner of the hayrack. Finally, they just started heading the bales in that direction and letting the girls pull the bales up onto the hayrack.

At that point, one of the girls decided, "Enough of this! You guys stack the bales on the hayrack and let us throw them up to you." They were used to doing it. They made it look easy. Supper at my house was very quiet that night. My boys were sunburned, exhausted, with aching muscles, and shamed faces."

His boys could not keep up with "those Charron girls." Very few can. No shame in that. No judging! They set the bar high. It is part of their lasting legacy. I know first-hand just how tough and talented they are.

Silence is not Golden

How did she get that black eye? If people noticed and wondered, they did not ask. Even when she went to work teaching inquisitive youngsters amidst a staff of mandated reporters of abuse, no one asked. This removed any hope she may have harbored for help. Not covering that shiner, not concealing it with makeup, not hiding it in any way was her silent cry for help. None came that day.

… and there I was, living the nightmare of domestic abuse. I had only known my husband for five months before we married. That was not long enough to expose the red flags, at least not to me. Because we attended many school functions and community events, or went to movies, we were seldom alone while engaged.

That specific situation made entering into marriage with no sexual experience an easy accomplishment. The real difficulties began on our wedding night. I planned the wedding. He planned the honeymoon. We had an evening reception, and then left for a "surprise" destination. This turned out to be a three-hour drive to a town hosting an annual celebration. Having no reservations meant the only room available had no air conditioning. It was a hot, sultry, early summer night. Too late I learned: *Do not marry someone if you cannot or should not follow their leadership.*

This first night together turned out to be disastrous for the process of establishing intimacy. Both of us were used to sleeping alone. Neither of us understood intimacy or true selflessness. How did this eventually lead to bruises and black eyes? Let us back up a bit.

Unless someone experienced in relationships and marriage is very frank with you, it is difficult to understand how much a marriage partner will impact your life in every aspect. First, it will impact you spiritually. It will affect the core of your very being. I actually had someone there for me, unexpectedly offering advice and counsel, before I said, "I do."

An older lady from the neighborhood who knew my future husband and his family well arranged a meeting with me. She spoke of pitfalls and related the certain consequences of "yoking" with someone unschooled in shared Christian beliefs and lacking faith. To illustrate, she likened it to a person with a red heart uniting with someone possessing a black heart, or a pink heart. She explained that events would nibble away at the red heart, leaving it ragged around the edges, with a bite taken out here, a shredded part there, until the red heart would not merely ooze, but would bleed, and eventually drain dry. She stopped by more than once to visit with me about my intentions. I heard her words. I felt her angst. I sensed her consternation. I downplayed the importance of her message.

As a young new fiancée, I judged this self-appointed messenger to be a crazy old lady embittered by an unhappy and unfulfilling marriage. I chose not to change my intentions to marry a non-believer. After all, we were planning a church wedding. It would be fine. My fiancé seemed open to change.

After we married, the roadblocks were many, from both of us. The scars grew, in each of us. I vaguely remembered the warnings from my earnest messenger but persevered on my path. Eventually, I realized that marrying an unbeliever did impact me spiritually. The health of my eternity was at stake.

I felt it was too late to be wise with my choices. I was stuck. It also impacted me emotionally. I wished I had married someone who would encourage me, be kind to me, and try to understand me. I needed someone to listen when I was struggling with a decision or to share the burden of shaping the marriage. I learned that any person who is uncaring about the other's feelings and self-esteem is selfish and should be left behind. A spouse can foster or cripple emotional health.

How about that black eye? I can now say with certainty that the choice of a spouse will affect you physically. It is vitally important to know if that person you chose will help provide for basic needs or if you will have to carry that burden alone. My husband jokingly said, "My job is to create the bills; your job is to pay them." It was not funny when it became our reality. It was frustrating and stressful.

A partner who will not care for the marriage will not care for your body or treat you with respect. Little outbursts, snippets of ridicule, and open insults will eventually lead to towering rages, unbridled verbal attacks, and punches to the face. I now knew this first-hand. When he split my face open just below my right eye with his wedding ring, I knew I was in mortal danger. Did I leave? No. In a calmer moment, I asked him to remove his wedding ring and put it away for safekeeping. The occasional black eyes continued, for no foreseeable reason, unpredictable and indefensible.

I began to realize why that crazy old lady appeared unstable. Living in this madhouse of volatile emotions will impact you mentally. Will your mate help you manage stress, or are you on your own? Will he value your opinions or disregard your feelings? Will he validate or repudiate? I ended up in a mental institution because he kept telling me I was crazy. I was not crazy. Maybe a bit neurotic, but I was not crazy. I was experiencing nearly continuous panic attacks because I could no longer keep everything under control. Our life was coming apart at the seams. My "red" heart was being drained dry. The neighbor lady's predictions were materializing as promised.

Meanwhile I had allowed the deteriorating situation to affect my other relationships. I was secretive and never shared with others. This merely magnified the effects of the stressors. I lived the nightmare of being married to the wrong person. One afternoon, we were alone in my car as I gave him a lift back to the ranch. He threatened to beat me to death with a two-by-four. I put a lock on my bedroom door after that. I immediately developed an exit plan.

When I finally left the marriage and moved away from the ranch, I moved into town. The entire community was understandably shocked. I hid the warning signs from most. Domestic violence is perpetuated by silence. Shame and fear kept me silent.

I realized how accomplished I had become at secrecy after I joined the morning ladies group that met weekdays in the back room of the local coffee shop. One of my neighbors had reached out to me, invited me to attend with her just to get me out of the house and back into civilization. That first week, I walked in and overheard a local businessman's wife sitting at the head of the table gossiping about the latest item, my impending divorce. The conversation did not stop at my entrance because most of the gossipers did not recognize me as the subject of the conversation. When they caught on, a most awkward silence ensued. I eased the moment by agreeing that it was a surprising development. Life went on. I became a valued member of the group. Most members did not gossip, but helped others in need. I re-entered community events with their support and assistance.

Why did I stay in that marriage so long? There is a payback from helping someone improve or better their life. That was my goal. The uplifting has to be mutual, however, or it annihilates self-worth. It expends good energy on others. I left nothing for myself. That month I spent in the "nut hut" let me recharge, rethink, and redefine. After I regrouped, I left. Sometimes the smallest step in the right direction becomes the biggest step of your life. **BREAK THE SILENCE.**

> Sometimes the smallest step in the right direction becomes the biggest step of your life.

Rivers and Rocks

And here I am, searching for self. Wherever I go, love will find a home in my heart. That is my blessing. I am to let that love shine. Perhaps I am one of the gatekeepers of this world, here to let others see the truth through my actions, to see hope and forgiveness, love instead of judgment. Love changes us, opens us up. Love sees through the heart, not the eyes.

I see myself as a complex maverick that can be flippant, friendly, insightful, brainy, decisive, sometimes hot-tempered, and always intense. I admit these faults while laying down the truth as I see it. I continue to be a generous and caring person seeking acceptance for myself and others and condemning injustices.

I seldom try to seek revenge. I will speak out when I see injustices occur. I try to turn personal injustices over to God and let Him take care of them. He will make things right. Whenever we try to get even, we just get in the way of God's working in that person's life.

Our lives are like rivers. The rocks and boulders in it are our difficulties. The water is our spirituality. The more water there is flowing, the smoother the ride. (Up to a point; sometimes floods occur.)

I have vowed that my life can never again be allowed to fall into a pattern where I just let it pull me along. If I do, it dashes me against the rocks of reality when I am least prepared, and crushes me.

I have learned that we have at least two choices. We can let life swamp us, or we can paddle with it, trying to see the rocks ahead.

I want to get to know the stranger that lives inside of me. If ever a person needs her own space, it's me—a financially independent, headstrong woman who, it seems, can be loved only in small doses. I am a real character, a piece of work, but a godsend to those needing help. Like my favorite flower, the rose, I have a beautiful soul.

CHAPTER FOUR:
The Road to Independence

Open to Interpretation

M R DUCKS.	Them are ducks.
M R NOT DUCKS.	Them are not ducks.
O S M R.	Oh, yes, them are.
C M WANGS.	See them wings.
L I B.	Well, I'll be.
M R DUCKS.	Them are ducks.

Breaking the Ice

And there we were, on needles and pins, hoping for the best as our new toastmaster gave her very first speech at Loup Valley Toastmasters. It was her icebreaker:

Let me formally introduce myself to you by telling you something about my life and how I have lived it. I have done many things in my *thirty-three* years of life. I chose to walk down the road of life searching for freedom and fighting for my independence. That path has included several detours, many commonly shared by other women. I would like to share glimpses of my childhood and its contributing factors, my adult life with its continuing trends, and my new life with its opportunities and its challenges for growth.

I spent all but the past year of my life on working ranches within an eighty mile radius of Ord, Nebraska. I like to tell my children that I was born on a horse. My earliest memories include my own special Welsh pony, Sandy.

My first eleven years were spent on a Platte Valley farm north of Central City, Nebraska. By the time I was four years old, I was breaking Shetlands to drive on a pony cart, or to ride—many of them for other people. Soon after, I began working in the hayfield, as well as helping with calving and feeding the Angus cow herd. By my twelfth birthday, when my folks moved to their Ravenna ranch, I was a full time hired hand and could operate almost any piece of equipment on the ranch.

My parents insisted that anything worth doing was worth doing well. It was easier to do something right the first time than to explain why I did not, or to suffer the harsh consequences. I learned to strive for perfection and excellence.

A family maxim—*When everything seems to be going right, it means you are probably overlooking something*—taught me the need for constant vigilance, to never relax. This became a way of life for me, a way to cope with the stifling lifestyle, the constant domination, the stress of living in a small three-bedroom house with eight other siblings and two parents.

We played as hard as we worked. Actually, we had very little unstructured free time. We played basketball, volleyball, and softball as a family, since we had enough for our own team. I have wondered if the folks planned it that way.

As the eldest, I became the designated ranch foreman and took ranch management very seriously. I worked on the ranch during my school years, summers, and for a full year before entering college. I was given no opportunities for social activities or personal relationships.

College life gave me more freedom, more opportunities for personal growth, more control of my own life. I went back to the ranch on weekends. I still let my work and activities control me.

Impatient to be independent, I started teaching school (on a provisional certificate) after two years of college. Soon after the first year of teaching, I married a local Sandhiller from near Brewster. I did manage to finish my formal education, earning my Bachelor's Degree over a decade later, while raising our three children. It was a long winding road to success.

During this time, I kept my horses and my personal herd of cattle. I continued ranching and breaking quarter horses for people. For self-fulfillment, I taught physical education, music, elementary education, Sunday school, and vacation Bible school in Loup, Blaine, Garfield, Greeley, and Valley Counties.

To keep busy, I learned how to garden, can, and freeze vegetables and fruit, do needlework, quilting, and woodcrafts. I filled my home with handmade quilts and embroidered pieces. I crafted handmade toys and built rocking horses. For many years, I gave handmade Christmas presents and "goodie" boxes. My idea of resting was to change activities.

I still felt manipulated, controlled, and stifled. To escape this, I joined and led many church, educational, and civic organizations. They included the Mid-Nebraska Reading Council, Valley County Home Extension Council, Wranglers 4-H Club (I was a leader), and Ord Music Boosters. I ended up a member of the AATP—American Association of Tired Persons.

One of life's ironies is that whatever we are, as we get older we become more so. For me, staying busy had become everything. I found I was a prisoner to the people and things I originally thought would free me. I ended up feeling like I had been run over by a fast-moving train. It was definitely time to make some changes in my life. I did just that.

Now I am walking down a different road, carrying a license to fly. I set three main goals for myself: to recognize and capitalize on the opportunities each day brings, to conquer the fears that control me, and to let go of the need to control others.

Today, I participate only in selected activities that I enjoy, like Toastmasters. I spend time developing special relationships with others. I no longer believe in "forever." I try to remember that all of us must think what we think, and live in our own time. Only then can our freedoms become real.

I have done many things in my life. I have accomplished much. Of more importance, though, are the things still left to do, the wonders still to experience, the lessons still to be learned. I continue to journey down life's road and to watch out for fast-moving trains sneaking up behind me.

In the Beginning

And there we were, at the local Toastmasters weekly meeting. Daughter came along as a visitor. She wrote the news article for the *Ord Quiz*, my usual task:

It looks like they have done it again! Who and what, you ask? Why, the Loup Valley Toastmasters have once again made professional Speechcraft more exciting than, well, dry toast.

During the October 5th theme meeting, "In the Beginning," the LVTMs went out of their way to take us back to the start of life, where everyone starts as an equal: wet, ugly, and naked. Table Topics Master, Dorrita Helm, bravely suggested "New Beginnings" for discussion and enticed intrepid club members and guests alike to share short accounts of their first moments.

Enthralling both seasoned toastmasters and those of "raw dough dialect" with stories of hope and horror on their "birth" day were: B. J. Axthelm, Alan Gross, Alma Bredthauer, Pat Turek, Art Duvall, and Linda Cone. Did the sharing of these experiences delight listeners, or just disturb? Well, you would have to ask special guests from the Thesaureans: Alma Bredthauer, Pat Turek, and Julie Spilinek.

Also providing entertainment was featured speaker, Bill French, with a six-minute account of his "beginnings," titled "Disaster on Christmas Eve," which was evaluated by Linda Cone and primary speaker, Zeke Lowery. Zeke shared an exciting ten minute review of the "Arch Over the Platte River Road" and was evaluated by B. J. Axthelm.

Spectators can expect more shenanigans this Thursday, October 12th, with topics surrounding "Columbus Day, The REST of the Story." Head breadburner, oops, Toastmaster, will be Judy Roggow. Chief Evaluator, Greg Jenson, will be calling team members, Art and Tanya Duvall. What will he be calling them? I guess that you will just have to come down to the Ord Drive-in at 12:00 noon on Thursday to find out!

— Kylie R. Cone, Reporter

Should We Act Our Age?

And here we are, in the midst of a roomful of people. It is break time. Everyone has a chance to kick back, relax, and enjoy the opportunity to share. We may have a close friend or two here. Others we know somewhat. And then there are those that are friends just "waiting to happen." We visit to pass the time.

Have you noticed, while visiting, how often we define ourselves by what we do, and then ask others, "What do you do?" "I'm retired," I answer. The response: "R-i-g-h-t ... You are too young to retire. What do you do?" My answer is, "I am retired and have been for nearly five years."

I have retired from my chosen professions, and from ranching and farming. I have relocated to the city and restructured many of my personal relationships. I have retired from civic and organizational boards, from nearly everything but life!

Retirement is a goal some of us look forward to and others dread. It may have been planned or totally unexpected. Retirement really is a new adventure.

Today, I will be sharing how I dealt with my first years of retirement. I will mention some retirement issues and suggest some possible solutions. I will continue to ask, "Should we act our age?"

Those who achieve the most in this world are those who make the best use of their time. What do you do? "Choosing the best task to do—and doing it the right way—that's effectiveness," according to Alan Lakein, who wrote *How to Get Control of Your Time and Your Life.*

To be effective, we need to plan retirement as carefully as our careers. Retirement always takes getting used to, especially the emotional turmoil, which is largely unplanned.

First of all, we may no longer have a job that identifies us. Anyone whose individual sense of self-worth springs from a particular job description may face difficult times. We need to figure out who we really are before we retire, then learn to enjoy our time off. (Put that on the to-do-list!)

Most people have interests and passions that define who they are much more than their job descriptions, if only they would realize it.

To those who worry that they will stop contributing and just roll over and die, I have two things to say:

1. You have contributed enough already.
2. You do not have to stop contributing just because you have retired. You just do not have to give at the workplace.

We have not retired from life. We are now teaching inspiration. We can broaden our expertise by first becoming clear about the direction we wish to go, then learning to reach for what we may have been putting off until later in life.

Mona Moon, a motivational speaker, says, "If you really get clear about what you want, even if you do not know how you are going to get it, things come to you." I am waiting; I am waiting! I had a fortune cookie this year that said, "All things will come to you." I was so excited, thinking, "Yes, this is it!" Well, it was a memorable week. Many things happened. Some pretty wonderful things; some situations I could have lived without. Then I realized "all things" does not mean "only good things."

A second major retirement issue is having no set schedule and needing to create one. Even if you have been a good planner, one of the great luxuries of retirement is trying out different schedules to see which one really works for you. We can develop a routine and then quickly change it if it gets stale. We can do something every day, just not always at the same time. I tend to vary my form of exercise, as well as the time of day. I want to feel active but free to come and go as I please. After all, I am retired.

The changing relationships with those close to us are a third major issue. Suddenly, we need to learn to respect their space and not get in their way. They may not have our freedoms. We may find more "little things" to share and need to find a special sharing time.

Relating to people who still have jobs can be intimidating, especially if they do not understand why we chose to retire. We are as important and interesting as we ever were. In fact, if we keep active and continue to explore new things, we are probably more interesting than we were before. Leaving our job is a big deal, but it is not the end of the world. "The best thing about getting older is that you gain sincerity," says Tommy Smothers. "Once you learn to fake that, there's nothing you can't do."

We need to learn the joy of keeping our options open; spend our time on our true passions, but also consider adding new things to the mix. Learn to keep our life fresh and new. Education is a lifelong proposition. As our lawyer friend remarked, we never have time to learn everything, no matter how hard we try or how many mistakes we make.

Sometimes it pays to remind ourselves what we are missing. I have always found mandatory meetings boring and largely unproductive. I do not have to attend those meetings anymore. I am retired.

At our family reunion, we were celebrating my very active Grandma's 87th birthday. My children asked her, "How does it feel to be 87?" "Well, I still get around, but I'm not making any plans for the future," she answered. "Don't say that," Son responded. "Look at Marc Chagall. Marc did some of his best stained glass windows when he was in the 90s." "I don't do windows!" she replied smartly.

To those who continue to ask, "What do you do," I can reply that I am a "personal finance manager," another necessity of a retiree. Sticking to a budget is essential when we are retired. That does not mean giving up our passions, but often doing them "on the cheap." Properly investing available resources is increasingly important; otherwise, we can outlive our resources. My official title these days is CFO for the Porch Sitters of America.

Lastly, we can really learn how to communicate. But whatever we say, we can still expect the other person to hear something different. To clarify what I have tried to communicate today, I will quickly review.

I have discussed these retirement issues:

1. No longer having a job that identifies us.
2. Having no set schedule and creating a new schedule for our new life.
3. Changing relationships with those around us.
4. Relating to people who still have jobs.
5. Learning the joy of keeping our options open.
6. Living on less money.

Many of these ideas were adapted from John Mosedale, author of *The First Year: A Retirement Journal.*

How many here today think we should act our age? Show me by signaling "yes" (pause) or "no." I am constantly being told to act my age. Daughter shakes her head and summarizes what she sees. "Mom, you are in your 40s, look like you are in your 30s, think like you are in your 20s, and sometimes act like a teenager."

I believe that is not all bad. My own mother was old by the time she was thirty (not by my standards, but by hers). She thought she was too old to wear shorts or put on a bathing suit; too old to go square dancing anymore or smile at silly jokes; too old to throw snowballs and outrun the "enemy"; too old to play in the family softball games.

By her personal choices, she was choosing to be old. When we make the choice to keep a positive attitude, be enthusiastic, keep learning, and use our sense of humor, we stay young at heart. Ironically, young people who have not made this choice are already old.

My mother, at age sixty-five, is much younger than she was at thirty. She can laugh and have fun with the rest of us. I am still waiting for her to wear shorts or put on a bathing suit. Some things just never change.

My advice to those growing older:

• Do not act your age; learn to compensate.
• Do not lose your enthusiasm for life; keep growing and learning.
• Develop your sense of humor. You may need it.

George Burns, who knows about such things, says, "With a positive attitude and a little bit of luck, there's no reason you can't live to be 100. Once you've done that, you've really got it made because very few people die over 100."

I am still looking for my "new adventure." Whatever it is will be done on my own terms, as free of stress as possible. I will probably continue to write, to speak, to occasionally tutor, to learn new dances, and to do volunteer work. My mind will stay active as I fill my days with activities I enjoy. But I will leave plenty of time to "do nothing." I have been told we are successfully retired if we can do nothing and feel no guilt. I may have arrived!

Life Plan

And there we were, listening to our fearless leader presenting a seminar on life choices:

Our topic today is "How to Take Charge of Life Problems You Thought You Could Not Change." How do you feel, personally, about making some major changes? Are you ready for something different? Let us shake things up. (Everyone take a deep breath.)

Most people have difficulty coping with change. In today's world, change finds us. If we do not take charge of our own lives, change will take charge of us. Things happen!

Performing our job well is not really a defense. We still may need a different set of skills to meet the needs of the future. In the 1990s and beyond, life planning is a survival skill.

Do you avoid change, even if it may be beneficial? People who cannot face change may be in a state of "Inner Kill." Prime symptoms include:

- Always taking the safe route.
- Reacting instead of taking risks.
- Avoiding decisions.
- Daydreaming and talking, rather than taking action.

Inner kill is closely related to fatigue—from overwork in a pressure-filled life, or from underwork while not really participating in life. Three examples of *Inner kill* candidates are:

1. Middle-aged people juggling work, personal and financial responsibilities, aging parents, and growing children.

2. Early retirees who have unexpectedly or involuntarily been removed from the workforce. Without careers to define themselves, they may find themselves bewildered and unable to respond to life meaningfully.

3. Young adults just graduating who begin careers, then find themselves in a rut. They wonder how they ever got into it. They may have allowed events to control them.

Not many of us ever plan to fall into these categories. These are for "other people." However, our lives are apt to get "out of square." Unless we wish to remain misshapen polygons, we must face change.

We can start shaping our life the way we want it to be. Oh, we think we are the only person who is frightened when on unfamiliar territory. Not true! All the people we envy, the ones who seem so self-assured and unafraid, feel fear, too. Everybody does.

The real issue is not fear itself, but how we handle it. Those who cope best have learned to accept fear as a given and go from there. Waiting for shakiness to go away before we jump into the pool keeps us paralyzed.

The trick is not to get rid of fear but to be more confident in ourselves, so we can go forward despite it. We tell ourselves, "We'll handle it."

Every time we push out into the world and stretch our abilities, take new risks to get where we want to be, we are going to experience some fear.

We will feel it less, and feel better about ourselves, if we go out and do whatever it is we fear. Even if we fail, we are sure to be less scared next time around because no matter what went wrong, we are still breathing, right? Let's take a moment to check …

We begin to reshape our lives by taking the initiative and engaging life. This requires overcoming our fears of criticism, rejection, betrayal, failure, and even our fear of success. We must re-script ourselves to trust both our own judgment and that of others who can help us. If we can decide to change, instead of escape, we may grow personally and professionally.

Yet, we must be prepared to take risks. Calculated risks for positive change require excellent information. We must utilize our sources. So take stock. Assess your quality of life. Answer these three questions:

- Who am I, really?
- Why am I here?
- Where am I going?

Then courageously create a vision for yourself. Using these ten fundamental areas, explore: 1) time, 2) values, 3) vitality, 4) purpose, 5) career, 6) talents, 7) spirituality, 8) health, 9) relationships, and 10) money. What questions should you ask yourself?

It is difficult to take stock by yourself. Discuss the questions with the people who know you best. Then listen to their answers. After taking stock of current activities and setting priorities, you are equipped to decide the changes you want to make for a better future.

Choose four major goals to pursue for the next twelve months. They might include one for your personal life, one for your work, one for your relationships, and one for your finances. Jot them down quickly. Then ask yourself these key questions:

- Do the people who matter to me support me in this goal?
- Do I have enough time and enough money to accomplish this?
- Am I flexible and willing to sacrifice lower-priority items?

If the answers are consistently yes, tell others about your plan; increase your motivation. Then develop an action plan for each goal, with deadlines.

Break the plan down into small, measurable steps. Put a date on each step to track your progress. This action plan will put you on the road to meaningful and productive change.

To summarize, we can do anything we set our minds to do if we believe in ourselves and approach the task with positive expectation. The first step, and the most important step, is to believe it is possible. Do that, and you will have started your journey!

When we actually develop an action plan, we will be able to take charge of life problems we thought we could not change. We will start putting our life back "into square." We will cheerfully engage life, assess risks, and create a vision. We will better understand the answers to the questions, "Who am I?" "Why am I here?" and "Where am I going?"

We will understand life planning for the present and beyond. We will survive. With practice, we will flourish.

Courage allows the successful person to fail
and to learn powerful lessons from the failure,
so that in the end,
it was not failure at all.

-Mayo Angelou

A Grain of Sand

And there we were, gathered at the Advent breakfast, preparing ourselves for Christmas. I was the featured keynote speaker. This was my message:

Which of these statements best describes you?

a. You are sensitive to others.
b. You know how to leave a great impression.
c. You are loved, accepted, and appreciated.
d. You are a grain of sand.

Welcome, all. It is wonderful to be among friends and family, to recognize familiar faces. My message today is designed to help us accept and appreciate ourselves and others.

We do not have to be born with an outgoing personality to leave a great impression on others. We simply have to understand two basic facets of human nature: First, people are quick to develop close relationships with those who seem similar to themselves. Second, people are more receptive when we treat them the way they want to be treated, not the way we wish to be treated.

Two people can seem to hit it off when they share thoughts, needs, opinions, and feelings. Taking the time to identify and respond to those needs works as a powerful motivator. Just be sensitive to others. Does this sound like something a grain of sand would do? No, a grain of sand constantly irritates.

Some time ago at a high school game, I was sitting among friends in the bleachers. Suddenly, fireworks of a sort exploded just behind me. The argument was about who would win the University of Nebraska at Lincoln's football game that weekend. It became nose-to-nose combat between longtime friends. Words flew, tempers raged. Threats were made. Bets were placed.

No one would believe the next time we saw these two characters they would be sitting together at the local coffee shop cheerfully discussing the chance for snow, upcoming hunting trips, or illegal immigrants. No sports contest, no matter how important, was going to break up this particular friendship. Never had, never would.

They have come to understand, through the years, that there are any number of things on which they will disagree. So they disagree, apparently getting some kind of perverse pleasure from it. But there are so many reasons they like each other that they are able to rise above the disagreeable periods.

When you disagree with someone and want to maintain a rapport without denying your own values, artful vagueness offers a way to respond without implying that either of you is wrong. Both parties' self-esteem is preserved. This is how it works:

Begin with the statement, "You know, I've been listening very carefully, and ..." Finish with, "You've got a point there ..." or "You may be right." Do not say you think they are incorrect. Artful vagueness defuses arguments, preserves goodwill, and allows you to present your own point of view at a more auspicious time, usually much later.

It is difficult to accept people who can be different from what we prefer them to be. They see life differently than we want them to see it. They laugh at different things. They handle problems in a different way and may even have different loyalties.

These differences may annoy us, especially this time of year when we are in the midst of holiday preparations. Someone may come to mind for you, even as I speak. There are some people who will always annoy us, simply because their personality clashes with ours.

Maybe we are messy; maybe they are neat. Maybe we are extroverts who process our thoughts by spewing them forth for all who want to listen, and for many who do not. Maybe we are introverts who process internally and wait for a quiet time to sit quietly, contentedly, and think things through.

Surprise! People used to really annoy me. Life has been much easier, much less complicated, less infuriating, since I have grasped that people will be who they are just because that is who they are. They really have no choice. Nor do I.

Difference is good. Every group, every family, every board, every committee needs people with different personalities, people who may annoy each other. We need the dreamers and the schemers, the creative types. We also need the practical people who say, "But are we covered by insurance when we do that?"

One of my favorite people, my youngest sister, is fond of volunteering, saying, "I can do that." Then she gets home, thinks things over, and says, "I can do that? How can I do that?" But she usually gets it done.

Organizations need people to discuss, compromise, and, yes, debate issues just to hammer out the best decision, much like an oyster needs to be irritated by a grain of sand in order to produce a pearl.

You have realized by now that this is not a talk about sports, politics, or religion. It is about kindly accepting differences in other people—differences we usually cannot do anything about—and, going one step further, learning to appreciate them.

My newest T-shirt reads, "I'm out of bed and dressed. What more do you want?" It was a gift from my favorite daughter. I am not a morning person, a "rise and shine and give God the glory" kind of person. I annoy people who are. I do not even want to talk until I have my glass of juice and a soft-boiled egg.

I may become alert around noon. I absolutely bloom during the evening hours, when my friends may be camping on their couches, watching television, or even trying to sleep. That is when I do my telephoning, my organizing, and become annoying.

I am convinced our behavior is somehow ingrained into our very being. To quote Henry David Thoreau: "If a man does not keep pace with his companions, perhaps it is because he hears a different drummer. Let him step to the music which he hears, however measured or far away."

There are many people whose drummer beats in double time. They survive and thrive on one speed, and that is fast, full speed ahead. They are high-powered people who work hard, play hard, and sometimes die young. But even if they do, they have crammed a lot of living into their lives. They would rather be a shooting star for five seconds than a lamp post for eternity. Other folks worry about these people and are always telling them to slow down. Instead, we can appreciate them.

When I lived on the ranch northeast of Ord, I could burn up the oil, or scatter gravel. When my son was very young, we hurried to town for parts. The work crew was waiting for them. As I darted across the road and zipped up the driveway, Son said, "Swo down, Mom, swo down!"

I smiled and glanced over at him, noticing he was white-faced and hanging on to the door. I slowed down, but his words became my family's message of caring, given to me whenever I needed to ease up a bit.

People have many ways of telling others to slow down. Of course, they usually tell them to slow down after they have talked them into serving on a committee, or delivering a speech, or helping fix up the church. They are sincere about getting this person to slow down. Sometimes, though, they just want you to sit on the couch with them. Be with them. Share with them.

You can tell the beat of someone's drummer as he or she walks down the street. Some people step out in march time, purposefully walking, almost running, to what we can only assume is an important destination. They are on a mission.

Others walk as if there is a waltz tune playing in their heads, gazing about, taking in the sights as they go. They may appear lost. The rest of us fall in between, sometimes marching, sometimes waltzing, sometimes skipping, and moving to the beat of our own drummer, peculiar though that may be.

As annoying as this may be when we try to walk with them or work with them, their way works for them. Differences are good.

71

My younger son is a true workaholic. His parents were excellent teachers. Never still, always planning or doing something, he stays busy from early morning until late at night. Some people just cannot seem to become a slug.

My daughter knows how to be still and listen better than anyone I have ever known. Yet, her quiet ways generate just as much, or more, productivity than those rushing around, who may be annoying her.

My older son likes to read and escape from the chaos and confusion of the world. His favorite day is "read in the bathtub day." He then returns to his realities completely focused and infused with energy. Three people. Three different personalities. Three different ways of doing things. Three sources of joy.

As I sift through sand here, sharing some personal insights, I hope to help us look at those people who may annoy us and see them in a new light. Appreciate them for the grain of sand they might be, or the pearl they may become if we give them time and love.

"Happiness," according to Adela Rogers St. John, "is a sort of atmosphere you can live in sometimes when you are lucky." Joy is a light that fills us with hope, faith, and love. Our smile lets an inner beauty come to the surface. Let us have our joy and appreciation for others show during this advent season.

We need that flaming extrovert. We need that somewhat disorganized genius. Messy people have interesting lives and the opportunities to "find" things unexpectedly.

No matter how successful we are or how good we think we are doing, we are going to annoy someone. Having positive expectations, and keeping those grains of sand in perspective, develops creativity. It encourages us to be our best.

In conclusion, people will be who they are because that is who they are. Are we still annoyed about that?

Let's review. Rather than be annoyed or irritated with others, remember:

- All of us have to be ourselves.
- Not all of us hear the same drummer.
- None of us sees things exactly the same way.
- Once in a while, we can agree to disagree.
- You and I can appreciate differences in others.
- Each of us may be that grain of sand helping to produce a pearl.
- Differences are not divisive. They are good.

We are not annoyed after all. We are sincerely appreciative. We are who we are, and we are never supposed to be who we are not. Let that be enough.

Secret Serendipity

And there we were, traipsing through the timber on an adventure together. Sometimes we need a place to just be, to feel ridiculously free, to look inside ourselves and see, a spot of secret serendipity. Her favorite place was beneath her special tree, nature's ideal spot for restoration and appreciating beauty. A lasting testament to her discovery, it will remain a precious memory.

As a confused and hurting youngster, she often escaped into the wilderness, following the deer trails, soaking up the solitude. When life became too much to bear, she sank down on her cottonwood log resting under an ash tree. She could see the river through the underbrush and hear its many moods. They varied nearly as much as hers and lent a sense of stability.

During adolescence, this special spot saved her sanity. She befriended the squirrels, the raucous blue jays, other scurrying wildlife, and the deer. They became her secret companions. She felt less lonely when they scampered past. They learned to trust her and be unafraid. She learned to trust her own instincts and became less afraid.

Struggling through her teenage years, she came to depend on the secret hideaway. She often disappeared for hours at a time, to the consternation of her parents. Nothing could entice her to reveal her special place of prayer.

If she craved uplifting, she climbed the branches and looked upon the world from her lofty perch in the deer blind. If she needed to relax, she stretched out upon the log and stared heavenward. If she needed to meditate, she bent her head in contemplation and looked inward. The calm introspection led to decisions, sometimes made in despair. She came to realize that nothing about life was really fair. She froze inside and appeared not to care.

After leaving home, she mentally returned to her secret lair. Her mind still seemed to work best in the open air. She struggled with her fears, her relationships, and spiritual growth, her heart laid bare. She held in her tears, not succumbing to despair. She felt crucified. Everything she tried became a snare. She became trapped in a life not her own. She stayed this way until her children were grown.

Finally deciding to carve a more fulfilling life, she left her many prisons behind. Unlocking the bars took persistence and time. She conquered her fears and left her troubles to time. She learned to forgive. She started learning how to live.

As a special treat for Christmas in 1994, she ushered her tumultuous twosome along the trails until they were there, in her special lair. They climbed the tree, sat on the log, rambled along the river, and glimpsed the beauty. They shattered the stillness with their giggles of glee. The sense of serendipity was not something they could see. But it was a very special sharing time for the three. They fit into her special spot of serendipity.

Weeds and Flowers

And here I was, wondering just where I fit into this life. Have you ever felt out of place, as if you just did not fit in, like a big, healthy dandelion in a lush green lawn? Did you then experience personal insecurity and anxiety, feel contempt from the ignorant or unknowing?

One of my favorite pastimes is working in the yard and garden. It is a marvelous stress reliever for those times in life when the unknowing express contempt for the insecure and appear ready to commit murder at every turn. Well, what would you do with that huge blooming dandelion in your yard? Yank it out by its roots? Sever it with a sharp blade? Spray it with a chemical that makes it curl up on itself, turn brown, and die? By a dandelion's definition, that is murder.

Dandelions were always the first flowers my children brought to me each spring. Shared gifts of love, carefully placed in a vase. These fresh dandelions were used to decorate the dining room table covered with fancy linen. Their magic brought peace to my heart.

Those first dandelions were soon followed by flowers from the garden and the yard. They were more beautiful, more fragrant, but never more special. To me, a dandelion is not just a weed. A weed may be a flower that happens to be blooming in the wrong place, like that dandelion in the lawn.

Sometimes life's circumstances make us appear to be dandelions when we want to be seen as flowers. This apparent injustice may make us feel sad, frustrated, or even unappreciated. If we are not recognized as a flower in life, we may become angry, bitter, or anxious. We fear the fate of the dandelion.

The magic of acceptance, understanding, and forgiveness allows us to bloom, to be seen as a flower, to be valued. Life seems to have a purpose. We fit in. Any experienced gardener knows the difference between weeds and flowers. Do you?

The Meanest Man I Ever Met

And here we are, practicing our "judging" skills. As a preliminary exercise, we are asked to be "members" of an award selection panel. We quickly jot down our nomination for the meanest person we know. What made this person memorable? How was our life changed?

OLD JULES is a classic written by Mari Sandoz. This is a book about the

74

meanest man Miss Sandoz ever met. He was unbelievably cruel to those around him. The book, *OLD JULES*, puts life's priorities in perspective while portraying the strengths of women confronted with this cruelty. Using this story as a backdrop, I will share my nominee's unforgettable qualities. This is a story about the meanest man I ever met, a man I call "HW," a man my brother calls "Harry," my sisters call "the Supreme Commander," my mother calls the "Warden," a man the neighbors never call.

The meanest man I ever met was—The Parent. Every child that survives childhood claims his/her parent was the very worst. There was no contest. Mine really was. The Parent's role—yes, this Parent's role—was to take raw innocent babies and turn them into independent-thinking survival machines. This person did it by repeatedly reducing each child to a blubbering bowl of bland bread pudding and then accusing them of having the backbone of a jellyfish.

No matter how correctly I tried to do something, I was told I could do better. My proud achievements were ridiculed and judged to be lacking. My well-considered reasons for actions taken were deemed unsatisfactory. My answers were usually ruled as incorrect. He scared the joy out of me. He insisted compromise was for weaklings. He often demonstrated the skills of one in a Mexican stand-off, stubbornness personified. He demanded I "act like a man."

The purported purpose was to teach me to have firm principles, strong beliefs, excellent problem-solving skills, never question an order, and show no fear. This person became the most important person in my life. Everyone else was compared to this man and found wanting.

Being the first born, an experimental model, I was the perfect goat. I refuse to share his nickname for me. He had many other names for me, too. This person was constantly correcting me, beating me with any available object, and never ran out of tortures—physical, emotional, spiritual, or psychological. I was more afraid of this man than of anything life required of me. School became a place to rest. Jobs became a playground of pleasure. Marriage to a comparative stranger appeared a heaven-sent opportunity for escape.

What was his secret? The Parent gave only two choices: do it his way or die. Now that is motivation. Not allowed to "leave home" until my twenty-first birthday, I left the very next day. I went straight to a job teaching school. I remember trying to tell this man "goodbye." He turned away, refusing to even acknowledge my leaving, and emotionlessly dismissed me from his life.

I thought I would never go home again, but I was wrong. I kept returning, trying to make things better, to become that perfect person capable of pleasing, finally able to get it right. Any later attempts at re-bonding, at nostalgia, yielded precious little. He taught my siblings to say, "We really missed you, but, oh, it was so good!"

After twenty more years of this self-inflicted hell, I could admit these efforts were futile, self-destructive, consuming, unloving. I became less frightened but was still in awe. Finally, I was able to begin trying to see things from his perspective.

Looking through his eyes, and then peering into his heart, I discovered a frightened, insecure, extremely unhappy man who tried to control his life with unending activities and could not stand to be alone with himself. This man was scared to die.

I realized he really did want me to be an independent-thinking survival machine. He thought I could do it if I learned how to be "a real man." As a man, he could not appreciate the fact that I could only hope to survive and enjoy life if I learned how to be "a real woman."

To my father, who tried to make a man out of me and failed miserably, a toast. To the woman I have become, I thank you, Dad.

A Return to Serendipity

And there we were, at a Toastmasters humorous speech contest.

Contestant #1:

"Tomb it making cern" (*"To whom it may concern"* in regular English), Utopia has a serpent! I am not referring to the cute little foot-long garter snake that likes to stretch out in the sun on the east side of my house. Nor am I referring to the much larger grass snake that hangs out in my back yard and continuously startles me by rapidly running for cover just as I am about to step on it with my bare feet. I am describing an imperfection, a defect, a fault, a blemish, an eyesore in my otherwise nearly perfect world.

By definition, *utopia* is a place of ideal perfection, sometimes an imaginary and indefinitely remote place. My utopia is the neighborhood on the Valley View Drive cul-de-sac in Ord. *Utopia has its serpent.* Without knowing something of the area I am describing, can you guess what form this serpent takes? Can you guess what most irritates some of the residents here? What issue here causes neighbors to request police inquiries, become experts on city ordinances, and engage in verbal shouting matches of disagreement? I will give you a few clues. (I hold up index cards with these letters on them.)

C   Can you think of something that just might be this significant, this consequential?

A   Are there situations on Valley View Drive that might incite this much passion, this much emotion?

M   Might there be a reason to get this involved?

P   Perhaps there is; perhaps there is not. It really depends on a person's perspective of the problem.

E   Enough already.

R   Review the clues.

S   Surely you have guessed it!

Yes, CAMPERS are the problem. Campers are this utopia's serpent. Recreational vehicles have invaded this otherwise beautiful area. They are parked on the street, in driveways, even on empty lots owned by Sack Lumber Company. They are everywhere. I tried to take a photo of my garden this summer. When the photograph was developed, it showed nice green foliage and vibrant flowers surrounded by, you guessed it, campers.

Campers, otherwise known as recreational vehicles, are …

Annoying. They particularly annoy one lady resident who relentlessly pursues avenues to alleviate the problem. If they are parked on the street for more than twenty-four hours, she calls the police so further action can be taken. If they are on vacant lots, she calls the owners or managers to request action. If they are known to belong to neighbors, she personally addresses the issue because, you see, campers are …

Magnetic. They attract other campers. If one person parks a camper somewhere, others feel they can, too. We have campers parked behind campers. We have campers parked across the street from other campers, creating traffic bottlenecks and a potential hazard to playing children. Some campers even migrated up here from other areas. It almost seems that campers are …

Permanent. Seemingly, despite the best efforts of all interested camper eliminators, campers are permanent. They are not seasonal menaces any more. They stay here all year long. They just shift positions at times, giving us false hope of disappearance. Campers are …

Eyesores. They ruin an uninterrupted view of our backdrop—scenic hills dotted with cedars and leafy trees. Who wants to look out the window and see a camper? Many efforts are made to find a different home for the camper parked next to my garden. The owner insists it is not an eyesore, that it is a beautiful, well-kept camper, forgetting that it cannot be seen through.

In this owner's defense, he pointed out my garden, which is also on this empty lot. I hope he did not mean that my garden was an eyesore to him. At the time, it was filled with beautiful blooming flowers and vines filled with vegetables. A garden does not effectively reduce vision. It enhances it. Campers do …

Reduce vision. You cannot go over them, you cannot go under them, and you cannot go through them. You can only go around them, which can be dangerous for walkers, children, and vehicles. Campers steal our …

Serendipity. They create irritations and upsets in our remote, nearly perfect little world on Valley View Drive. They become targets of conflict between the neighbors.

Campers are annoying, magnetic, permanent eyesores that reduce vision and steal our serendipity. What can we do with this unwelcome serpent?

We can COMPROMISE on the issues. We can be aware of the needs and feelings of all concerned. We can AGREE to accept the presence of other's personal property. We can MANAGE to find good things to say and better ways to say them. PROBLEMS, once major, then become less threatening. Working together EARNS respect, promotes trust, and builds community pride, which becomes its own REWARD. So the serpent slithers off. SERENDIPITY returns.

It is almost autumn. The flowers in my garden are fading, the vegetables are harvested, the ground cleared and ready for another season. The campers remain, even after advertising the one for sale on the vacant lot, to the owner's surprise!

What really happened here this summer was an attitude adjustment, a renewed effort to enjoy one another, a return to utopia, because serpents like this are of our own making and can be undone, with caring, trust, and cooperation. This little "serpent" concerning campers on Valley View Drive disappeared, but my garter snake just got a little longer. It is part of my own special serendipity.

Color Life Beautiful

And there we were, with a blank piece of paper and a box of crayons. We were invited to express ourselves and our feelings. There would not be a "show and tell" session to follow. I was the workshop leader. This is the gist of my presentation:

Is your life a rain cloud, or is it a rainbow of color? Listen to yourself sometime. Listen to your speaking voice. It expresses color, emotional color. Your voice coloring conveys feelings. The emotions and vocal colorings you express can arouse similar emotions in others. Just watch international contest speaker, Jim Otto, as he presents. Connecting, as this master speaker does, must be a giving and receiving ability. To fully connect with others, emotions must be recognized and understood. Feelings have faces, colors, sounds, and smells.

Today, I will briefly touch on our feelings. It may take both sides of the paper, but plan space for these eight emotions: fear, frustration, loneliness, pride, happiness, joy, love, and forgiveness. Sketch as we go. This is a doodler's paradise.

I have provided crayons to add color to our emotions. I will add sounds and mention specific smells or associations I attribute to each emotion. You will most likely have other reactions. Let us begin by using this simple color wheel. (Set up display of color wheel.)

If emotions are not recognizable or are allowed to run together, they form the neutral color gray. A gray life may appear as a rain cloud, dampening emotions. If you have ever experienced depression, you know something happened to your world. All the bright colors faded away. (Put away color wheel chart.)

Can you remember the day the music died in your life, the day you stared at the face of fear? Of hurt? Of anxiety? What did it look like? Show me. Sketch it. Color it in. (pause) Sometimes it is not the song that makes us emotional. It is the people and things that come to mind when we hear the music.

I remember the day my music died. It was a Friday morning, April 29, 1989. My world as I knew it changed forever. I walked out of my classroom knowing I would not be able to return any time soon. I damaged my voice and was no longer able to continue teaching my beloved fourth graders. At the time, teaching was my world.

(Display picture of fear.) It felt like this song by Dwight Yokum, *There Should Be Music*. (Play the song as sketching is being completed.) Life was not just a rain cloud. It was a thunderstorm, with frightening flashes of lightning. (Put away display picture of fear.)

This anxious time was immediately followed by frustration. I could not understand what was happening to me, or why it was happening. It seemed like I was at the bottom of the circle, a definite violet. What does frustration's face look like? How does it sound? (pause) Frustration is not pretty. It really stinks. (Display picture of frustration.)

When something is destroyed, or a dream is lost, it must be replaced with something new. I chose to "reinvent" myself. I left my abusive marriage, the ranch, and my adored horses. I began to experience freedom. I could take the clothespin off my nose and breathe again. Rebirth is reflected in the chorus of the song "It's Independence Day," sung here by Martina McBride. (Put away display picture of frustration.)

Hand in hand with freedom came loneliness. I had left so much behind. I was uncertain who my "real friends" were. Even my children's loyalties were understandably divided. Draw your version of "lonely's" face.

My face of loneliness is long, plain, and painful to see in the mirror. What color is loneliness? I chose variations of blue. The music of loneliness has a compelling, throbbing beat. Today, I chose the song *I Was Just Standing*, another Dwight Yokum tune. (Display picture of loneliness as it is playing.)

Inaction was never my thing. I used this time to make new friends, play recreational sports, and rededicate myself to God and family. I began coming to Toastmaster meetings as a visitor, for six months.

Slowly developing confidence, I rediscovered the face of pride. Every day, I listened to Christy Lane's *One Day at a Time*. (Put away display of loneliness.) (Display picture of pride.) Life still did not smell so sweet, but I was reawakening. I needed to "Learn to be Still," as excerpts from that Eagles song tells us. (Put away display of pride.)

What was just over that green hill? Was it happiness? Well, I kept on running. I spent more time heeding the road signs of life. Wearing the face of happiness again, I joined Toastmasters and made the commitment. I learned to insist on my place in the scheme of things and to live up to that place, to empower others in their reaching for some place in life's plan. To do this is to make dreams come true. But we cannot miss the signs.

A poignant five-line poem relates:

> I missed the point; I missed the signs.
> I never asked; she never said.
> That made them easy to ignore.
> I paid no attention to what mattered most.
> My God, what did I do?

Happiness depends on listening to those voice colors, seeing the signs. (Display the picture of happiness.) Like Ace of Base, *I Saw the Sign*. The sun came out. That day, everything changed again. I let go. I started enjoying life.

We can learn much from children. My Sunday School children led me to joy. They are inspirational. The youth group sang this song, *We are the World*. Listen with me. (Turn up the volume.) (Put away the picture of happiness.)

Children like to build, to experiment, to share. They know about giving. From them, I learned to assemble the best that is within us and to give it away, to gather together with those we love and to rekindle joy. Activities with Toastmasters and my volunteer work accomplish this for me. (Display the picture of joy.)

"In our life there is a single color, as on an artist's palette, that provides the meaning of life and art. It is the color of love." So says Marc Chagall. What is the color of love? Would you recognize the face of love? Can you draw it?

A quote from Anna Trego Hunter tells us: "If we are to make a mature adjustment to life, we must be able to give and receive love." The three principal postures of love are explained by Albert M. Well, Jr., "It gives with joy, receives with appreciation, and rebukes with humility and hope."

A voice filled with love is warm. (Display a picture of love.) I also picture love as slow-dancing in the arms of someone I wouldn't want to have to live without. Love is dancing to Eric Clapton's *You Look Wonderful Tonight*. (Put away picture of love.)

To complete the circle of emotion, we reach forgiveness. "Forgiveness is the fragrance the violet sheds on the heel that has crushed it," quips Mark Twain. (Repeat the quote for emphasis.) The voice of forgiveness is gentle. The face of forgiveness is softened. Forgiveness is a state of grace. Join me in singing *Amazing Grace* by Christie Lane.

Now look at your sketched faces. What colors did you choose? I used the color wheel to reflect the spectrum of emotion: (Set up the color wheel.)

- Fear was gray, sometimes deepening to black.
- Frustration was violet, deepening to purple.
- Loneliness used all the variations of blue, signifying sadness.
- Pride became the hues of green.
- Happiness was sunny yellow.
- Joy was bursts of orange.
- Love was a wide range from deep rosy red, to pink, to the purest white.
- Forgiveness returns to the palest violet.

"The world is a looking-glass, and gives back to every man the reflection of his own face." This quote by William M. Thackeray may help you when you look at the faces you draw or the ones you present to the world. (Put away the color chart.)

In conclusion, sometimes we fail to connect because we approach the problem or the person with the wrong attitude, miss the essential emotions, or do not recognize the faces.

It seems to me that a soul that is in extreme pain shrivels up, closes in upon itself, loses the ability to hear the birds singing, the children playing, or to see the best parts of life. It becomes time for a change. Change does come in many colors, and it is anything but blue. It is beautiful.

When we destroy something, grieve a loss, or leave something behind, we must replace it with something new. The ability to cope with a range of emotions determines how satisfying and productive a person's life will be.

The ability to reflect emotion in colors with our voice determines how effective a speaker we will become. Let us give one another a smile with a future in it. When we speak, let our voices reflect our feelings, express those emotional colors, and connect with others. Keep our lives a rainbow of color. Color life beautiful.

Acceptance

And there we were, seeking the perfect gift. Self-acceptance makes the best personal gift. In it, we may find what we have been searching for. I have learned the consequences of living a false life are frustration, joylessness, and depression.

My faith is founded on knowing I have been placed here with certain gifts and certain goals. I am going to end up where I am supposed to be, no matter what I am going through right now. When we have faith, we cannot help but accept ourselves.

I remember feeling joy the first time I realized there was no reason to be hard on myself. Suddenly, I did not care what other people thought of me. That fear no longer controlled my life.

I was free to be myself, without the false faces. Whatever I chose to do next, I could face the possibility of failure, and it was okay. I was okay.

If we have been hard on ourselves, we may be hard on those around us. We want to take control because we want to feel safe. This constant test of faith teaches patience and trust. I have real moments of joy now. I know it will continue because I am committed to life getting better.

Sometimes We Stumble

And there we were, at the local Rotary meeting, waiting for the keynote speaker to begin:

This message is for those of you who have been through an awakening. To let you know a bit more about me, my awakenings, and my life's turning points, I have adapted one of Erma Bombeck's articles. It now contains my personal observations and insights. It ends with a call to positive action.

According to Erma Bombeck's advice, "You have to stumble on the path to wisdom." When I was a little kid, I didn't know anything. I knew that was true because everyone told me so.

People wanted to help me get smarter. They helped me by picking out my friends, my college, my career, and by telling me how I should live my life and avoid making mistakes. I did not listen to any of them. I figured how hard could learning about life be? All I really needed to know I learned in kindergarten anyway. Let me tell you what I mean.

I started kindergarten on my fifth birthday. I was too scared to stand up and join the other children in the pledge to the flag. I huddled in my desk. This was not a good beginning to the school year, but it was my first public speaking experience.

When I was almost seven, just learning to drive a tractor, I was helping my father pick up bales off a very wet meadow. That light tractor's front end kept slipping around toward the left because the bale loader was pulled behind an offset hitch. My dad told me to step lightly on the right brake to straighten the tractor. When we got on the other side of the field, it did that front-end slide thing again. I thought to myself, "other side of the field, other brake." We were suddenly done hauling bales for the day. We needed a new left rear tire. That bale loader had a tined bale flipper. I pierced the tractor tire and ripped a huge hole in it. (Big goof.)

All my life, if someone claimed something was white, I would question if it might be black, or gray, or something else entirely. If they indicated something was not good for me, I just laughed and did it anyway. When it was suggested I wait for more help before doing something, I went right ahead. This led to many unpredictable "pickles."

Yes, I was getting smarter every day, but I seemed to be paying the price for it. In high school, the friends I liked the most were the ones my parents liked the least. Their definitions of appropriateness never came close to mine.

I still listened to no one else. Instead, I constantly tried to improve "standard operating procedures." I expected special treatment and often got it. I enjoyed "beating the system." During my entire life, I have stubbornly clung to bad decisions that, in a weird way, enlightened me and made me a little wiser. For some of them, you just had to be there, especially that unforgettable year when I reinvented myself. But that is a story for another day.

When I had children, I thought, "I will use all this experience and hard-earned wisdom. I will protect them from hurt, pain, disappointment, stupidity, and embarrassment." I quickly discovered what my mother knew all along. As Erma defines it: "There are two things you must do by yourself: Give birth and live your own life." If you do not do these by yourself, you will never mature, develop resilience, be responsible for your own actions, or learn from your mistakes. I questioned my mother a short time back, seeking reassurance, asking her, "I wasn't such a bad kid, was I?"

"You always had good intentions," she replied. My answering thought was "Excuse me, but I have always had a mission."

Most of us know more good than we do. Most of us *know* more than we *do*. We generously evaluate ourselves by our intentions, instead of our actions.

We may ask the wrong people the wrong questions. Someone always has an answer to our questions. But we must ask the right questions, and then listen for the answers. What happens next depends on us. We may stumble, but we learn how to live. Life can be snazzy snapshots of splendor!

Defining Success

And there we were, searching for success. Where was it? What did it look like? Some of us are raised with the Midwestern work ethic. It lets us believe we must have a job and earn money to be a productive individual, contributing to our society. What happens if, through changed or mitigating circumstances, a person is no longer able to contribute to society or to reach personal fulfillment by earning money in a job or in a career?

How can that person become worthwhile to self or to society? What can be done to carve out a fulfilling, satisfying lifestyle? In what other ways could we define "success"?

What is success? Is it something nearly everyone strives for and very few of us realize we have achieved? I suggest that success does not so much involve knowing the right answers as it is asking the correct questions.

To answer the question "What is success?" I offer ten pillars of success in life. These pillars will support a positive attitude, which promotes hope and fosters strength. We can then enter into the world of exuberant joy, boundless love, and unlimited potential. Also, I will ask the defining questions. The answers, of course, are up to you.

Ten Pillars of Success in Life

Choosing, writing, giving, doing, praying, being determined, being joyful, forgiving and making amends, dreaming, and pleasing. The ultimate success is pleasing the One who created us, by being the one He intended us to be.

I cannot always change the world, but I can always change myself and my attitude. When I change my attitude, I change the world.

I leave you with these thoughts: Some of us are fueled by incredible confidence,

The Ten Pillars of Success in Life

Pillar 1 is "choosing." We have opportunities every day while walking down the road of life. We can choose to fall into a hole and become lost. To fall in and climb out again. To walk around the hole and continue on. Ask: *Which do I choose?*

Pillar 2 is "writing." We must believe in something enough to write it down. Ask: *Am I willing to put it in writing?*

Pillar 3 is "giving." Every gift I give to someone else is a gift to me. Doesn't that astonish? It is ultimately rewarding as well. Ask: *What gifts can I give?*

Pillar 4 is "doing." Trying does not guarantee success. Not trying, however, absolutely guarantees failure. Ask: *Do I choose success? Will I try?*

Pillar 5 is "praying." We each have the power to fill our cups with the spirit of life; to become calm and serene as the quiet waters of a beautiful, calm mountain lake. Ask: *Do I give myself permission to choose peace? Will I pray?*

Pillar 6 is "being determined." This is like saying, "I can win, and when I do not win, I will come back again, better than ever." It is being tenacious. Ask: *Do I believe in me?*

Pillar 7 is "being joyful." My joy is a celebration of life—my life, and yes, yours as well. If I keep offering the world my joy, I will touch people. I may change someone's life. When facets of life get me down, I can write them off and let them go. Ask: *Will I write myself a prescription for daily joy?*

Pillar 8 is "forgiving and making amends." To err is not to fail. I can admit my mistake, ask for forgiveness, make amends, then forgive myself and get on with life. Ask: *Can I forgive myself?*

Pillar 9 is "dreaming." Positive dreams are highly motivating statements of loving and joyful desire. The future belongs to those who believe in the beauty of their dreams. Ask: *Do I believe?*

Pillar 10 is "pleasing." Now is always the time to give. This is always the place to give. I choose to remember it is the love I have inside of me and project to others that brings me the gift of love. Ask: *Can I expand my world with love? Will I choose to be lovable?*

others by nothing more than deep desire. We succeed because we do not know how to surrender to failure. We ask the defining questions. We search for the answers known only to us. We utilize the ten pillars of success in life.

Our definition of success: *Success comes when we feel good enough about life that we are willing to give a piece of ourselves away.*

A Place of My Own

And there I was, out in the yard in front of the barn with my dad. My first memory in life is of a small girl terrified of heights and horses. I was being thrown into the saddle of a Morgan mare that danced around nervously. I felt so alone, so unprotected, so vulnerable.

I grew up in a part of the Midwest where girls were not cherished. We experienced life's harshness, learned to expect nothing from others, and worked ourselves nearly to death trying to please. I craved affection and love. I grew to love my horses, who gave me what they could.

My favorite garb was well-worn boy's denim jeans, usually too big for me because I never did grow enough to fill them. I partnered them with denim shirts, long-sleeved during the winter, and then ripped-out to be sleeveless during the summer. I preferred boots to high-tops and wore an old straw hat until frostbitten ears forced me to cover them. Still, I managed to carry myself with dignity. Inside, I was a lady.

School life found me trying to express my individuality. It took a very special teacher to show me how to strive for excellence, achieve positive results, and help others along the way. I found approval and acceptance at last. I became a teacher and mentor to others.

When twenty-one, I married. I picked badly. A man who appeared adept socially became a tortured man who would fly into rages and strike out at whoever was near. I was forever absorbing his cruelty. Eventually, it undermined my self-confidence.

Desperate to protect myself and my children, I moved out, found a house in town to rent, and began piecing together my shattered life. I began reaching out to others, listening for ways to improve my situation. I figured I deserved a chance to get even with life.

My dream was to have a place of my own. I looked at many houses over several years' time before I found one that touched my heart. My children felt it was our dream home. We filled it with special mementos of life's special moments. We pieced it together carefully. We filled it with friends and with love.

This home of mine is decorated with precious plants and flowers, given by friends and family. A hand-made quilt decorates each bedstead. Heritage linen covers each table.

If my soul needs restored, I tend my lawn or spend time in my garden. If my spirit is troubled, I write or share ideas in speeches or essays. I am continually reminded that Someone watches over me and guides my thoughts and actions. I see the wonderful miracles of life.

Though my children live in their own homes now, the love remains. I live with quiet dignity, thankful for the support of my friends, surrounded by the love of my family. I still wear shirts, jeans, boots, and a hat on occasion. I no longer feel alone, vulnerable and unprotected. I took the chance and got even with life. I created a place of my own.

"How Nice"

And there we were, the autumn of 1997, scattered about the world, living our lives. I jot down these thoughts:

How nice to be …
An independent woman
Answering to no one
Able to be free.

How nice to be …
One of the landed gentry
Living in God's Country
With acres to see.

How nice to be …
Living atop this high hill.
There's such a lovely view
With plenty to do.

How nice to be …
Owner of an empty nest
Accountable to none
Catering to one.

How nice to be ...
>> Surrounded by friends, much loved
With bonding things to do
>> And memories of you.

How nice to be ...
>> Dancing away a Saturday.
Triple two, line dance, waltz,
>> Rock and roll, and swing.

How nice to be ...
>> Parent of college students
Searching for what to be
>> —a mother of three.

How nice to be ...
>> One of God's special children
Committed to living
>> Faithful and giving.

How nice to be ...
>> Calm and serene, free of fear
Willing to share and to feel
>> Able to be real.

How nice to be ME!

Boomerang (Daughter's Tale)

Sometimes situations have a way of circling around that you least expect. It is even more surprising when that circular flow takes years to occur. I have a true appreciation for the humor in that moment of realization.

My mother stuffs her car trunk so full that it is essentially unusable. She insists that each item contained in the boot of her car is necessary in a crisis. All of her children concede that items, such as a spare jacket, must be carried at all times. Needing four different types of blankets and silverware seems less likely. One day, my brother Rick was helping with an engine problem that occurred while we were traveling to Kansas. He pulled out her "women's" tool kit. It had items like a hammer, measuring tape, and a screwdriver. It contained nothing that a person could use on an engine. A long conversation followed as to why this was even necessary to carry in the car, especially the screwdriver. What possible use could there be for that? Obviously, no one is able to sway this woman on logic, so the toolkit stayed in the car for many years. Whether that kit was ever useful is still not known.

About ten years later, I found myself in a spot of trouble while traveling from the west coast to Nebraska. It was winter, and I had been driving in a literal blizzard the entire route. Somewhere along the line, my wallet had been taken or misplaced. I was in Wyoming, needing one last tank of gas to finally get home safely. The required spare jacket and blanket in my car had already come in handy. Growing up, my mother insisted we include those items and a spare twenty dollar bill in our vehicle. She called it "mad money" for reasons I am still not sure of. Mad money has saved my life numerous times, and this day was no exception. That would buy just enough gas to get me the rest of the way home.

However, nothing can be too easy. Fighting exhaustion and weather for twenty-two hours and losing my wallet would not be enough to qualify this as a proper "Cone" trip. While unlocking my gas cap, the top broke off, and I was not able to pull the plug out. Quite the conundrum. I tried several different things, but nothing was of use. I went into the gas station to see if they had something that I could borrow. In the end, the only thing that helped was a screwdriver. One little turn, and the plug popped right out.

I was fortunately able to purchase a new gas cap and just enough gas to pull into my driveway at three o'clock in the morning and stumble to my bed. The next day, I had to take care of some serious business—replace my money, cards, driver's license, and buy a screwdriver to leave in my car.

Regifting (Our Hero's Tale)

My mother, bless her heart, is an inveterate regifter. No gift is safe from being recycled for future holidays and celebrations. The most egregious infraction was on my birthday, 2009. I received a gift-wrapped horseshoe set—a very nice one.

This would have been wonderful if my Grandmother Charron had not gifted me with this very set of horseshoes for Christmas 2001. At that time, I was in the military and could not take it home with me on the airplane. I left it with Mother until I came back through Nebraska in a car.

Ironically, not only did Mother regift me, she regifted me with my own gift. She had not even received it as a gift herself. She claimed it was a huge joke. I beg to differ.

Mother brought this "Regifting" to a whole new level the Christmas of 2015. Apparently, she rummaged through the closets, cupboards, and cabinets to find what can only be labeled "White Elephants." She carefully wrapped them and placed them beneath her brand new Christmas tree decorated with treasured family ornaments.

When it came time to open gifts on Christmas Eve, she had each of us draw a number to determine the order of selection. The best number was the last draw. She went first. No one wanted the slipper socks she picked out. We moved on to the next person. A spirited session of "dirty" gift exchange with loud groans and sinister "stealing" began.

The joke was on us. Since we do not believe in regifting, the "white elephants" will not find their way back to mom's house, with one exception—the creepy doll with exchangeable heads. Sister insisted it stay with its original owner. Next year, it may appear again.

We decided it was so much fun that we will bring our own selections for the "dirty" gift exchange next year. Paybacks are a bitch! White elephant, anyone?

CHAPTER FIVE:
SPRITES AND SPROUTS

It is amazing when you read something that perfectly touches on feelings you cannot easily verbalize.

"Be patient toward all that is unsolved in your heart and try to love the questions themselves, like locked rooms and like books that are now written in a very foreign tongue. Do not now seek the answers, which cannot be given you because you would not be able to live them. And the point is, to live everything. Live the questions now. Perhaps you will then gradually, without noticing it, live along some distant day into the answer." – Rainer Marie Rilke

A Moral Equivalent for War in Vietnam

One of the biggest controversies of the present day (November 1967) involves the situation in Vietnam. Nearly everyone can agree it is unfortunate we are involved in such a struggle. Yet, there is a lack of consensus on what our nation should do to better, or to alter, the murky situation. Our war efforts could be replaced by internal projects to help educate the people of Vietnam so they can adequately feed, clothe, and care for themselves.

We know that our military is not in Vietnam just to help the South Vietnamese. It is also evident that we are not helping them as we could or in the ways we should. Instead of directing our forces against an "unseen" enemy, we should fight against forces we can see only too well—poverty, sickness, and illiteracy. If we had as many teachers, educators and doctors in South Vietnam as we have soldiers (5,200 according to the latest release), their problems would be resolved far sooner than they will be under the present policy.

To achieve this end, our nation would need to work for the welfare and interests of the South Vietnamese people instead of ours. The present concern of the United States is mainly to stop the spread of communism. If we would approach it somewhat indirectly, the end results could be more satisfactory. As it is, we are losing the battle.

If all our billions spent on this war had been funneled into educational and health programs, the South Vietnamese could stop worrying about where the next meal was coming from or where clothing and shelter could be found. The main appeal of communism would dissolve. With adequate education, the South Vietnamese could detect the falsehoods and pitfalls of the communist line. Education is a more indirect route of arriving at self-rule for their nation.

This suggested moral equivalent would help to build and develop the character of the persons working in Vietnam far more than do the activities of the military. It requires dauntless courage and relentless patience to teach anyone, especially someone harboring such diverse basic beliefs and with a cultural background foreign and contradictory to our own. The progress often tends to be disheartening because it is not readily observed. There is essentially no tangible evidence of learning. It often takes much faith to continue, but the results are more satisfying than to those of a soldier who, when fighting, tends to display the more primitive drives rather than the traits that would lead to personal happiness. The broken lives of our returning military personnel are a direct testament to this.

Our nation should, therefore, substitute teachers, educators, and physicians for soldiers, marines, and sailors. If we chose this more indirect but more effective method of resisting the communist threat, everyone, except the Communist Party, would benefit. It would also reflect, on the part of the United States, an unselfish interest and an honest desire to help the underprivileged people of the world. A nobler course would be difficult to choose.

Should Abortion Laws Be Liberalized?

The year is 1967. The question of liberalizing abortion laws is being high-lighted in the nation's spotlight more each day. The American public is increasingly supporting these liberalized abortion laws. This, to me, seems wrong. Abortion laws should not be liberalized because the practice is immoral and, in most cases, unsatisfactorily justified.

Officially, the abortionist exists beyond the reach of organized medicine. Yet, growing numbers of physicians believe there are often good reasons for terminating pregnancies. The American Medical Association recently changed its stance on abortion and adopted a new policy that permits therapeutic abortions under three conditions: when the pregnancy threatens either the life or health of the mother, when the infant might be born with a disabling physical deformity or mental de-ficiency, or if pregnancy resulting from rape or incest threatens the mental or physical health of the mother. Colorado, North Carolina, and California have adopted laws similar to the revised AMA policy. The general consensus is that countries with legalized abortion have sanctioned unchangeable social custom.

Despite the fact that abortion is, as a general rule, illegal, there were an esti-mated thirty million induced abortions last year as compared with one hundred fifteen million live births – a ratio of one to four. Many of these abortions do not qualify under the AMA policy and are performed in the privacy of a physician's office or in even worse conditions. They are morally and religiously wrong but not necessarily socially wrong. Despite the strong religious resistance, the growing tendency for society to accept abortion is increasingly apparent.

The various reasons of selfishness, inconvenience, or poverty often serve as reasons for abortion—legalized murder. A woman who considers herself a member of higher society, or someone with a demanding profession, often finds a child to be a great inconvenience. Unwilling to make any necessary sacrifices, she may then resort to abortion. Conversely, a woman living in such dire poverty and unable to adequately support another child often employs abortion as a method to resolve the situation. When abortion laws are liberalized, this practice is increasingly accepted and even used as a birth control option.

The new AMA policy permits many unnecessary abortions. The first condition, when the pregnancy threatens either the life or the health of the mother, should not apply very often. A woman capable of conception will, in most cases, be able to survive a pregnancy even if the child will not. Abortion, in this instance, is therefore unnecessary. Those women with cancer or other life-threatening situations are the exception.

The possibility of the infant's being born with a disabling physical deformity or mental deficiency is listed as a second condition. Abortion in this case is very difficult to justify because who, besides God, has the right to decide which cripple will die? In many cases, no definitive proof of the mental or physical deformity is seen until after the actual birth. (This was before the extensive use of sonograms.) Who wants to sit in God's judgment seat? (Author's footnote: When faced with this exact scenario, I elected to have the child despite the odds and delivered a healthy baby who continues to bring joy to this world.)

Pregnancy resulting from rape or incest also qualifies as reason for legal abortion under the new AMA policy. Since an infant conceived under these conditions would, in fact, be undesirable, I would suggest, rather that resorting to abortion, putting the child up for adoption at birth. There are many childless couples in the world today that would cherish a little one, regardless of the parental background. Instead of immorally murdering a child, the victim could bring joy into the life of someone else. A grievous sin is thereby converted into good.

Since abortion is, in most cases, actually unnecessary, not to mention lacking in justification and morality, there is no need to liberalize the present abortion laws. An acceptable substitute for many situations is to put the unwanted child up for adoption. To encourage this alternate method of contending with unwanted children and to discourage immoral practices, the present abortion laws should definitely not be liberalized.

Finding Freedom

" *We should never allow our fears or the expectations of others*
to set the frontiers of our destiny.
Our personal choices determine our destiny."

—Author Unknown

After reading the conclusion in Katherine Mansfield's *The Daughters of the Late Colonel*, one wonders when the best opportunity for breaking the bonds that tied the daughters to their father's dominance was offered. How could they have better resolved their conflict? How could they have escaped their father's overbearing and fearful dominance? The situation could have been better resolved by definitely deciding to fire Kate instead of postponing that decision and living the rest of their lives essentially under the influence of their father's dominating personality.

Dismissing Kate would have been a huge step toward freedom for the two sisters. After having once made a definite decision, other decisions would be easier to make. Like crossing a swift stream, once begun, there can be no turning back. Instead of bowing to what their father would have wished, they would then be compelled to continue making their own decisions. That is the only way to bury the past and to move forward.

If Kate was not there to take care of them, they would necessarily have to develop some self-sufficiency. They would be more likely to develop some outside interests. Instead of letting Kate decide what they wanted (the incidence regarding the fish, for example), they would have to make their own decisions. As the ocean is composed of little drops of water, each necessary to the whole, so is each morsel of self-confidence necessary to overcome the fear of the father's dominance and the feeling of inferiority derived from it. Each time a decision is made, more self-reliance is achieved. This is another step toward their personal freedom.

Kate was actually a symbol of the colonel to the two sisters, a constant reminder of his dominating personality. If Kate would not have appeared exactly at the times when they would nearly overcome this fear of their father, it would not persist. Consider that they saw her watching them just before they went into their father's room to go through his belongings. This gave the sisters an irrepressible feeling of guilt and insecurity that ultimately led to the venture's failure. Without Kate's actual presence in the home, they would not be as inclined to feel the presence of their father. They would not feel they were being watched with his critical eye.

Without the colonel or Kate to supervise and criticize their actions, the sisters would eventually look to one another for approval instead of wondering what Father or Kate might consider to be proper. Free from this fear of criticism, they would develop more confidence in their decisions and in each other. They would not feel they had to answer to anyone else. They would be free to live a life of their own.

If the sisters would have taken that first step and dismissed Kate, they would have been able to live a new life, a life free from their father's dominance. By postponing their decision to some future time that will actually never come, they have elected to keep on living as they had in the past.

After writing this, it took me another thirty years to take that measurable step toward freedom. The following is worth repeating:

"We should never allow our fears or the expectations of others to set the frontiers of our destiny.
Our personal choices determine our destiny."

—Author Unknown

Blonde Moment (Pink's Tale)

And there I was, living on the Air Force Base. I believe I was about ten years old. We could play four-square on the corner or roller skate up and down that street. We used that fairly isolated street as our playground. There was a bus stop across the street from our house with a small wooden shack and a bench. The shack had a hole in it that I could look through and secretly spy on my house. One day while skating by, I stuck my finger through that hole in the shack to waggle it at those sitting inside. I could not get my finger back out. The harder I tried the more swollen my finger got. I started to cry.

Mom saw me through the kitchen window. I had been standing outside the bus stop for some time, not moving. She came out to investigate. First, she laughed at my predicament. She tried soap and then lotion on my finger to loosen it. It would not come out. She fetched Dad and his jigsaw. He joined in the laughter. Everyone else was laughing. I was still sobbing, but now it was from hurt and frustration. Dad cut a 4x4-inch square around my stuck finger. I had to skate home with that block of wood still on my finger. I was more "blonde" than "Pink" that day.

A Chilling Narrative (Daughter's Tale)

And here we are, curled up on the couches, creating our own horror stories. This story is to warn you and others against something terrible, something sinister. Please heed this as a warning. This is not a true story, but it could be. Every statement included in this document is fiction, at this moment. Corresponding names are pure coincidence.

It is a cold, blustery night. Chilling. She feels it all the way to her bones. Objects float in front of her as she walks, slowly moving down the sidewalk. Litter is everywhere. One object in particular sticks in her mind—a McD's carry-out bag. Strange ...

The street is clear and dark. A light mist covers the air, making the street lights softer, darker. No lights remain on in the desolate houses. Only darkness prevails. Bitter darkness. Still, her feet carry her forward. Stillness. The only sounds are those of a gusty wind and the light trickling of water down into the sewers. Quiet. Ominous quiet. And the occasional bark of a dog.

Down the road, she hears a car approaching. Closer and closer. Fright courses through her. Where to go? What to do? Suddenly, she lunges into a nearby alley. Hiding behind convenient bushes, she peers out into the street. Slowly, the car passes by. A red Ford Probe. It moves so slowly. She wonders why. The car finally reaches the end of the block. It pauses. She waits … and waits. Why doesn't it go away? she thinks irritably. Finally, when her tension has nearly reached the breaking point, it pulls forward and slowly moves off. She stays behind the bushes until it disappears … into the darkness. Relief finally flows through her. She again feels comfortable enough to finish her journey.

She realizes that she is tired. She hopes to be asleep soon but realizes there is no sleep for the weary. She starts to sing … "All by myself … la la la … Don't wanna be … la … all by myself …" Down the street she moves, pausing here and there to study inanimate objects.

She comes upon a large blue house. She notices a swooping roof and a light on upstairs. The house creates a strangely disturbing feeling of familiarity. She ponders this for a bit, but her thoughts come up empty. She can hear dogs running around in the background, making their existence known. Suddenly, she feels the awareness of a close presence. A shuffling noise develops in a large nearby bush. Her heart pounds. She acknowledges a strong feeling of fear. She has nowhere to go, nowhere to run. Quick, she thinks, RUN! All of a sudden, a small figure appears. Her heart leaps into her throat. Should she scream? Should she run? Or is it too late?

Wait … wait … a feeling of hilarity passes through her. Stupid, she thinks. Out of the bushes appears a small white cat. Little brown smudges cover it in various places. She chuckles aloud, then says, "Hello, kitty … you're sooo cute." Slowly, it moves toward her. After she pets it for a while, it begins to purr. Finally, she realizes that she is late and needs to be going. Moving away from the big pale blue house, she says goodbye to the small cat.

A block later, she realizes that it still follows her. "Go home … home!" she quietly but sternly orders. The cat pauses but continues to follow the wearied traveler. Again, she turns to reject it. One block later, she stops. The cat is still there.

Standing there, staring down at the white cat, a sudden feeling shoots through her. A cruel feeling. One that would produce fear in most people. *Why should I return it?* she ponders. *It obviously doesn't want to go home.* As her thoughts run repeatedly around in her head, her outer features change. A stranger watching her would notice the definite blackening of her already dark eyes, the tightening of her facial features, the malicious line of her brow. She comes to an abrupt decision. She is no longer all by herself. The cat jumps into her welcoming arms, and together they continue down the dark, cold street.

The wind picks up a bit, so she cuddles the little feline even closer and picks up her pace. She continues on through the dark, frightening park and on by the empty golf course until she stops in front of a large, brown house. It is hidden behind much foliage and skirts a small stream. Finally ... home!

Up the front stairs and into the house she walks, quietly sneaking upstairs to her room. She takes the cat to her room in order to avoid annoying the feline of the house, Toutset. Touts is a strange cat, and the black-eyed girl is afraid of how it would respond to the new little kitten. Touts has many strange attitudes and activities. She never knows whether to cuddle it or leave it alone entirely.

She makes a small bed for the white cat in an old shoebox, and places the cat inside, tying the top on, so that it cannot escape. Tomorrow night she will return it, but for now, it is hers. Tired, she collapses onto the bed, and her thoughts slowly fade ...

Meanwhile ...

Frantically, a young girl runs about, loudly calling out a name. She runs back and forth. Tears start to slowly run down her face. She is experiencing pure misery. Finally, she gives up. It's gone. Sadness completely envelopes her hunched over form. She feels bile start to form in her lower regions. The moment finally passes, and she moves back to the large blue house. She will look again tomorrow.

She stops in front of her door, and faintly calls out one last time ... *Skittles*. She pauses and then turns to go inside. Upstairs, she collapses onto her bed. A stranger watching would notice the tears spilling out of her eyes, the pain on her face, her shaking shoulders. Exhaustion finally takes its toll, and she slowly drifts off.

The Next Day:

The girl with the black hair and even blacker eyes wakes up. She looks at the clock and notices that it is two o'clock in the afternoon. She stretches and then forces herself to get out of bed. After she slowly dresses and stumbles downstairs, she notices that, strangely enough (actually, one of the few times in her life), she is alone in the house. Where are her parents and sisters? Did they go to grand-mother's house without her? After a short time, happiness takes the place of dis-appointment. After she puts Touts out and makes herself a cheese sandwich, she goes upstairs to let the little white cat with the brown smudges out to play.

After watching it run around for a while, she sits down and works on making bead necklaces. "Infernal beads," she grumbles about five minutes later and puts them aside. After making another cheese sandwich (this one out of cinnamon raisin bread because of the lack of wheat bread), she puts the video Pocahontas in and sits down to watch. As she watches the film, her mind wanders through many different subjects and finally comes to rest on the little white cat. She knows she has to return it tonight but dreads doing it. Dark thoughts start to cloud her mind …

Meanwhile …

A brown-haired girl sits in the crew room in the back of McD's. Tears are running down her face. Her wonderfully thoughtful friend Calamitee is trying to calm her. This friend is always so considerate of everyone else's feelings. There should be more people like her in the world. The girl, however, is not thinking this. She is thinking about her little white cat with brown smudges, which disappeared last night. "Don't worry," her friend said, "I'm sure Skittles will come back. It's just a matter of time."

Calamitee then has to leave, however, for her grotesque boss, Kirk (who is reportedly gay, which is no excuse for being a jerk) comes back there and screams at her, ordering her to get up front and run the register. Then he yells at the crying girl, telling her to stop crying. This, of course, makes her cry even harder. She wishes that she could leave. She wishes more than anything else that her little cat would come back.

Later in the day:

The black-haired girl has come to a decision. She loves the little white cat more than anything else in the world, except for Toutset, of course. She feels that if she has to go without the cute little kitten, the owner will as well. Her stormy black eyes reflect vicious thoughts that would make any man turn cold. Suddenly, she springs up off the sofa and starts enacting her evil plot.

Meanwhile …

The small brown-haired girl is finally free from the suffocating confines of that wretched McD's. Tired, she stumbles out of her car. All she wants to do is put on something comfortable, put in a good movie, and cuddle up with her best friend in the world—Skittles.

Then she remembers. Skittles is gone.

Gone. Not to return. Missing. Gone.

Later on that night:

The dark-eyed girl has finally completed her tasks. Everything is complete. The job is done. Finished. Over. She feels a short flash of sorrow, but it soon dissipates. Looking back at the cat for the last time, she feels the sharp pang of pain. *If only life didn't have to be like this,* she thinks.

She doesn't seem to realize what she has actually done. Her mind has finally tumbled over the edge. She is somewhat psychotic. Some would attribute it to job stress. Some might say it is because of her parents. Some have other theories that lay quietly, disturbing them privately, in their own minds.

Meanwhile ...

The brown-haired girl is upstairs doing her hair when a phone call comes. It is Calamitee. She wants to go to a movie. The girl sighs. Not another night spent with that strange person ... her "friend." Sometimes she thinks she might just kill her because she is so weird. Oh, well, she has nothing better to do. She agrees to go. "I'll meet you at McD's," she says. She loves going to McD's. It's her favorite place in the entire world ... so far.

She is walking toward her car when she notices that her two dogs remain quiet. Strange. Really strange. As she approaches the vehicle, she notices a form appearing out of the darkness. It appears to be attached to her basketball hoop. *What in the world is this?* she wonders. She moves closer. The object becomes clearer. Closer and closer she moves until she finally distinguishes what the dogs have been staring at so attentively ...

Bile rises in her throat. She runs to the other side of the car and throws up. The bile just keeps coming and coming. She fears that she will never stop puking ... and then it ends. After pausing for a couple of minutes to compose herself, she moves closer. It is horrible!

It is Skittles! Someone has taken the time to string up her cat by all four legs. They have shoved a fry scoop through its ravished chest. There is a note hanging on the scoop's handle, fastened by a bead necklace. A black, blue, and white bead necklace. It seems somewhat familiar. She lets the thought pass as she approaches and reaches for the note. It is stuck. The dried blood has reacted like glue. She pries the note off the cat's terrible corpse and opens it slowly ...

Meanwhile ...

Up at McD's, Calamitee is upset. The brown-eyed girl is late ... as usual. Calamitee is never late. She wishes her friends were as considerate. Oh, well. Since her friend has not arrived, she is forced to speak to the strange black-haired girl. *Oh, great,* she thinks, *she'll probably say something weird, and I'll have to play nice.* Calamitee decides to make conversation. "I wonder where that so-called 'friend' of mine is."

The dark-haired girl blandly responds, "I have no idea what might be delaying her." Calamitee notices she never actually makes eye contact. *Oh, well,* she thinks, *she's probably just mad about something.*

"I guess I should go see what her problem is now," Calamitee announces demurely, for she does not know how to make a quick exit. The comment works, and the black-eyed girl murmurs, "Bye!" though there is a strange light in her eyes … Disturbing.

As Calamitee pulls into her friend's alley, she has the strange feeling that something is not right. She sees the small brown-haired girl squatted down on her haunches by the side of her car. She runs over to see what is wrong. All her small, brown-haired friend can sputter is "Skittles … Skittles … Skittles." When asked to explain, she makes no response, except to repeat the previous answer.

Calamitee decides the girl obviously has a stomach ache and needs to be left alone. No movie tonight! As she is leaving, she notices that the black-eyed girl has waited until she left, then drives into the alley herself. She decides not to let it bother her and goes home.

The black-eyed girl walks up to the small crouched form. She asks, "Did you receive the note?"

"What?" the brown-haired girl cries out in shock. It is at that moment that she recognizes the cruel and malicious features on the face of the other girl. Fear suddenly becomes very evident inside her. The words in the note came back to her, one by one …

Hi. How are you? I am fine. By now I suppose you have noticed the gutted cat hanging from your basketball hoop? I did it. Yes, I admit it. It was me. And I am very proud. I have decided to go on a crusade. No one in this world will own a pet but me because no one else loves their pets like I do (rowr, rowr). This is the end of your pet. Unfortunately, your life now has to end as well, for you know too much. Goodbye, friend.

The note is sinister. It radiates evil. And it says all that the brown-haired girl needs to know … As she tries to strike out and hit, the black-eyed girl ducks and rips the fry scoop out of the dead cat. Almost instantly, it is over. Decapitation by a fry scoop; not a pretty sight. She gets rid of the evidence, and returns home …

The next night:

The black-eyed girl is out for a stroll. Again, it is chilly. For some reason, she has the strange urge to walk up by the hospital. She makes it to the top of the hill and starts back down. She notices a small brown puppy. It is near a white clapboard and brick home that seems familiar, but she does not let that thought bother her. "Hello, puppy ... You are sooo cute ..."

There Are No Coincidences (Daughter's Tale)

And there we are, seniors, getting ready for our high school graduation. One night, a strange coincidence occurs. It is one of those little events in everyone's life that reminds us we are connected in the tapestry of life, if we just take the time to notice. It begins just like any other: working the night shift at McD's, staying late to close and clean, chatting with my friends, tossing around ideas for afterwards. We are thinking of going for a drive, just to hang out and chill. We are seniors, and graduation is this week.

Suddenly, Mom charges in to McD's, clad in PJs covered by a coat. She appears somewhat frantic, insisting that I return home as soon as I can. I promise to come straight home when I get signed out of work, wondering what is up with this woman.

Arriving home, I find my mother still in a state. She insists she was sleeping soundly when a voice told her: "Find your daughter!" She claims she did attempt to ignore the summons, but the voice returned even more persistently, insisting, "Find your daughter." Overcome by a strong understanding of urgency, she rapidly walked the few blocks down the hill, cut through the hospital, and found me working as usual. The sense of urgency remained. Thus, the impassioned pleas to return home quickly. None of this is her normal behavior. I decide it is just another pesky annoyance.

The following morning provides surprising answers. My two friends had been waiting for my shift to end so we could go on a late-night ride with someone else. When I went home instead, they went on that ride without me. They lost their lives that night as their vehicle rolled while speeding around a sharp corner on a country road. I cry when I remember that I could have been with them. Was it just a strange coincidence?

My mother reminded me there are no coincidences. Someone was looking out for me.

Next time your morning seems to be going wrong—you are slow getting dressed, you cannot seem to find the car keys, you hit every traffic light—do not get mad or frustrated. God is at work watching over you.

When I am stuck in traffic, miss an elevator, turn back to answer a ringing telephone, all the little things that annoy me, I think to myself, *This is exactly where God wants me to be at this very moment.*

I pray that God continues to bless us with all those annoying little things, those frustrating people, and may we always remember their possible purpose.

Fire in the Hole (The Heir's Tale)

And here I am, learning car mechanics through experience. Our Hero sends money to build engines for him while he is somewhere on the East Coast defending our country's freedom. A junior in high school, I am learning how to assemble engines. Today, I drop a 327 Chevy engine into Our Hero's black '56 Chevy. I put a carburetor on it with a fuel bowl on top and a vacuum line on the bottom. The lines are about an inch apart. It is a red electrical pump that will pump forty pounds of pressure and shut off when the fuel bowl is full. I run it for about ten seconds and notice the bowl is not filling. I realize my mistake. It is hooked up wrong. It fills the motor with gasoline.

I pull out the fouled spark plugs. I try to crank it over to push out the excess fuel. This is a special car with a push button start. The push button is not working, so I short the starter across with a screwdriver. When the #8 piston reaches the compression stroke, it blows compressed gas out the spark plug hole onto the short I create with the screwdriver to crank the engine. The spark ignites the gas. Now the car is on fire.

I run into the house and ask Mom for the fire extinguisher. We do not have one, she says. I run back to the garage. The cardboard underneath the car is on fire. I drag it out, throw it outside, and let it burn. The car is still on fire. What to do?

I pick up the air compressor hose and try to blow the flames out. They burn higher. I try to blow the gas away from the car. Huge flames follow the air. Flames are hitting the side of the garage. While I am busy trying to disperse the gas, a can of ether on the floor explodes and creates a huge fireball. It burns the hair off my legs from the knees down.

I believe the car is blowing up. I dive out of the garage and land on the concrete driveway next to the burning cardboard. I have skinned elbows and road rash on my arms and hands. I look back. I see the car is still there and is still on fire. I run back in and put out the fire.

Now there is a cloud of smoke two feet from the floor. I open up the overhead garage door to let the smoke escape. I stand outside the garage, dripping blood.

Smoke billows out. Someone going down the street at 30 mph sees me, locks up his brakes, and runs over. He wants to call the fire department. I tell him the fire is out; everything is A-OK. I have it handled. He looks concerned but goes on his way. Using the air hose saved the wiring on the car. Nothing on the car is hurt. I change the fuel connection and finish the job.

The next day, several neighbors make house calls to express concerns. Everyone seems to know about the car fire. We buy a fire extinguisher for the garage.

My Life on the Farm (Our Hero's Tale)

And there we were, trying to make a living on a poor dirt farm in rural Nebraska. One of my most vivid memories of childhood is when I was sixteen or seventeen years old. Since we sold our cowherd, we were taking in cows. This particular herd was Maine-Anjou, bred to Charolaise bulls. This mix produced five hundred of the meanest, worst calving cows we ever encountered.

One day in March, after school, I rode out with Dad to check the cattle. Of course, one was having calving problems, which was the reason I was riding along. We gently herded the cow into a pen and ran it into the chute. Things weren't progressing. The calf was approximately ten percent out, but stuck.

Closer inspection revealed the calf was breech, coming out backwards. A cow usually cannot have a calf by itself if it is a breech birth. It must lie just right in the uterus. This meant we were going to have to assist the birthing process by providing the "muscle." Otherwise, the calf certainly, and possibly the cow, would die.

Being the designated able assistant, I ran to the pickup and returned with the calf puller. A calf puller is basically a come-along on a pole. The pole is braced against the cow's hindquarters, and the come-along winches the calf out of the birth canal. Since I was the more petite of the two, (my dad weighs 205 pounds and has arms like a bodybuilder), I was elected to place the pulling chains around the calf's legs just above the hooves.

Ignoring the cold, I stripped down to my jeans and T-shirt. Putting a loop in the chain and hooking it over my thumb, I worked my arm up the birth canal. The average bovine birth canal is about halfway between elbow and shoulder length. Partway in there, the cow contracted. I thought my arm was going to break. There is nothing to do but take it until the contraction weakens. If you move, your arm will surely suffer. Soon, the pressure eased, and I placed the chains around the two closest hooves. They felt awfully big for a newborn calf. Perhaps it was overdue.

I hooked the chain to the calf puller, and Dad started to crank away. As the calf's hooves reached the cervix, I guided them out so they wouldn't tear anything. Baby hooves are very sharp, never having been walked on. The cow started bawling hard. We eased up slightly to let the contractions work.

Dad was slowly cranking, and the calf kept coming. I had never seen a calf this long in my life. An average calf weighs sixty to seventy pounds at birth. This one was going to weigh between one hundred and one hundred twenty pounds. Then, my dad ran out of puller length. The calf was right at the shoulders, the widest part of the calf, and the one place the pullers were really needed.

The cow, under severe duress, began to collapse, no longer having the strength to stand. The calf had not started breathing yet. We were going to have to hurry, or we were going to lose them both. So we did what we had to. We grabbed the chains off the winch, and we pulled. We pulled until we were sweating and our joints were cracking. And still we pulled. We got down in the mud and pulled "tug of war" style. And we pulled some more.

The calf started to come. Now it was putting pressure on everything internal to the cow. The cow was screaming with pain. We were grunting from the strain, and the calf started bawling. All that pressure caused a bowel movement, and the vagina tore alongside the calf's shoulder, showering us in feces, blood and piss. After an eternity of pulling, the calf's shoulder popped free, and the calf, covered in slime, landed directly on top of us. We just lay there, covered in manure, blood, mud and piss, slime and sweat, ready to pass out from exertion.

It is not over. We still have a job to do. We stagger to our feet, get the calf to stand and start breathing on its own. Then we work on the cow until she is motivating under her own power. We turn them both out into the little catch pen to get acquainted.

It is truly amazing how quickly an animal can recover from such a strenuous experience. As the calf gets up and starts to suck, and the cow starts licking the calf clean, you feel a little pride. A miracle, a creation, and you were part of it. As I look down at myself and see the excrement and mud covering my body, I realize I am shivering uncontrollably from the cold. Somehow it does not seem to matter so much.

Now, when I am given a task with something onerous that I detest doing, I look back on this time and realize how small the present task really is. After experiencing so much, putting this situation and this place into perspective makes me realize how insignificant it all is.

We have been building our particular situation up in our minds until it is a giant. Once it is put into proper perspective, the importance we attach to daily events seems so silly. One day, I caught myself grumbling about standing extra watch, plus working on some broken equipment. I was working with next to no sleep and was feeling no small measure of self-pity. But as I think back to a muddy feed lot in Nebraska, I realize that this is nothing. Taken into perspective, this is just a den of lions. A bit of perspective will beard them in their den every time.

The Lady (Our Hero's Tale)

And there we were, simply staring. If you saw her from the street, you would agree she was quite a looker. You might even whistle. A closer inspection, however, reveals the inescapable ravages of time. Her classic features still give evidence of the undeniable beauty of her youth. She is a testament to a better age. As she lies there in repose, you sigh. Preparing to move on, you think on lost loves and simpler times.

But deep inside her lurks a weapon of destruction, wreaking havoc on all who oppose her. Almost at the flick of a switch, the veneer of civility melts away. A growl emanates from within. Where a lady had stood, a fierce warrior maiden prances proudly in her stead.

The tiny frisson of fear crawls up your spine. Your mind races, searching for escape. With almost an animalistic grace, she makes her exit. You escape unscathed. This time. You can't hold back the sigh of relief.

What a combination of aging beauty and savage grace. What strings of hate became entangled in her destiny? The volatility only enhances the beauty. You entrench yourself once again in the stable environs of your ritualistic life. But, irrevocably marked, you fantasize the exciting world you glimpsed only moments ago, only eons ago. That is the Lady.

My Summer Vacation at Age 24 (Our Hero's Tale)

And there we were, somewhere under the sea. The birds are singing, the sun is shining, and we are underway on a fast attack nuclear submarine, making the world safe for democracy, saving it from the innumerable forces of evil.

We join Our Hero as he stands watch, ever vigilant in his mission to rid the world of those three villains: dirt, bilgewater, and oil. As boredom presses during the interminable hours, Our Hero yearns for the one glimpse of happiness that brightens his life, that one speck of illumination in the whirling cesspool of murky confusion—his antique car. Yes! Happiness is a '56 Chevy in powder blue with 625 screaming, kicking ponies under the hood. Is she a feisty Bess or an aging Jezebel? He loves her all the same!

As he emerges from that gloomy haunted region known as "The Hole," his comrades congratulate him on surviving yet again. He lets his mind wander, recalling the nightmares residing within, nightmares that could loosen his ever weaker grasp on sanity.

He drops in at the local joint, drinks something stale, and swallows something slightly rancid. It is best not to look too closely! He stares through his glass. Finally, his consciousness makes its way back to his body. He struggles to make his way out of the teeming mass of humanity that is the galley.

On his way to his personal domicile and its blessed oblivion, reality intrudes yet again. "We need you and your team to do transmission checks on the weapons," the technician informs him. A sigh … He gathers strength for yet another battle.

The High Chief gathers us all round, intoning solemnly, "We must tighten up the discipline. Informality is the enemy." We look at one another and ask ourselves, "Isn't Communism the enemy?" The hierarchy seems to fabricate enemies as required to manipulate us into doing their bidding. How does one tell where the enemy really lies? Around every corner, he may lurk. Maybe Chief is the enemy? How can we tell? Reality leaves no lasting impression here. It is like trying to walk a highwire in a crosswind.

The latest battle begins. Our Hero settles down into the rhythm and ritual that is loading and unloading weapons. His team taps into the lulling cadence and performs like a well-oiled machine. His personal presence does not even seem required here. *Do I have a purpose?* he wonders. *Or am I just another drone in the beehive that comprises society? Will my deeds ever make their mark?* Best not to continue that train of thought …

Task complete, the machine finally regresses to its components. "Yes, Cross, you can go eat." "Go to the rack, Burkhart." "I will meet you on crew's mess, Jim." He cleans up all evidence of the evolution. A place for everything, everything in its place!

Savoring a solitary precious cigarette, he quietly listens as the remaining team members discuss topics that have no bearing on the current situation. Past memories, future goals and plans. Never the present! After everything else they accomplish and endure, asking them to face it would just be asking too much. Our Hero bids his companions *adieu*.

Now ensconced in his personal domicile, he reflects that it resembles a coffin. He lets his mind escape again, once a solemn promise is given for its return in the morning. As blessed oblivion closes in, he ticks off yet another day from that mental calendar that marks the journey to freedom. Twenty-six. Counting makes time go faster, and yet infinitely slow.

Finally, darkness descends. The body restores itself, as does the mind in its flights of fancy. Tomorrow is another day, with new battles and new enemies. No taint of yesterday must cling to tomorrow's consciousness. Soon, any accumulated load would overcome the strongest defenses. The breakup would not be pretty. Our Hero survives the best way he knows. "It ain't nothin' but a thing, and things never last." That is his only hope.

The Perfect Christmas Letter — Christmas 1997

And there we were, sending out our annual Christmas letter to family and friends. Doesn't time just slip by? I know the holiday season is here because the Christmas cactus is blooming, the one Daughter said we did not really need because we already had a cactus. She meant me.

We had an eventful year. The Heir stumbled into the house, once again asking for a fire extinguisher. He was mumbling something about a propane bottle that fell over, and these mammoth flames coming out of a kerosene heater he had lit. He has not raised the roof out there in his garage yet, but I have considered it.

Our next door neighbors are finally speaking to us again (if we happen to meet them while shopping in Grand Island). You would think our dog had chewed up his wallet, family photos, and credit cards on purpose. After all, he was the one that fell down while out back trying to untangle the mutt (Yes, it was our mutt). To keep the peace, we farmed the dog out to a friend who now claims that dog is eating him out of house and home.

That same well-meaning friend brought me an article on how to cope with hot flashes. (Retribution?) I mistakenly thought I was always "hot." I guess not.

After celebrating the Parent's fiftieth wedding anniversary, Our Hero noted that I would be half a century next birthday. (I am only "33" and still in college.)

Speaking of college, The Heir, Daughter, and I took turns taking college classes this year. The Heir finished his Southeast Community College at Beatrice classes, I renewed my teaching certificate, and Daughter started a four-year program in Business Administration at the University of Nebraska at Kearney.

While traveling to college, we each made the intimate acquaintance of our fellow church member and State Patrol Officer who admired our driver's license photos and remarked how well our vehicles performed. I do not know why he was in Sherman County anyway.

We made choices. When I announced my decision to get engaged to my dancing partner, my "friends" impishly remarked, "I thought you were smarter than that." One of my co-workers (no longer counted as my friend) told the aforementioned, "I admire your courage." My sister advised me that I would need to change the wedding date, so it would not conflict with their trip to the state bowling tournament. Now everything's perfect!

It was a pretty wonderful year, even if we did not get to see Our Hero for most of it. We hope 1998 will be just as rewarding. Enjoy the holidays and have a great Christmas.

Love always,
The Cones

"A Conversational Quilt"

And there we were, chatting on the telephone.

"Hi, Mom! Just making my monthly check-in call."
    Special words, special chat-time …

"You will never guess where I am, what I am doing, who I am with."
    Sit down time, special stories …

"What's the news from home?"
    Sharing time, bonding, joshing …

"I just wanted you to know …"
    Planning time, scheduling, calm …

"I don't know how to tell you this…"
    Panic time, problem-solving …

"I appreciate the way you listen."
    Uplifting, rewarding time …

"You have done the right things, helped me learn."
    Requital, a giving time …

"I have so many things to show you when you come."
    Accepting, adventure time …

"Well, it had to happen, and today it did."
　　　Resignation, sighs, a time for praying …
"I just want you to know that I love you."
　　　Heartfelt love, a touching time …

"Happy Valentine's Day, Son! I will take your calls, anytime."
　　　Now it is time to make some calls of my own.

On Life and Society (Our Hero's Tale)

And there I was, watching for the train. Life is sort of a journey from point A to point B. There is no prescribed route, although there are some tested and tried trails that will get you there. One of these is a social standing in society.

Social standing is like a train on a track that runs down the pathway of life. Once you get on that train, everything is pretty cut and dried. There is a certain way to do things. You stop at certain places at prescribed times and arrive at your destination at a scheduled time.

There are different ways to get on that train. Some people have parents that put them on it when they are born. Others see everybody else getting on and do so, too. Some decide the train is the best way to get to their destination and climb on.

Once you get on that train, life changes. You do not have to walk in the rain, cold, or blazing heat. You cross big ravines and can tunnel under mountain ranges with ease. Life is much easier there.

But you also miss the smell of the trees in the morning, a field full of butterflies, the miracles of nature, sunlight on your face in the springtime, and the symphony of nocturnals at twilight. The lows are higher, but the highs are lower.

One problem with trying to get on that train is that it does not stop and let you on. You must take a running jump at it as it goes by. The longer you wait, the faster the train goes, and the harder it is to get on.

If you decide later that you want to get on, it is so far ahead of you that it is nearly impossible to catch. If you do get on, the good seats are already taken. You get stuck with the seat next to someone totally disagreeable. There is gum on your seat, and the cushion is worn out. But you are on the train.

Somehow, when I was little, I was either not looking, did not hear it coming, or was not told to watch for it. I missed the train. But now as I see it going by, I look at it and wonder if I did not inadvertently make the right decision. At least the right one for me …

Postcard to Nebraska (Our Hero's Tale)

And there we were, far from Nebraska. Welcome back, true believers. We catch up with Our Hero in the sleepy port town of Haifa, Israel. Next door to the Gaza Strip and the West Bank of the Jordon River, the streets are fraught with danger. However, the archeological delights of Bethlehem and Jerusalem beckon to this wary traveler like the sirens did to Ulysses. Women with guns are everywhere he looks. What is in store for our intrepid wanderer of foreign shores? We wait, breathless with anticipation, for word on his next exploit.

Our Hero pauses a moment to reflect on the last port call, Souda Bay, Crete. In a word, it sucked. The winter months find this tourists' paradise barren and deserted, a ghost town on an arid rock in the middle of the ocean. He finds his name as a Navy man both exalted and vilified on boat pictures in several establishments of the dark smoky alcohol-serving kind. Relics of a previous visit assail him at every turn. After restocking his larder with contraband liqueurs, he retires to the relative safety of his submarine. The world has left this place. There is nothing here for him now.

Greetings from the USS NORFOLK:

Try writing your life like a comic book or a dime novel. It actually seems exciting that way. I'm going to tour Jerusalem and see all that religiously historical stuff on Saturday. Other than that, I do not have many plans for here. Our submarine schedule has been torn asunder. 132 days.

Get your orders in for Christmas presents, or you are not going to get anything until I return. You know what the great thing is about Europe? No two-to-four hour a day sessions with nothing but Christmas songs on the radio. To all of you I intended to read this, take care. I will try and write again soon.

Missives from the Mediterranean (Our Hero's Tale)

And there we were, reading the letter from Our Hero, still at liberty port in Israel.

Hello again!

I spent a couple days in Haifa, Israel, enough to tell you about it at least. Received the photos you sent. That seems fairly rapid as far as mail in the military goes.

In this port I have mostly been walking around and shopping a lot. I had to buy some sunglasses. It is winter. Why would I need sunglasses? I splurged and bought an expensive pair of RayBans. I have vowed not to sit on them or lose them this time. We will see what my resolve amounts to. I looked at a leather jacket. It was very nice, lined, and fit like it was tailored to my body. But at 1600 shekels ($390) I decided to pass. I will wait till next fall and get one exactly like I want at Wilson's. It will not be as nice, but, oh well. They also have some very inexpensive diamonds here, but I do not have anyone to bring one home for, so I will pass on those, too.

I was going to go on a tour of Jerusalem and Bethlehem. I figured since I was in the area, I might as well make the effort. But the tours were cancelled due to some shootings in the area. Israel is very civilized on the surface, but underneath tensions swirl. I guess it just was not meant to be. Amazingly enough, all my friends seem to be afflicted with the same malaise that has affected me. We seldom go out and do anything and are generally home early, before the night life really gets started. Old age and hard living are taking their toll, I guess.

I should be flying back sometime in March to process out by April twelfth. I did not get some of the qualifications that I need to really make myself marketable. If I have problems getting a job, I might take my GI Bill and go back to college to become a high school English or History teacher. I could still play with race cars during the summer. That would not be that bad, would it? I had all these high hopes, but I think it is time to face reality.

By the way, let Sister know that garter photo you sent has developed a loyal cadre of devoted admirers. They are all slightly confused by the bowling shoes, though.

I have been looking for some nice crystal for you for Christmas, but everything over here is silver and mucho dinero. I will wait till Spain, I guess.

Swagelok (Our Hero's Tale)

And there we were, on liberty port call in Israel.

Good morning!

I figured it was time to tell you exactly what happened so far, except that it is all classified. You will just have to use your imagination. We stopped in Haifa, Israel, for six days. The big deal about Israel, of course, is Jerusalem. We toured it in one day, which is not quite long enough. But to spend too much time there is probably not a good idea, as it was rather tense from the different factions there. I spent the rest of the time walking around and shopping.

Israel is fairly civilized, consequently everything is quite expensive. The other stop of interest, rather similar to Jerusalem in a twisted, convoluted sort of way, was the Elvis Presley Café. Some guy loved Elvis Presley so much that his diner has every Elvis Presley concert bill, album cover, commemorative plate and memorabilia ever made. It plays Elvis …

> *Hello from Atlantis. This is a message from the superior alien race that has taken over the body of this frail pitiful human. I will use him as a speaker until his usefulness to us, the master species, has ended. Their pitiful excuse for an underwater vessel. Bah! We scoff at it derisively. Using primitive nuclear power/steam turbine propulsion plants*
>
> *in steel shells—Planet Zorkon has not even used them for thousands of your earth-years. Our instructions to you are these: Go to the leaders of your country and tell them exactly how bored your submariners are. Explain to them how this makes them susceptible to mental takeover by an alien species.*

… Presley music twenty-four hours a day, and has the world's largest Elvis statue outside. Look it up in the Guinness record book, you will see.

Other than that, this run has been really boring. When we actually do our job, it always is anticlimactic. If anything exciting happens, I will be sure not to tell you, as it is classified. I will correspond after our next liberty port, which will be in an undisclosed location on an undisclosed date. So, until then, be good. I may be home sooner than originally thought. I will try to see you then.

The College Coed (Daughter's Tale)

And here we are … It is that time of year again! Hopefully, the holiday season is treating you wonderfully as the onslaught of Christmas cards and letters hit. Since I do not see anyone very often, I thought a brief rundown of my life at the moment would help you catch up a little … yes I know (groan) … So I guess I will hit the four basics:

School: Yes, the same old drivel every day. You have been through it, too, so you know what I am talking about! Other than dealing with the dreary boredom of constant redundancy in my classes, everything is as fine as could be expected. In one moment, graduation seems to get closer and closer and, yet, farther and farther away. Moving on in my life will be a godsend!

Work: I now work at Herberger's but am retiring this work-front during my future school semesters due to a need for greater concentration on my studies and less time on my hands. I have to resort to extreme measures due to workaholic tendencies passed down from my mother (tee hee). An article of literature said it best: "Why should I let this toad work squat on my life? Can't I use my wit as a pitchfork and drive the brute off?" I am not sure how accurate the statement is, but it always makes me laugh and, thus, serves its purpose!

Life/Relationships: What in the world to write here? I guess that I will just have to say that most of my life is concentrated on school and work and leave it at that ... I don't have time for much else!

Family: My family is doing great this year, which is a profound relief to me. In fact, we have not had any significantly dramatic happenings for a while, which, of course, means that there is something MAJOR coming around the corner! May God let me meet it with grace!

So there you go ... my life in a nutshell! I hope that your year was just as good and the New Year will treat you even better! Have a Merry Christmas!

Greetings from the Landless Down Under (From Our Hero)

And there we were, refurbishing the fast boat.

Greetings from the Landless Down Under!

Once again fickle fate has presumed to place our mighty warship in that most coveted of working ports, La Maddalena, Italia. As we watch five weeks of work get crammed into three weeks, then get crammed into one week, the work day has been steadily extended until nearly 10:00 pm. The dead of winter has closed nearly every attraction available to the tourist. Ah, Europe! Where we walked around the narrow cobblestoned streets, pummeled by the din of motor scooters, and inundated by the sneers of disrespectful locals tired of our intrusion.

Europe! Where gasoline is more expensive than wine per liter. Europe! Where the clubs do not open until 1:00 am, but liberty is secured at 2:00 am, so we can never meet any local people.

But, on the other side, there is always the boat. I have never been so ready to get out in my life. Today, an admiral toured our boat. He asked me if I was going to re-enlist. I just looked at him strangely. Is he on crack? I told him I was going back to college to become a high school history teacher. He asked me if I was married. Like that is a reason to keep doing what you hate. You know something? There is no way I could stay in. I have blown my career by being too outspoken and making too many political mistakes. How could I have failed at the Navy?

114

Trained monkeys could do this job well. How could I not? I do not understand.

Tomorrow is country night at the enlisted club. There are a lot of "big-boned" women who need to be swung 'round the dance floor a time or two. I think it is my civic duty to perform this public service, regardless of the personal sacrifice involved.

Last time in port, there was this cute little blond chick that was definitely the reigning beauty of the evening. I had danced with nearly every woman in the place except for her, mainly because I am so intimidated by confident, attractive women. Thanks, Mom. So anyway, we (our group) had gotten fairly well lit as the evening progressed, and we were discussing her merits from across the bar. They all said I should dance with her, and I said, "No. Good-looking women never dance with me." The evening wore on. My friend Jason from Texas danced with her, so they said that I had to dance with her. Well, I bet them a beer that she would say no. So, of course, she said yes. Then she complimented my dancing.

When the place closed, she gave us a ride home. The next day she came down to the boat and talked to me. Now I am all nervous. What is her deal? You can never trust them, and I have not figured out her ulterior motive yet. Also, I met a girl from Pratt, Kansas. Small world, huh? She is much more appealing to me, and a brunette, besides.

Now I am signing off because everybody is reading my email while I type it. Only the XO should read my email. Speaking of which, how are you, XO? I just want to say how much I love the Navy, this submarine, and my chain of command.

Love,
Your Hero

The Clean Sweep (By Our Hero)

And there we were, after more than nine months away on a "Med Run," entering the harbor at Virginia Beach.

… Our Hero, submersed for weeks at a time under the massive waves of the Atlantic, arrives in port aboard the USS NORFOLK proudly displaying the broom (signaling a clean sweep). Being met by the Commander-in-Chief himself, and hordes of family and friends, helps give meaning to the many months of depravation, meager rations, and personal sacrifices. It is enough to persuade him to re-enlist for another tour. Who knew?

Those who happened to catch his re-enlistment ceremony on that early morning CNN television show knew. It became the worst kept secret ever.

Dear Mom:

And here we are, still underway. Mom, I know you will not get this for a while, but I am going to write anyhow. I am fine. Do not worry about me. We are okay.

I am re-enlisting on April 1st. There is a chance it will be tax-free because I will be re-enlisting in a combat zone. Money in the pocket!

I will probably be home in early May for a speed run to get my stuff out of the garage. I am leaving the Maroon car there, since it seems that Brother needs it for a spare. Ideally, I am going to bring the blue (used to be black) '56 home and mothball it (evil car, keeping me down). The guys on the boat have named it "The Blue Sponge" (for what it does to your extra cash and some you do not have). Then Dad or Brother will load up the stuff I need in their pickup and take me back to Norfolk. Then we can go to a NASCAR event or an amusement park or something. If they are too busy, I will pull the '56 home with my '55 (my new car) and pull a trailer back. I might make it home for the Rod Run, too. We will see.

Anyway, I hope you are doing well with my decision to re-enlist. It was all much more anticlimactic than it looked on television. Mostly, we cleaned up dirt and caught up on sleep. You would not believe how much dirt can collect in a place with no windows, and doors that are locked and watertight.

More to come! Introduce the idea of taking me back to Norfolk to those two. Actually, you could drive one of their vehicles out here. I would be doing most of the driving. You have never been out here to see my house, you know, although I will not be living in it when I get back. My renter has a lease until November.

Love,

Your Hero

Tiger Cruise

And there we were, honorary submariners on the USS NORFOLK. Daughter and I went to Virginia Beach, gingerly boarded Our Hero's submarine, and spent the day under the ocean. We did not actually go under the water until we had wallowed and rolled on top of the water for thirty miles. Time enough for Daughter to become extremely seasick, despite the anti-nausea medications. She spent much of the cruise in Our Hero's bunk, trying to keep from heaving. Our Hero was back at the base, on crutches from his most recent motorcycle mishap. We traveled on the tiger cruise as "temporary family" of another submariner.

We did special activities, ate at mess, and toured the non-classified parts of the sub. Eventually tiring of this, I discovered a fairly small room with only a couple of Navy guys in it. I politely asked if I could join them. I did not realize they were officers; I invaded their private room. They asked who my submariner was, as he was not escorting me at the time.

Understanding the situation, they politely asked about Son. The more I related, the more interested they became. They began asking some really detailed and personal questions, like: "How did your son become interested in joining the Navy? What did he do in high school? He actually attended college? What was his field of study? Tell us more …" I enjoyed relating stories about his activities and interests. The time just flew.

We then did the DIVE, and shot up to the top of the water at a 30 degree angle. Dishes rattled. Everything that was not secured rolled around. It was exciting. Before we returned to base, I had an official photograph taken while operating the periscope. I descended to the unfathomable depths of their mysterious realm and successfully completed all assigned activities. I was an Honorary Submariner, a scavenger of the sea. For me, the tiger cruise was awesome.

After docking, Daughter and I climbed up the steps to the bridge, climbed out of the submarine, and strolled down the pier toward Our Hero who was waiting to take us back to his house. I was joined by my two submariners from the small room. They could hardly wait to visit with Son. I really had no idea why. They started relating some of the details I had shared with them. Their smiles got broader and broader. Son got quieter and quieter. He later referred to this moment as his worst day in the Navy. I thoroughly blew his cover as a dumb hick from Nebraska. His superiors expected much more from him after that. Too bad for him; the hero only wins in comic books!

"This Car" (Our Hero's Poem)

THIS CAR IS WHY STREETS HAVE SPEED LIMITS.
THIS CAR IS WHY YOU LOOK BOTH WAYS BEFORE CROSSING THE STREET.
THIS CAR IS WHY YOU DON'T LET CHILDREN OUT AFTER DARK.
YOU'RE AFRAID, AND YOUR FEAR MAKES THIS CAR STRONGER.
WHY DON'T YOU GET OUT WHILE YOU STILL CAN?
GET BACK INTO YOUR CHEAP PLASTIC GRAY LITTLE IMPORT
WITH ITS AIR BAGS AND CRUMPLE ZONES AND
TELL YOURSELF IT WAS ALL A BAD DREAM.
BUT DON'T LOOK IN YOUR REARVIEW MIRROR.
YOU MAY NOT LIKE WHAT YOU SEE.

Fuzzy Dice

And here we are, parked alongside Interstate 90, about a half-mile ahead of Our Hero who, we notice, has just been pulled over by one of South Dakota's finest. The flashing lights alert us to the crisis. We nervously wait to see if Our Hero will be carted off to jail.

Why the concern? Apparently our "caravan" has been clocked traveling five miles per hour or more over the speed limit. We are on a deserted stretch of interstate somewhere between Spearfish and Rapid City, South Dakota. This should not be a major concern.

What is freaking us? Our Hero is driving on a suspended driver's license. His S-10 pickup has no tags, so he is using fictitious plates (ones taken from his '56 Chevy he left garaged back at the ranch in Nebraska). This is a major concern.

We are on the way to Washington State, relocating Our Hero for his latest deployment at the Naval Base near Bremerton, Washington. The Heir is towing a heavily-loaded six foot by twelve foot U-Haul trailer with his new charcoal gray Chevy crew cab. Being adventurous, I come along for the ride, which does not preclude driving duties or helping to unload. Our Hero is just trying to keep up in his S-10 pickup with no working clutch.

The patrolman takes his time. He runs the plates, researches the license and registration. He happens to notice Our Hero's sea bag stowed near the tailgate of the S-10. He asks where we are going and why? Sighing heavily, he strongly suggests Our Hero get these infractions remedied as soon as he arrives in Bremerton. He then gives him a warning for having fuzzy dice hanging from his rearview mirror. In South Dakota that offense is ruled as "impeding vision." The kind officer also advises him to tell the lead vehicle to slow down, so he can keep up without speeding.

Meanwhile, we, the Ollie and Ollie movers, are freaking. After waiting nearly a half-hour to see what Our Hero's fate is, we are mightily relieved to see the lights on the cruiser go out, the S-10 pull out and continue down the road. He signals us to follow him.

With an incredibly long ways between marked gas stations near I-90 in this stretch, Our Hero stops at a picnicking area to pour in another five gallons of gasoline. His S-10 is a racing pickup and has no gas gauge. He just stops about every 250 miles and fills it. He carries an extra can of gasoline for the longer stretches.

It is a nice sunny day in May, so we munch on our packed lunches. We are eager to hear the details. Obviously, fuzzy dice dangling from the rearview mirror

118

is not condoned in South Dakota. Laying the fuzzy dice aside, Our Hero intrepidly continues westward.

Lookout!

And here we are, just about to enter Idaho. Ollie and Ollie's moving company is at it again. This time we are moving Our Hero from the east coast to the west coast. He re-upped.

As a reference point on trips, we take photos of the "Welcome to…" state signs. Heading west on Interstate 90, we reach Lookout Point. I have the passenger window rolled down, the camera ready, and we scan for the sign "Welcome to Idaho." Just at the top of the grade, we see it. The Heir slows "slightly" and pulls to the edge of the roadway. I snap the photo, and we are on our way, down the mountain.

I look to the right and see the tips of majestic pines waving in the wind, and stare down the mountainside. It looks to be about a mile down a steep cliff before I see where the ravine might end. I look up. We are careening down the highway about 55 mph. The Heir applies the brakes to slow our descent. Either the trailer brakes are not hooked up or they are not functioning properly. The back of the pickup slides toward the ditch. If he does not let off the brake, we will jackknife the rig. We pick up speed. "Look out!"

The Heir begins to "NASCAR" the pickup and trailer back and forth across the three lanes of traffic. With his S-10 pickup, Our Hero blocks the faster traffic so they do not get in the way and perhaps cause a collision. By now, I am screaming, "Oh, my God! We are going to die." Repeatedly, non-stop! We are gradually picking up speed, in spite of his best efforts to keep the rig on the road. I cannot seem to quit screaming, "Oh, my God …" The Heir, holding hard to the wheel and steering for his life, says, "Mom! Your screaming is not helping." I cannot stop screaming.

After five miles of this, the highway levels out a bit, and he gets the pickup under control. He is red-faced, sweating profusely, and visibly shaking. We finally find a friendly shoulder and park. After ten minutes, we start off slowly and creep into the town several miles ahead. We stop for lunch and regroup. The Heir has a nervous stomach. Each of us is very emotionally fragile. Son asks if I got the picture. I nod. Yes, of course, I got the picture.

On my way back to Nebraska, I return to Lookout Point. I park on the shoulder provided to chain and unchain tires. I want to see what the posted speed limit is going down that hill. I see the sign! It says "6% grade next 4 miles.

Trucks 15 mph." OMG. No wonder we lose control. We are so busy looking for the "Welcome to Idaho" sign that we miss the important one.

Welcome to Idaho (The Heir's Tale)

And here I am, looking for the state sign for Idaho, so Mom can take her photo of it. I finally see it, 75 feet ahead on the right. We are cruising about 60 mph, but I get off the road a bit so she can get it in frame. Out of the corner of my eye I see a sign that says 6% grade next ... miles. I guess that must mean 40 mph. When I pull back onto the highway, the back end of the trailer gets loose. The trailer is swaying back and forth. I speed up to get away from the weave.

There are three traffic lanes with shoulders on each side. I take the curves all the way from the right side to the left side, NASCAR style, to cut the speed. I drive with one eye on the road, one eye on the swaying trailer, and one eye on the green tips of the trees as we rush past. Mom is in the passenger seat screaming, "Oh, my God, oh, my God, we are going to die."

I ask her to stop saying that. For five minutes she does not stop screaming, not until we get off that steep part of the mountain. Brother is driving 80 mph just to keep up. My nerves are shot. We stop so I can get them under control. Mom wants to push on. We are burning daylight. I insist that we stop for a half-hour. They eat. I do not. I cannot. Oh, Idaho, you fickle fiend. Is this a welcome?

Our First Power Tour (The Heir's Tale)

And there we were, two guys in an S-10 pickup with roll bars, fictitious plates, a shifter that would not shift, a clutch that would not work, and a transmission that kept going out. We ran down to Bakersfield, California, to join the long haulers. The first day was fun.

On day two, we went through Death Valley. It was about 135 degrees. The soles of my shoes were melting just from the heat of the exhaust under the floorboard. To stop that, we bought a couple big bags of ice and poured them on the floor. Others keep stopping us, letting us know we were "leaking" water. It was 128 degrees with 40% humidity when we rolled into Phoenix that evening.

Since it was unbearably hot, I wore shorts. My legs had not seen the sun since last summer and were so white they could blind a person. The pickup was cramped. I had to lean one leg against the shifter. Somehow, I burnt a patch on my left leg. I thought nothing of it.

That night we stopped at our friend's place for the night. We were parched.

He gave each of us a 32 ounce Gatorade. We pounded them down in seconds. He refilled the bottles with warm water, and we put them down like we were chugging beer. He refilled them a second time, this time with cold water, and told us to "sip those things."

Since we were driving without benefit of a shifter, he helped us pull the transmission. We planned to fix the truck overnight. He finally found some gaskets that would work. He had to pull them out of a Bendix air conditioner from a refrigerator truck. The next day it was still 113 degrees. It took us until 6:00 PM to get the truck back together and get on the road to Albuquerque. We had 280 miles to go to reach the rest of the long haulers. We needed to get there before 10:00 PM to get our book stamped for the "long haulers" award.

We were traveling through the desert. It was dark. The highway was posted "65 MPH CARS / 55 MPH TRUCKS." The trucks were traveling 80 mph, so we were following them, occasionally passing them at 90 mph. There was no car traffic, just truck traffic. We were cruising along and came up on one truck with a shiny blue look. We thought that seemed different. I was driving. Suddenly, Our Hero shouted, "Oh, s--t!" Four cop cars were coming up on us, with their cherries on. Our Hero told me to give him my wallet, phone, pass codes, and anything else I thought he might need. We figured I was going to jail.

The four cop cars went past us like we were not even moving. We decided to follow them at their speed, just a mile back. Now we were doing 120 mph. A fifth cop car came by in the passing lane. He was traveling 120 ½ mph as he passed me. I looked over at him. He did not even look at us. A half hour down the road, we saw the big wreck. A truck was on fire in the median by the weigh station. Cops were diverting traffic through the weigh station. I could feel the heat of the fire on my face as we slowly went past at 20 mph.

We resumed our 90 mph speed until we hit the next gas station about thirty minutes down the road. We had to fuel the S-10 about every 200 miles. It was my turn to buy the gas. Our Hero pumped the gas. I used my ATM card to get cash to pay for it. The ATM machine was inside. That area was closed off. One person had been thrown from her vehicle at sixty mph and looked really bad. She was waiting there for the ambulance. Cops were everywhere.

Our Hero was leery about hanging out in the midst of all those cops because we were still running those fictitious tags. He pulled the S-10 out of the lot and parked down the street a bit while I went to pay for the fuel. They would not let me inside. I walked up to a cop and told him I had to get to the ATM machine so I could pay for the gas. He went in with me. The accident victim was on a bench right beside me, knees all busted up, limbs angled the wrong way, and with really bad road rash. I tried not to stare. I got my $200, paid for the gas, and walked back out. The cop said, "Man, I don't know how you can do that." Then he walked over to the trash can and puked. I walked down the street, crawled in the S-10, and we went down the road. After all that, we did not get to the stamp station in time. We found a motel room.

The next day we were traveling again. It was 90 degrees, and I was still wearing shorts. My legs were white on white except for a spot the size of my hand. It was red as could be. At one of our stops that day, we noticed a red '50 Olds with its left door all dinged up. We were looking at it. The driver was a nurse and noticed the burnt spot on my leg. She said, "You need to come over to my car." She got out her kit and started swabbing crap on my burn, wiping it down, and applying salve.

We decided to get a tent and camp out that night. While we were there buying our tent, we got some poster board and made the good nurse a sign. We wrote: "Looking for a husband with parts for a '50 Olds car door." She hung that sign on her car every day for the rest of the tour.

Oklahoma City was 72 degrees. I was back to wearing jeans. That day, our Nurse walked up to me and said, "I want to see your leg." I replied, "My jeans don't go up that far." "I can solve that," she said, as she unbuckled my belt and dropped my pants to the ground. I was standing there in my underwear with my pants around my ankles in front of about a thousand people. She was wiping on antiseptic cream, cleaning it off, putting on more salve. She was concerned about my leg, mainly because I was not. Red-faced, I pulled my pants back on and declared, "Laugh over!" Then we were on the road again.

On our way to Tunica, Mississippi, we had to go through Memphis. They routed us through the worst part of Memphis. There we were with 20 mph streets, constant stoplights, and no shifter. We had to shut off the motor to stop, start it and speed shift to go, ease up to the next light. Do it again. On one corner, we saw this guy with an Uzi and a thirty-round banana clip, so we went through a light that was just turning red. Others followed. Someone with an AK-47 was at the next light. It was red. We went through it anyway. Three more cars went through it with us. Another mile took us out of town.

We found a gas station, and filled up. It was only a few miles to our next overnight stop. We decided to take the "caps" off the exhaust to make it sound loud and mean. The car show was at a casino. The entrance was on the east side with a big half circle to get to the parking on the north side. We made a nice loud entrance.

We parked three or four cars away from the GM repair shop provided to assist the long haulers. Once again we jacked up the truck. This time we were missing one specific wrench we needed to take the transmission out. We asked them for one and fixed the truck again.

Since we had a two-day stopover, we got a hotel room and carried our tools inside, so they would not get stolen. The alignment setup on the S-10 was eating the right front tire. We bought a new tire, found someone with an alignment shop that used mirrors instead of lasers to do the re-alignment. The guy there gave us the keys to his brand new Suburban, so we could eat and go back to the hotel. By four o'clock, he had the S-10 ready.

At six-thirty, we decided to find a laundromat and do our laundry. We only had one change of clean clothes left. It was a small town. We asked for directions. We were told, "You can't miss it. It is just on the right side of the road." We drove slowly down the street, looking for the laundromat. We could not find it. We passed McDonald's. About seven cops came out. We decided it must be donut time. We turned around and asked a couple of girls for better directions. They pointed it out. It was the building behind the building on the street, two blocks up the street. We pulled into the laundromat parking lot.

Suddenly, there were cops everywhere. One of them had his pistol out. Four guys in an Excursion had just come out of the laundromat. They were parked next to us. The cops pinned everyone in. We could hear them running the plates. A '56 Chevy owned by Rick A. Cone. Our Hero began handing me his money, phone, keys, everything. My right hand was up on the roll cage. I was using it as an armrest. Our Hero advised me not to make any sudden moves.

The cop walked up and said, "Your stereo was too loud." We showed him the dash. We did not even have a stereo. That part of the dash was removed and thrown in the back of the truck. The passenger had a Walkman with ear buds to listen to music. No stereo. Then the cop said, "Did you know your license plate lights don't work?" Our Hero said, "I just paid someone $500 to wire this rig and fix every light. Let's take a look." We walked back and looked; the lights were working. Then the cop asked, "What are you doing here?" We answered, "We are here to do our laundry."

We were on the Power Tour. It had been nine days. We were out of clean clothes. "Oh, what is in these bags?" "Our laundry." "Why are they in garbage bags?" "Because it rains and we wanted to keep them dry." We asked them not to get our clean clothes dirty. They went through the bags. The clean clothes were thrown on the ground. They were kicking them around, looking for drugs. Even our good, clean clothes were now grungy.

Then the cop wanted to know about the posts for the remote battery hookup in the back of the truck. By this time we knew we were being jobbed. We patiently explained the setup. We pointed out the stickers from the Power Tour stops. We talked about the NASCAR transmission. Our Hero asked if they wanted to see the engine. They popped the hood. Our Hero droned on and on about his truck. Then the cop asked, "Do you think this thing would do a hundred?" Our Hero cagily answered, "I have never seen a place where the speed limit was posted at a hundred, but I think it would do that, no problem." It was now forty minutes into this pull-over. The cop asked, "Are you guys going to be here for a while?" We replied, "The last time we checked, it took a couple hours to do laundry." The cops left. The four guys in the Excursion left. We picked up our clothes and decided to get out of there. We would do laundry later. We could wear our dirty clothes one more day.

We ran into the guys in the Excursion at the car show. They told us how scared they were. They saw the whole thing, cops with their guns drawn, and heard the questions. They thought a drug bust was going down. We were happy to move on down the road.

At Talladega, the transmission on the S-10 went out again. The organizers wanted the long haulers to park on the grass in the infield. We wanted to park on the concrete so we could jack up the truck and work on it. We lost that battle. The rear main was out, so the S-10 was taking a quart of oil every hundred miles. The undercarriage was coated with oil. It dripped on us as we were under there trying to work on the transmission. We drove 400 miles that day, so the tranny oil was hot. We could only jack up the front or the back because we were on the grass. We did not have much room to work that way. Our Hero tipped the transmission as he was removing it and poured hot oil down my back. Half of me was now covered in stinky, smelly, burnt transmission fluid. Our Hero did not fare much better.

We were wearing the special shirts provided by that day's sponsor, as requested. They were now filthy. The free lunch for those on the power tour was served between two and four PM. It was then three-thirty. We had to leave the truck and get over there, filthy shirts, oily hands, and all. They were already packing up lunch so we grabbed what we could. The sponsor for the day was gabbing on the microphone. As we walked past, I said, "Hey, man, I've got your shirt on." I heard, "Thanks a lot, ya f**king a**hole!" over the mike. Everyone looked over at us. Someone commented, "Dude, you guys need to take a bath, bad." We found a place to eat with the least amount of people around us. We knew we were stinky, and dirty, and oily. Fifteen people got up and walked off.

While we were eating, some guy from *Hot Rod* magazine sat down and talked to us. He said it seemed like we were having some trouble. We said, "Yeah, but we are getting through it." We were grungy to the max. In spite of our protests, he introduced us to three or four really "big" people because he thought we could use some help. The current GM of Chevrolet was there and asked about our specific situation. He offered ideas on how to solve the problem in the future and told us how to make an external slave cylinder that was outside the bell housing. We would still be able to shift. He was very understanding and helpful.

The Power Tour ended at Panama City. We decided to go swimming in the Gulf of Mexico, just to say we had done it. There was a tropical storm near Texas, so the waves were heavy, some six foot. By the time we noticed that we were gradually being swept out to sea, we were a long way out. It took us two hours to swim back to shore, fighting the undertow. We were exhausted after that swim and sat on the balcony during the dance that night. Most guys at 24 and 27 would be out raising Cain. We decided we could not party like rock stars anymore. We had aged ten years just from the debacles of life.

The Day I Apologized to My Parents (See Rule #50) (Our Hero's Tale)

Every child that grows up eventually apologizes to their parents. The day comes when that adult child realizes why the parents were so "hard" on them and "unfair" and "ruined their teenage LIVES!" We join Our Hero on the day the light came on, it all made sense, and he made the call to let his parents know the message was finally received and acknowledged:

That light came on for me in January of 2001. My submarine was hosting a "Tiger Cruise." Long ago, before the era of Al-Qaeda, a boat would occasionally invite the crew's family members on a one-day trip to see what happens on a submarine and what their son/husband/brother/father did all day. My mother and sister had gone on their Tiger Cruise when I was on the USS Norfolk (SSN-714) in 1997.

My first boat, the one my mother and sister rode on, was a fast attack submarine. In 2000, when I reported to my second command, a much larger and roomier ballistic missile submarine, they came out to visit. I took the two of them on a tour of a ballistic missile sub while they were there. The crewmember tour guide was showing us a berthing area, and explaining how little space each crewmember had. My mother exclaimed, "Really? That seems like quite a bit to me." The tour guide looked at her quizzically. She drew herself up and replied

125

loftily, "WE are fast boat sailors." The tour guide made eye contact with me. We managed to keep straight faces for the remainder of the tour, but it was not easy.

It was my dad's turn to ride on a Tiger Cruise. He came with me on the USS Michigan (SSBN-727). This was a special cruise because it was going to be three days long, something that almost never happened. The guests rode out on a "small boat" to meet the sub and were transferred over to us. I got to go topside and escort him below. It was a rare beautiful clear day in January, and I enjoyed the scenery and the stillness of the crystal clear Puget Sound for my brief moment topside.

Well, Dad did not agree with me about the stillness. He remarked multiple times how much the boat was rolling. It was so stable I had to close my eyes to feel any movement. I mean, the Sound had looked like a tabletop when I was topside. Dad had ridden a troop ship to Germany when he was in the Army; he should be used to this. I began to get concerned. My concerns intensified when the Commanding Officer announced that our submergence would be delayed due to a waterspace management error by squadron. He assured us it would be taken care of quickly, and just to hang tight. You see, every submarine gets a "box" of water they have to stay in. The boxes account for navigational error, right of way, shipping lanes, ocean depth, and several other factors. Unfortunately, there wasn't any room to give us a "box," so we were stuck on the surface until the powers that be moved some boxes around. Submarines are shaped like a cigar, and don't do well on the surface.

While we were waiting, a monster storm rolled in. Now there was no doubt that the ship was rolling. I was now alarmed. Dad was green. I mean, green. Heck, half the crew was green. The boat started rolling. I mean, rolling. We needed to dive for stability, and do it right now. Just then, the CO got on the horn, and told us there was not going to be a "box" for us until morning. We were stuck on the surface all night, with all these seasick landlubbers, in a storm so bad I was having trouble getting enough guys together to man a full watch team.

We spent the night rolling, and tossing, and turning, and twisting. Quite frankly, I have been to some places I cannot particularly discuss where it is winter and stormy all the time. I even rode out a hurricane once. Never had I experienced anything on this scale. Over half my division was so seasick they could not stand watch.

My poor Dad. He lay in my bunk, retching and heaving into a bucket with a trash bag in it for hours upon hours. And me? I had to sit there, helpless, wondering what to do. He would hand out the bucket, and I would dump out the trash bag in the head (toilet). Of course, the plastic bag can't go down the toilet on a submarine, because the Navy cares for the environment and sends no plastic overboard. That meant I had to squeeze the vomit out of the bag into the head, then dispose of the plastic bag. It was a rough go. Then I had to go back to the berthing area and helplessly sit on my hands while it happened all over again.

That was the moment when I realized why my parents were so pissed the day I announced I had lost my full ride scholarship to the University and was quitting school. After that disaster, it felt like they barely put up with me while I worked a few dead-end jobs until I ran to the military along with all the other people who could not make it in the real world. Today was the day I figured out why they cared what I made of myself. I thought of the many times they cleaned up MY vomit, nursed me through multiple ear infections, pneumonia, chicken pox, a hernia operation, and numerous near-death childhood experiences. I could almost hear them saying, "I didn't suffer through all that, just to see you amount to nothing!"

Finally, morning came, the boat had waterspace, and we mercifully submerged. Dad immediately found his sea legs and whistled his way around the submarine, striking up conversations with other guests and talking to off-duty crewmembers. He took part in all the activities, bought a command ballcap to wear, and never took it off. He had the time of his life in those three days. It is the one story I have heard every single time I have visited him, no matter how deep into dementia he has fallen.

When we pulled in, I called my mother and apologized for everything I had put her through in my youthful ignorance. I took Dad out to dinner and apologized to him before he returned home. I remember that day as crystal clear as any I have lived. What day did you realize the sacrifices your parents made for you?

Oww ... (Our Hero's Tale)

And there I was, tooling down the highway on my way to the base. Well, it had to happen someday, and today it did. I had my first wreck on the motorcycle. I was on the right side of the lane on a long left turn, where the highway intersected with a gravel road. At the outside of the turn was scattered gravel. The bike skidded. I went into the ditch and flew over the handlebars. I do not remember much after that, but I hit my head at least twice, of that I am sure. I have the lumps to prove it.

When I came to, there was a busload of guys standing over me, asking if I was "okay." I replied, "Just a minute!" I stood the bike back up. It started, so I said, "Yeah, I'm fine. Good to go." They looked at me like I was crazy, but let me go on my way. The bike and I were covered in mud from head to toe. I rode in to work that way.

About that time, other guys from my division rolled in and asked, "Gee, what happened? Did you wreck your bike?" Duh! They were like, "Really?" Yep. "Oh... my... God! Are you okay?" Yep. "Good Lord, have you seen the Doc?" Nope.

I have a bit of a stiff neck, a bruise on the top of my head, one near my hip. The bike has some serious cosmetic damage. Apart from the veritable hay bale of grass I pulled out from under it and the mud everywhere, we are both fine.

That entire day I heard stories of guys breaking collarbones, femurs, losing all their skin. I attribute my "good luck" to wearing quality motorcycle gear and to tucking in my arms and staying limp as I went ass over teakettle, so to speak. I will be catching rides to work for a while. My nickname on the boat has been officially proclaimed, "Evel Cone-nievel. Even the officers were calling me that by the end of the day.

Remember, there are two kinds of riders: Those who have laid it down, and those who are going to lay it down. The cool biker terminology for this is: "Son laid down his ride, but his leathers saved him from too much road rash. His brain bucket did its job, so he's fine."

Yes, I will continue riding. Like the old saying, "If you don't get right back in the saddle, the horse will know you're scared and buck you off every time after that."

Your loving, but stiff and sore, son ...

Cycling (Our Hero's Tale)

And there I was, cycling. It turns out it wasn't a race, just a ride. I did not finish last. However, I am hurting badly.

I was going to do the fifteen mile loop with a guy from work, but when I went out to load my bike this morning, it had a flat tire, and I had to do some improvising to get it fixed, so I missed him. I said to myself, "I feel pretty good. I got good sleep last night. I am going to ride the thirty-mile loop.

Unfortunately, the guy at the registration tent did not know the color codes, and was telling everyone riding the thirty-mile loop to follow the blue arrows, which were actually for the sixty-five mile loop. So several others and I got a little more than we bargained for. I can barely stand, my knees hurt so bad.

At about the forty-three mile point, I was going to quit and call a cab, but then a guy who was paralyzed and pedaling with his hands passed me, so I felt lazy, slothful, and overall just like a total loser, and buckled down and made it to

128

the last stop. I did cut some corners toward the end just to get done with it, as did many others, including the paralyzed guy, so I felt justified. My leisurely fifteen-mile morning turned into a fifty-two mile festival of torture.

They said sorry, but I do not think that really made it okay. Punching that idiot in the nose, that would have come closer. Two Japanese massage therapists to massage my knees, that would have probably been suitable reparation, but only if they did not speak English. And I got sunburned. And, yes, my lower lip is sticking out. It's sunburned, too. Leave me alone! A hero today I am not …

The Birth of Blue Sponge Racing (Our Hero's Tale)

And there we were, discussing the birth of Blue Sponge Racing. Back when I was working on the Blue '56, I was complaining to my neighbor about how much it cost to drive a fast old car. We talked about what money pits hot rods were, and he christened my car a "wallet sponge." It was blue, so the car's name was changed from Ole Bess to the Blue Sponge.

Then Jimmy and I hooked up as racing buddies. His 1970 Nova SS was also blue, so it became Blue Sponge Two. Then I bought the S-10, and it became Blue Sponge Three. Now my neighbor just bought an Olds Cutlass, and guess what. It is Blue. So it is Blue Sponge Four. As soon as Brother paints his two '55s, which he has determined will be, guess what color. BLUE. They will be Blue Sponge Five and Six. Also, unbelievably I am sure, the Mustang is light blue! That means it will be Blue Sponge Seven.

Jimmy was fabricating a bracket for his nitrous system, which ended up being a short piece of 1" aluminum angle iron with some holes in it. We were talking about how he could sell it for twenty dollars to some idiot like us, only with money, and Blue Sponge Racing was born. So anything we have to fab for our cars is a custom Blue Sponge Racing piece. Like my oil pan (a custom Blue Sponge Racing deep sump pump oil pan for '82-'93 S-10 with small block), his handmade traction bars, the nitrous bracket, my clutch setup. They all command outrageous prices because they are so specific and so well made, well, except for the clutch. But I am working on that. Since we know the owners, we get ours for less.

Anyway, here are the rules for Blue Sponge Racing: Any make of car is allowed, except for five-liter Mustangs. No new import cars. All cars must be painted some shade of blue. No idiotic graphics are allowed. No hood scoops; flat hoods are the rule, unless the hood scoop came from the factory. Frames must remain stock, no tubing for pro-street style cars, unless they run 7s or quicker in the quarter mile. You can run as much tire as will fit in the stock frame, although you can notch the inner fenders. No stickers. Stickers are for people who want to go fast but cannot. Nitrous is not required but is encouraged. Engines must run on pump gas; we build actual street cars.

We at Blue Sponge Racing recommend the B F Goodrich Drag Radial. Billet and chrome must be minimized to what parts only come in those materials. Some hard core people at Blue Sponge Racing paint over their chrome pieces. Semi-flat black is always an appropriate color. "When in doubt, weld it shut and paint it semi-flat black." Loud exhaust is not in vogue at BSR but seems to be the inevitable result of high horsepower engines. Also, we run to small-block as opposed to big-block power, but there is no set rule regarding this. However, if it is a big-block, it better be a BIG one, it had better run on pump gas, and it had better fit under the hood! Also, cheap wine and Taco Bell food is the choice for sustenance. On a final note, if your car looks faster than it is, it is probably not a candidate for inclusion on the Blue Sponge Racing Team. If it is faster that it looks, you are definitely on the right track. If you hate Mustangs, some allowances can be made, however.

Relief (Our Hero's Tale)

And here I am, feeling relieved. Outside of the financial world, everything is good, I guess. I am desperately searching for something to do in this place, though. I do not want to go to Seattle, but Bremerton/Silverdale seems only slightly larger than Ord, like Ord with stoplights, or something. There is not one dirty rundown biker bar full of hard-faced women with tattoos and no bad seventies bands, either. I thought about going to the theatre but found out their season just ended.

I am NOT working on the truck. I have even started eyeing the motorcycle. So I have been spending my time researching for the Mustang project that will take place in February, I think. I am going to be the most knowledgeable person ever regarding '71 Mustangs with late model Mustang suspension and 460s in them. That way I do not have to make all the mistakes I have with my other cars. Maybe it will be cheaper that way.

Also, I am gathering pictures for the Blue Sponge Racing official website. Tell Brother to send a picture of him in front of his ugly orange car for inclusion in the site. I am getting everyone that has helped and putting their photos on the website. Brother is "Blue Sponge Racing, Midwest Division." I am Blue Sponge Racing West. Jimmy is Blue Sponge Racing East. I get a free website with EarthLink, and that is what I am going to use it for. We have nationwide coverage! How many race teams can say that? We should all get BLUSPNG on our license plates. Since we are each in different states, we could. Then we could drive to a central location and get a picture with all our cars sitting next to each other. Very Cool! And then, and then … You know.

Anyway, I am going to go now and find something fun, exciting, and cheap that does not involve alcohol. See you and the girls in August. I will come up with some air mattresses for you gals to sleep on. Everyone will be sharing the basement. Hopefully, I am going to have the area scouted out enough that I can be a decent tour guide.

Your Hero

Chutzpah

When you are the second son, you may try to stand out from the crowd, excel, and get attention any way possible. I introduce you to my favorite middle grandson. This kid took the training wheels off his bike when he was three years old. He was a dare devil at the very least. Mostly by necessity, he would play with the older kids in the neighborhood. This made him act a little older than he really was.

One day the Kid went on a bike ride with his older brother and his friends. At the top of a huge hill, the Kid started down without a second guess. Halfway down the hill, he knew he had messed up. It was OVER. It was just a matter of time before he crashed. The Kid alertly spotted a pothole ten feet in front of him. Crucial! He pressed the brakes to stop, and he did just that. Stop. By pressing on the front brake lever, he made the bike's front tire stop. The Kid did not stop. He flipped over the handlebars, smashed his chin into the asphalt, and now remembers little of what happened next.

The nearest hospital was two hours away. His mother cried more than the Kid. He was in shock, yet held a bloody towel to his chin during the hectic ride. At the end of that day, he had stitches.

You would think after such a horrible experience, the Kid would learn his lesson. He did not. About a year later, he went down a different hill. This time he was on a big wheel. Halfway down the hill, the plastic wheels lost traction. The Kid started spinning in the big wheel, hitting a car parked on the road. Luckily, the Kid did not get hurt, but he never learned the lesson.

When I arrived for my annual visit when he was six, he challenged me to a footrace. He proudly informed me he was wearing his fast-running shoes. Unexpectedly, he did not win. He never quit trying.

When he came to visit a couple years ago, the Kid was sporting a walking cast. It was the result of a skateboarding trick gone awry. Today, he admits he still does that same skateboarding trick. He did not learn the lesson. To live continuously on the edge takes chutzpah. He has it in spades.

Mexico(ish) (Daughter's Tale)

I am blessed with a natural inclination to humor and adventure. Given a fifty-fifty decision, I will say yes seventy-five percent of the time. Unfortunately, this occasionally puts me into experiences that I would not have chosen for myself upon more foresight and less courage.

So there I was ... in Austin, Texas, co-leading an AmeriCorps team that was helping flood victims get registered for assistance with FEMA. We were working sixteen to eighteen hour days, six days a week, and only a few people had a day off at a time. Since there's only one fifteen-person van for everyone to use, and the commute is over an hour, this means we spend our off-day sleeping, doing laundry, and catching up on bookwork. Did I mention there is very little public transportation? Oh, and we sleep on cots in small shared rooms that do not really even allow us to shut the door to change, and we have no air conditioning. Not very exciting, considering Austin is a huge cultural mecca, and none of us had really had the opportunity to explore it yet.

Nearly two weeks in, the enthusiasm for the project is waning a little, and that is when it happens. In trying to find some motivational humor, I remark that the team leaders working the project should just go to Mexico on their day off. Why not? You only live once, and it is relatively close. Seven hours or so is nothing compared to driving halfway across the country. The only difference is that this time I made the joke in front of someone just as adventurous as, and slightly more reckless than, I am. I just giggle along until I find myself tagging along en route to a car rental. So this is happening, then? Ok, sure. I really have no one to blame but myself for bringing it up, and I am certainly no welch. The adventure is on! I have some horrible feeling of foreboding when we have to put the rental car under my name, but I am embracing life, so bring it on!

The first little difficulty that I have is with a customer service associate at the dealership. I make sure that she writes down every little dent and scratch on the vehicle. I have learned some things throughout my life. She keeps insisting that if the car comes back to them it will not matter if every little thing is listed. I have to be a little forceful to make it happen, and I am completely grateful that I did because that car did not make it back to that little dealership. But we will get to that later.

We finally convince the third team leader to join. She is trying to be rational ... the audacity. In convincing her to come along, I knew not what I did. That comes later, though. As we leave Austin after a work day, it is night driving the whole way there. No problem. I have at least one other person to keep me awake and help drive, right? Five hours of driving later (while the other two sleep), I pull into the San Antonio airport to pick up insurance for driving into Mexico. The original rental place recommended it and said it would help in case of emergency. We will come to that later, as well. For now, it is two more hours of me driving before we pull into a hotel at Nuevo Laredo. We will cross the border after a few hours of sleep and head into Monterrey. It is now four in the morning, so we make plans to leave at nine.

Actually, I do finally manage to get some sleep and wake up feeling kind of okay, considering I have worked an entire shift outside in ninety degree plus heat and then driven for seven and a half hours. After all, I am on this once-in-a-lifetime adventure, so I am feeling no real pain yet. Except about one issue ... This is when I should mention that I have somehow forgotten my passport. After serious debate of the issue, we decide to just go for it, and if the border turns us around, we will go to South Padre Island instead. No biggie. What is an anal cavity check or an aggressive law enforcement pat down in the long run?

We get packed up, decide to grab something to eat and—this is when I make the single most ridiculous decision of this experience—I ask the other Team Leader if she would like to drive. Only two of us were able to put our name on the rental application without paying a much higher amount due to age. I had ridden in vehicles driven by this person before and seriously feared for my life, but, hey, I am growing and branching out and accepting people where they are in the world. Sure, her driving makes me shriek in my head, but that is not an uncommon situation during my AmeriCorps term. Most people have little to no driving experience, especially with fifteen-passenger vans, and by this time, I have developed something of a callous over my terror. Besides, YOLO. It always comes back to You Only Live Once.

We stop off to get some food at a small grocery store where hardly anyone speaks English, which thrills us because their presence means this trip is legit. What did we get? Buffet style Chinese food. Yes, we drive all the way to the border of Mexico to eat hours-old orange chicken, apparently. Quite the cultural immersion. After this stop, the trip really gets to start, and I cannot wait!

To reach the border, we have to backtrack about twenty miles, then take a highway that put us at the crossing. I am on my best behavior but a little nervous about my lack of passport. The other driver has apparently zero rural driving experience and is driving through, literally, every single pothole on the road, of which there are many. I gently and kindly suggest she consider moving a little farther over on the roadway, as there is no traffic besides us, and we do not want to pop a tire on our grand adventure, do we? Giggle, giggle. No, we surely do not. Instead of moving over the eight inches or so that would have fixed that issue, she starts driving completely on the other side of the road, which is in the wrong direction of traffic flow. I am flummoxed, but, okay, no big deal. I think about my Uncle Dan's phrase, "but did you die?" and shrug it off. After all, YOLO.

We get to the Mexican border sans my passport, something that has been a matter of intrigue for all of us since the beginning of this journey across the bridge into Mexico, and we are on our way. They basically just ask if we have fruit. I have received a more difficult inquisition each time I cross the state border into California than I did while entering a different country. I am not complaining, but that was a little deflating after all the worry. At least, we did not have to worry about strip searches until trying to get back into the country.

I have been in Canada a couple of times in my life. Other than worrying about using the term "water closet" in place of bathroom, there is not much adjustment. The roads are in good shape. Most times, they post both kph and mph, and the road signs are generally in English. Mexico is a whole different ball of wax.

Since we did this trip on the fly—based on the thought process that Monterrey is basically a tourist trap, and one of the team leaders said they understood Spanish relatively okay—we did not plan for road names or even purchase a map. This immediately became an issue. Tourist trap or not, Mexico does not feel the need to oversell its main cities, or mention them on any signs. We handled this okay and eventually headed in the right direction at what we kind of felt was the legal speed. As I was in the back and had not driven out of the country in years, I forgot that kph is also on the speedometer in your dashboard. Apparently, the team leader driving never knew that and did not observe it. Five minutes of math computations later, we feel certain that no Mexican police will be pulling us over. One more hurdle overcome!

Finally, we are on the highway to Monterrey, and nothing will stop us now! Who cares if Sarah is driving literally five inches from the bumper of the car in front of us? That is just her way. We have already talked about how following distance increases safety and visibility and about how important missing potholes is. Besides, I am her friend, not her parent, and this is supposed to be a fun trip. So I suck it up and pretend it is not happening.

Less than sixty seconds after that relaxing thought process, the car hammers what must be a pot hole the size of Cleveland. We hit so hard, my teeth crack together and the windshield wipers start going. It takes less than fifteen seconds after that for me to know … popped tire. Darn it! This car is rented under my name, something I really did not want to do in case something like this happened. How did I get talked into it? Next time, I am paying the fifty extra dollars for someone else to rent the car. All this is running through my head, but outwardly I just say, "That's okay, but we need to pull over." Sara is still driving and says she thinks it is fine, nothing hurt. Kayla agrees. Sometimes I forget that not everyone has driven since they were seven years old, and things like this do not happen to them. I kindly ask twice before I just say "Pull the car over, now!" She was driving on the rim … city girls!

Four kilometers into Mexico, and we will be changing a tire. This is what I think until I step out and realize that she has hit hard enough to pop both the front and back passenger side tires. Crap. Obviously, we only have one spare tire, and we are in fricking Mexico. It is not like a Goodyear is going to be right down the road.

Our one major fortune on this journey is to end up at a run-down little truck stop. We are fortunate because, even though we cannot speak Spanish, and they cannot speak English, the people here are incredibly kind and do not let that burden get in the way of helping. Kayla has said prior to the trip that she can understand Spanish pretty well. In reality, she can understand about five words. None of them are helpful. One lady that works there uses her cell phone to translate our conversation to each other. Ah, modern technology is amazing. I try to use the contact number for the car rental company, but they keep routing us to a Spanish-only department, then to a number that disconnects us. Awesome customer service, Avis. Top notch. Long story short, three hours of trying to reach someone on the phone and some options later, we have a decision to make. That insurance that we were told to get covers absolutely nothing, especially in Mexico. I have no idea to this day what its purpose was. During all of this, the other two leave me and walk a half-mile down the road to a convenience store. Apparently, they think that the convenience store will sell tires, especially one in Mexico. It didn't.

When it came down to it, we had three choices: 1. Have the car towed across the border for $650 and then contact Avis for a switch; 2. Have the car towed to the border for $150 (but not across the border where someone can actually help us); or 3. Pay some local Mexicans to find a couple used tires and put them on for $125. That does not leave us much of an option. Despite the fine print saying any changes to the vehicle will be charged to us, I am pretty sure that is going to cost less than $650. And that option still would not have given us an operational vehicle. So, we have a guy who can speak a little caricature of English be a broker of sorts for us and put the deal together. Afterwards, he says we were charged double since we are young, pretty women that look rich. (And silly, apparently.) If only they knew that each one of them probably makes more per month than all of us combined. I mean, we are volunteers. We do not make anything. That is my point. But I digress. Apparently, it will take the Mexicans about forty minutes to drive wherever they are picking up the tires. We have to give them $100 dollars up front and the remaining money after they finish. I am just hoping I am not handing our last cash away to someone that is just going to run off with it.

Our tire broker says they will make us up a plate of food for free if we wish. There is no way I can eat anything at this point, but the other two say, "Sure." We go inside the little bare café attached to the truck stop to sit and watch telenovelas while we wait for them to return with tires. He sets a plate of mushy brown stuff, quick cook rice and an enchilada sort-of thing that probably had been frozen. I am in Mexico and have yet to get any legitimate Mexican food.

We have been here a while, and I finally have to succumb to the need to pee. I have been holding it because this place was not what you would call sanitary. And, trust me, I have pooped outside numerous times while backpacking. They take me to a cement building with a toilet inside that does not have a seat. Black flies are biting the whole time I am in there, and there isn't any toilet paper. I cannot shut the door either, or it becomes pitch black darkness. It is like a toilet in an abandoned jail cell. This is everything I expected from Mexico and more.

Once I finish, I walk outside, and that is when I notice the little Chihuahuas that were barking at me the whole time I was trying to squeeze liquid out of my body. This trip just became official! There is an obese, older man lazing by a dirty pool that has a cheap carport over top of it. He is yelling at the dogs. For some reason, everything in this moment just strikes me as really funny, and that humor continues for the rest of the day. I think the stress and shock was completely gone, and reckless acceptance has finally set in. Kayla and Sarah did not seem to care if we lived or died in Mexico, and I finally arrived at the point of finding the hilarity in the situation.

I get back inside, and the tire broker hands us a bill for the food. Apparently, free food in broken English does not actually mean free. So we pay for it by handing over random bills and hoping that the people working there are honest. Did we take any time to learn about money conversion rates before making this jaunt into another realm? Of course, not, silly! Why would we have done something practical like that? That was not befitting our traveling style at all.

The group of guys that went after the tires finally get back. We have been at this place over five hours now. They proceed to use hand tools and wood blocks out of the back of their rundown Toyota to pull our tires off and replace them. Sarah hit the pothole so hard that the rim was actually bent in. They have to use a sledgehammer to bend it back in order for the tire to even hold air. I am pretty confident that we are going to die while driving, but I have ceased to feel anything but amusement at everything.

The whole time a couple of guys are working on our rental, various people are walking up or riding bikes up to talk to the guys doing the work. They are obviously laughing about the situation, and I cannot blame them. I have no idea where they all came from because, other than the two buildings in the area, it is only sage and cactus for miles. They finally finish up, and in our difficult manner of communicating, they try to reassure me that the tire will hold air and not kill us all. I just shrug, smile, and pay them with our last fifty bucks and a thank you. At the end of the day, this is just something else that I will have to trust them on. I am happy that a way out looks possible and that they returned at all, much less actually got the tires on without any modern tools or equipment.

I am fully embracing how screwed I am, financially and otherwise, at this point and ask the other two girls if they just want to keep going to Monterrey anyway and who cares about anything anyway? Kayla is game, of course, but Sarah—consistent buzzkill of the "Not Quite Mexico Trip 2015"—just wants to head back to housing in Austin. Awesome. So head back we do. This time I am driving.

This is the part of the journey where it becomes relevant that I did not bring my passport. I did bring my AmeriCorps ID and FEMA ID badge. The Border Patrol is under the same governmental department, so I am hoping for a little family forgiveness. It takes us a couple of tries to figure out where to exit, as you are only allowed to leave in a couple places, as the Mexican police told us. I pull up and tell them a short version of our sob story, explaining the tires and saying that I lost my passport, which was technically true, as I was not 100% sure where it was at that point. Apparently, purchasing tires is considered consuming a service in Mexico, and that is a no-no without fees or permits. I had our helpers put the old tires in the truck, however, so it is obvious we are telling the truth.

Basically, the big tough border patrol agents realize we are incredibly unlucky and kind of stupid in how we are going about our little adventure. They tell us that we have to get a permit to travel more than five kilometers into the country, and we would have been turned around anyway. They roll their eyes at us, tell us never to do this again, and wave us out. Pretty funny. I am sure we gave them something to laugh about with their co-workers for the rest of the day. Or week.

I drive the car back to the San Antonio airport, where we fill out an incident report and exchange our vehicles. No imploding tires during this leg of the journey, thank goodness. When we exchange vehicles, they tell me that Sarah is no longer an authorized driver, as if I would have let her near the steering wheel of a vehicle I am in again. I have to drive the eight hours from Mexico(ish) to Austin, Texas, by myself. Of course, the other two sleep the entire time.

After we arrive back in Austin, I have a moment to realize that on our one day off, I have gotten four hours of sleep, driven fifteen hours, not seen Mexico beyond the border crossing, only eaten bad Chinese food and bad microwave Mexican food, and I am now more broke than ever. Awesome. YOLO??? The celebration has lost some of its appeal.

I took the car back the next morning, and the rental workers asked how the trip went. We gave them a condensed version, and they said "Yeah, you should never drive a car in Mexico." Well thanks, Avis. Glad you share that after the fact. But I am definitely convinced that this advice is actually good, unlike the insurance. There is no way in heck that I will ever be driving a vehicle in Mexico again. For me, it is the bus next time ... after I pick up my travel permit, show off my passport, and convince a fluent Spanish-speaking friend to join me.

Do I count this trip to Mexico? Not really. Outside of the hilarious Chihuahua experience, I am not actually sure it qualifies. Seven hours I spent inside the country, four kilometers from the border. Did I learn anything from this trip? Possibly. I will definitely never travel anywhere without doing at least some language and cultural research ahead of time. And I definitely will not ignore my feelings about someone's ridiculously bad driving in the interest of maintaining a fun atmosphere. Will I be more cautious next time I have to make a decision on embracing an adventure or playing it safe? Umm ... uhh ... I would like to say yes, but let's be real ... that is probably not going to happen. After all, the YOLO philosophy may be beleaguered, but it is still thriving.

The most powerful thing in your life
is your hour of opportunity ...
it is also the most irretrievable.

– Author Unknown

CHAPTER SIX:
NEW BEGINNINGS

To make a difference in someone's life,
you don't have to be wise, rich, or beautiful.
You just have to be there when they need you.

— Steven Aitchison

I Have Come to Believe ...

And there we were, District 24 toastmasters gathered together on a special Saturday evening waiting to welcome our new District Governor. First, we were treated to the farewell address of our current District Governor:

Welcome to this very special evening. Rarely do we have the opportunity to surround ourselves with people who mean so much to each other. Thank you for this opportunity to briefly touch upon some high points and some turning points of this past year. For the most part, I have decided not to mention specific names, to protect the innocent.

It has been a year like none other. Both District 24 and I celebrated the big 5-0 this fall. With this "coming of age" and the seasoning of experience during this year as your District Governor, I have come to believe in the value of friends, in the importance of letting others find the way, in the benefits of toastmasters.

I still do not believe the best time of day is early morning and that the thrill of the day is seeing the sun break over the horizon, though I have seen that happen many times on my way from Ord and Grand Island to meetings in the Lincoln and Omaha areas. *(Dan, maybe someday I will come to believe. We do learn from our friends.)*

First, I have come to believe in the value of friends. Real friends. Friends who will stand by us even when we are wrong, even when we say something we would really like to have never said. On more occasions than I care to admit, I have needed real friends this year. They came through for me. This has been a year of growth and change for me. Immediately after I was elected to office, I met the man I decided I just could not live without. That change in my life involved a change of name, a change of address, a different office location and email account, and a major lifestyle change. I had to develop a lot more flexibility. I learned to reach out more, to make myself more accessible, and to be patient with those less accessible.

Second, I came to believe in the importance of letting others find their own way, the best way of doing things for them. I am not going to say this was easy! If definitely was not! But the rewards of watching another person grow and learn is worth the anxiety it causes those who know another way might work better. In the end, these people become our real friends. A real friend knows that it is not a friendship until after you have had a disagreement and then found a way to resolve it. Those kinds of opportunities came to me this year, as well. Did I mention that this was a year of growth and learning?

Third, during my experiences developing new clubs and helping others find what works for them in the toastmaster program, I discovered the many benefits of toastmasters and the value in serving the district in a leadership role. Watching a club add a number of new members, hearing about dedicated toastmasters like Rod Dolton, who personally recruited nine new members and is working on recruiting even more, sparks my enthusiasm.

Working with toastmasters who think and speak in another language besides English redefines what sharing and learning together is really about. It is very uplifting to see people work together and help each other gain confidence, try new things, develop new approaches to life's many situations.

I will summarize my thoughts with a poem I wrote earlier this spring, "Requiem to PDGs" (Past District Governors), since I will soon be joining their ranks. I am truly thankful for the many people who helped, encouraged, and supported me. I especially wish to share my appreciation for the leadership team and for our area and division governors. Without them, this year would not have been as enjoyable, or as rewarding.

It delights me to know that the leadership is ongoing, that reliable toastmasters help train those who are learning the skills of leadership. We have a very seasoned leader taking the reins. Your new leader has shared many of the responsibilities of leadership this year and will continue to develop and share the benefits of the Toastmaster program. I encourage you to support her journey.

Once again, I look back with fondness and ahead with confidence, seeing all those who made the connection, reached out and gave to others, who showed me the way, who taught me the value of friendship, who shared the benefits of better communication and leadership skills. Thank you, all of you, for making a believer out of me!

Your Soon-to-Be Past District 24 Governor
May 15, 1999

"Requiem to PDGs"

As we ease into our PDG years,
And our banner year is o'er,
When our leadership dues are finally paid,
We ponder what purpose there is left
In our toastmaster lives.

There's still one important thing
We must do before we're through.
With the generous gift of these last gracious days,
We must show those that follow
How life's song can be sung.

They must see us accept what cannot be changed,
Yet battle on for a cause worthwhile.
They must see us forgive, and even forget.
Make attempts to heal old wounds,
And be unafraid to risk friendship again.

They must see our shining light right to the end:
For we give the leadership a brave light to follow,
One that never goes dim.
I believe that Toastmasters will give me an ongoing purpose for life,
Even as a PDG...but for a little while, my heart will feel hollow.

The Roast

And there we were, at the advanced toastmasters' monthly meeting. These are excerpts and snippets from the toastmasters' roast of Immediate Past District Governor Linda Cone.

Dan Monroy:

When I first met Linda, she reminded me of my Marine drill instructor. I did NOT want to look her in the eyes. They seemed filled with fire, passion, and cool condemnation. They hid a heart of gold and the sterling character of a warrior. I always wanted her on my side. I learned to respect her and see through the toughness to the gentle person inside.

We enjoyed many sunrises together on our trips from Grand Island, Nebraska, to wherever. It was a constant battle for her to even keep her eyes open. A morning person she is not. I delighted in waking her and showing her the beautiful sunrises. They were special moments in some very long days. I will remember Linda as a cherished friend and cohort.

Jim Dawson:

Our first encounter was chartering Strictly Speaking in Grand Island. Such enthusiasm! She reminded me of Dolly Parton's bra strap. She knew what she had to do, but really had no idea how to do it! It was refreshing watching her grow into a leader.

Gene Deyoe:

I remember this statement of hers, "This is the way it is!!! Now let's make it better." She was never satisfied until it was better, for as many people as possible. Hard work did not frighten her at all.

Her short term memory loss meant things needed to be precise and to the letter. This took some getting used to for the rest of us. We did make things better in District 24. It was not even that painful …

Jackie Gfeller:

Together, we learned to be organized. We conquered the paper monster that was living in my house. That paper monster had control over two big rooms and an entryway. We sorted, filed, tossed, gave away duplicates, and used the rest as resources. It only took Linda a couple of days to show me how. I found my house again. Since she is reputedly always searching for studs, I now present her with a stud finder. We wish her luck.

Linda has a reputation for being frugal, especially in airports. I present her with a care package (of nuts, raisins, candy, and snacks). This is to partially repay her for all the snacks she shared with me so I did not have to pay those exorbitant airport restaurant prices.

Her housekeeping skills are thorough and unrelenting. I share the story of the ironing board that would not fold up so she could put it away. We could not leave our motel room until we accomplished that (in my thinking, completely unnecessary) task. She liked to say her house was always ready for a party for forty people. I let her know my house usually looked like I had just had a party for forty people.

Working with her was something like working with a tiger and riding it so we would not be swallowed. I tried to tell her Rome was not built in a day. Her response: But I was not foreman then!

I can attest to her sensitivity to suffering. I just point to my throat. She once threatened to slit it! She did not appear to be joking at the time, but with her dry humor, who could actually tell.

To my friend Linda, who is tolerant, compassionate, and forgiving … a huge hug!

Computers for Cowards

And there we were, coeds in Computers for Cowards class. This is our take on it ...

It is "back to school" time. I am a student, freshly enrolled. I just got back from my Computers for Cowards class, and guess what I learned? I learned that I am a coward. Yes, a computer coward. Those darn little things called computers scare me to death.

If you had heard what I heard today, I swear you would run home right now and hide in the closet! Do you know what those harmless looking little boxes can do? No, I mean do you REALLY know what those "harmless-looking little boxes" can do? Today, I am here to share the *truth* as I learned it in my "Computer for Cowards" class.

The synopsis for this course assures me that I am spending my hard earned dollars to relieve myself of the anxiety I have over entrusting my entire being to a metal box full of unidentifiable gadgets, gizmos, thingies, and assorted wires and cables that go "here," "there," and "WHERE?"

Because I am open minded, I am willing to try this, but I hereby reserve the right to drop kick the silly thing out the window at the first sign of trouble. I will not, repeat *will not* allow this instructor to try and fool me into believing that my life will be better just because my computer tech brother can now send me intricately detailed e-mail (and expect me to understand it).

On the positive side, today our instructor did make a feeble attempt to lure us into a state of complacency by sharing "the truth about computers."

Truth #1: Computer nerds invented computers. Big surprise! Can one honestly envision seeing Bill Gates WITHOUT the glasses?

Truth #2: A bigger surprise comes with learning the "sole" purpose of computers. The "truth" is, computers serve primarily to remind us regular, every day, normal people that "techies" really "rule" the 21st century. (The "techies" of the world can twist numbers and letters into the most glamorous of databases, and make 65,536 different colors simultaneously appear on a piece of paper halfway down the hall, and do it only to remind everyone else that WE cannot do that.)

Once we come to grips with this reality, computers become much easier to tolerate (or so says my instructor). For example, I cannot

144

begin to tell you how many times I have been annoyed by a silly pop-up message right in the middle of my document that I am composing. That pop-up message MUST be dealt with because it will not go away until I do something with it. I cannot continue typing while it is there. The "techies" win again. My friend Mags says, "When in doubt, 'X' it out." But what if I need it later on? Where did it GO? Only the "techies" know.

Truth #3: Every computer has a "mood chip." A mood chip can detect your mood from the pressure you use to push down on the keys, and it senses your temperature through your fingertips. As your temperature rises and keys get pushed harder, the chip adjusts all internal components accordingly. The system will react to your mood by simply matching its speed, accuracy, and overall temperament to yours. In other words, the more frustrated you become, the more frustrations it causes. Ultimately, it will "freeze-up" altogether because you have quit typing and have begun to shake your fist at it. The mood chip cannot be removed.

I consider my instructor to be a "trusted" expert. So, I believe him when he says, "Computers do have feelings." But what about *my* feelings? Well, if you can't lick 'em, join 'em. I have decided the best answer for me is to take more lessons, to learn more truths. Perhaps I should become a computer tech!

With this in mind, I am planning to go back to the Computers for Cowards class. The instructor promised me that the mouse will not crawl up my pant leg. The random access memory will not randomly access my memory. Besides, I am looking forward to next week's class. He is going to present a lecture about inoculating my computer against viruses. I am anxious to learn where we are supposed to stick the needle.

The Year That Was ...

And there we were, newly married. During "the year that was," my goal was to learn to love honestly, deeply, and passionately unreservedly. That is what I attempted. That is what I did.

There are many who have known and loved my visage and my soul. They respond to the light within and to the love I can give. My grief arises from not being able to create this same connection, or an even closer one, with the man I gave my love to unreservedly.

No matter how much I enjoyed the time we had together, the fantasy of romance, our season of love, I eventually had to choose to return to the real world, to be with real people, those who recognize and tolerate imperfections and appreciate them, and me for having them. I returned for healing and for the support of my real friends.

I have as much passion as ever, but I am more relaxed, less driven. I have decided that intimacy turns on trust, and dies for the lack of it. A real relationship requires being trustworthy and real.

Most people with power say they trust people. What they mean is that they only trust them as long as they can control them. True trust occurs only when we have no control. My partner and I entered that state: no control over one another. It terrified us.

What about love without trust? In that respect, we were well-matched. I eventually reduced that barrier and continued to love, unreservedly, completely. He chose not to yield, not to trust. It became apparent that he did not deserve me or my love. I left him, though it broke my heart.

Friends concerned with my feelings, my state of mind, asked if I would do it differently if I could. If I regretted the experience? I believe if I had missed the experience, I would have missed the lessons. The point is I lived, I loved, I learned!

We were the conflict between order and chaos, between those who would force order and those who could not, between those who follow logic and the lessons of war and those who follow the spirit. We were not good to each other. Eventually, neither of us could nurture the other's self-esteem because we had been too badly damaged. The relationship died.

I can make a decision. I can let this shadow hang over my life forever, or I can move on with my life.

It is time to reach for the "big brush" and splash some color across the landscape of my life.

"The only real failure in life is failing to move in the direction of your dreams."

— Katina Kefelos

"Winter Comes Early"

Snowflakes gently drifting down
Covering trees, roads, roofs, and ground,
Masking features, softening lines.
Quietly swallowing nearby sound.

Snowscapes, bringing peace of mind,
Letting us share some quiet time.
We are here to stay, no place to go,
Ignoring even clocks that chime.

Cancellations set plans aside,
Opening up opportunities
To think or write or look outside
Observing all those white beauties.

Phone calls from precious family
Checking in, yet warning—stay
Cozy and safe, secure inside
Enjoying this unstructured day.

A Time to Speak

And here we are, confronting the bullies, standing up for justice. Sometimes we dance around things, afraid to speak. These may be the times we need to soldier on. When potential misunderstandings are present, it is often best to openly confront and discuss, to address the issues, not let fear keep us dancing away.

What do we do in the face of injustice? This is a time when we take up the sword of truth to do battle for justice. This is the time when we courageously tackle situations and resolve differences. This frees us from the yokes of worry, weariness, and evasion. It helps protect us from bullying and abuse.

A TIME …

More than most people I know
She left little doubt
About her position on any issue.

She studied the figures
Then looked into her heart
Made the decision, took a stand.

She never wavered, rarely backed down
Weathering the fallout, taking the flak
Accepting the outcome, not looking back.

Always outspoken about her convictions,
She preferred open disagreement
To those who merely pretended to please.

She followed her calling,
And saw that as the greater gain.
It cost her some profit and pain.

... TO SPEAK

But her efforts brought conviction
That whatever the struggle
She was not alone and could be strong.

Sometimes the odds were so great
She almost gave in
And silenced the brave words inside.

Yet, once called to action, she had no choice
But to follow the light and
Speak up for what she believed.

The battle took her many places
She never expected to go
It made her see things inside her unknown.

But for those challenges
Both accepted and thrown
Those victories would never be.

A Toast to New Beginnings

And here we are, as the year ends, welcoming in a new year. She raises her glass:

I would like to make a toast to New Beginnings. As the last few days of this past year fade away and join the passing days and years of our life as only a memory, we look forward to the New Year as a new beginning. We put aside our failures and mistakes and look expectantly for the good things to come.

With the wide-eyed wonder of a young child on Christmas morning eager to open presents, we look to the New Year, anxious to see what joys and pleasures await us. The events of the last year, whether good or bad, joyous or sorrowful, large or small, are woven into the fabric of our lives and form the foundation from which we launch our New Beginnings.

If our past year has been fraught with trials and tribulations, we look to the New Year to discard bad habits, start new traditions, and move forward with renewed enthusiasm and energy. If in this past year we have been blessed with success and prosperity, we look to the New Year with enthusiasm and energy.

Last year is history; the future lies before us. I would like to make this toast to New Beginnings.

Stepping Out in Faith

And there we were, sharing inspirational messages at our weekly meeting. Just last week, I heard myself described as "a driving force for Toastmasters." I smiled to myself and said, "Thank You, God."

When I first attended Toastmasters, I introduced myself as a broken person on the run from disappointment and despair. Today, I have an extraordinary assignment—to share the reason behind that driving force that renewed my belief in me. It is simply this: God answers courageous prayers, if we step out in faith.

For me, this journey started with a simple directive: *"Follow your heart. It will lead you."* I stand here today as a case in point for the hypothesis that God chooses ordinary people with loyal hearts and instills core commitments. These core commitments lead to confidence and to the expectation that what we ask for will happen, sooner or later, if it is meant to happen.

Please note that I said, "what we ask for." The Prayer of Jabez is an excellent tool for making prayerful requests. It reads:

And Jabez called on the God of Israel, saying, "Oh, that You would bless me in-
deed, and enlarge my territory, that Your hand would be with me, and that You
would keep me from evil, that I may not cause pain!" So God granted him what
he requested (1 Chronicles 4:10 NKJV).

Please join me as I incorporate the elements of the Prayer of Jabez into our
journey through life today, to help make it more resplendent. Stretching in front
of us are fields of blessings, if we step forward into another life. We must want
nothing more and nothing less than what God wants for us. What happens
next? Our life becomes marked by miracles. What's the catch? We must ask to
be blessed. (*Oh, that you would bless me indeed ...*)

We must passionately want to make a greater impact for Him. When we
feel that something is missing in our life, that our purpose needs to be redefined,
our vision clarified, we can ask to be blessed and for God to enlarge our territory,
give us more influence, more responsibility, more opportunity to make a greater
impact. (*Oh, that You would bless me indeed, and enlarge my territory ...*)

My family and friends, this development absolutely delights our Father. He
cannot wait to give us opportunities to grow and to touch the lives of others.
Things get exciting, interesting, involved! This little prayer can totally remap
boundary lines.

Are you feeling lonely or lost? Try saying the magic words: "Send somebody
who needs me." With this simple invitation, opportunities emerge. Then we
encounter the tremendous thrill of God working through us and carrying us along.
Pretty soon we learn to pray: "Send somebody who needs Him." Right away, we
have a front row seat to see miracles happen. A miracle is defined as "an intervention
by God to make something happen that would not normally happen."

When we take "little" steps of faith, we do not always need God's strength.
It is when we jump in, all the way in, relying on His strength to guide us, that
miracles happen. What is the catch? We must put His agenda before ours and
then go for it! We must give with everything that we have. (*Oh, that You would*
bless me indeed, and enlarge my territory, that Your hand would be with me ...)
What happens when we are suddenly out of our depth, when we are in over our
heads? Do we falter? Are we afraid? Sometimes. Do we get angry? Sometimes.
Do we question our abilities? I sincerely hope so.

Please let me explain that last comment. This feeling of crisis, of being
unequal to the job before us, is actually a feeling of dependence. It means we are
walking with the Lord, letting His Spirit fill us. It means we are truly living in
faith. The times we are not feeling dependent are the times we have backed away

from our true calling.

We are expected to attempt something large enough that failure is guaranteed unless God is working through us. This is when the seemingly impossible is accomplished. We are given unlimited opportunities to let Him become great through us. What's the catch? We must realize we cannot do it alone and ask for His help. What follows? Check out the handout: Incredible Blessings. Impossible Tasks. Unforgettable Experiences of Completeness. Tremendous Results. A Decision for Salvation. Incredible Blessings! See the cycle ...

This Cycle of Blessings Spirals Upwards. If we remember to ask ... (*Oh, that You would bless me indeed, and enlarge my territory, that Your hand would be with me, and that You would keep me from evil, that I may not cause pain!*)

Most importantly, all this success must be safeguarded from evil. What is required of us? As my friend Yolanda might say: *It is best to stay out of the arena of temptation.* We are challenging evil's turf with our new choices and their tremendous life-changing results. We try not to cause pain for ourselves or for others. Sin causes pain. Falling away from our blessed life causes pain. The cycle of blessings can be broken by sin and by evil.

We must ask Him to keep evil or impropriety from spoiling the blessing He desires to bring about through us. We must remember to keep our legacy of a blessed life safe by asking God to help protect our spiritual investment.

Stepping out in faith is a spiritual investment. This "sometimes challenging" journey calls to us first because of the immediacy. It is exciting! Second, we thrive in the present. It is something we can do now, to help make a different ending. Third, we place the focus on serving others by asking, "How can I help You?" We end up walking more closely with God.

On this journey through life, we are asked to surround ourselves with people who want to walk with us in the Spirit of God. Thank you for joining me on that walk and for being my flowers in the field of blessings.

Even when we do not understand exactly what He is doing, we can trust that He is doing it right. I will forever be grateful to those I met along the pathway. May we always be blessed, in this season and into the next. Let us step out in faith.

"R U A G.R.?"

And there we were, at the Lenten breakfast, preparing for the Easter season." As your keynote speaker, I posed this question: "Are you a G.R., or are you a Grrrrr?"

One of my life's most valuable lessons came as a surprise to me. I was being a Grrrr, instead of a G.R, a Gracious Receiver. I am here to remind you that nice things happen to us when we actually accept compliments and blessings others shower upon us and become gracious receivers.

Mr. Hermsmeyer, my principal at North Loup-Scotia, kick-started this journey for me by explaining that positive feedback was a gift, and the proper response was a simple and sincerely heartfelt "Thank you." That was a new beginning for me.

Have you ever tried to give someone a gift, or a favor, or even a compliment and instead of having it accepted, have it waved off or deprecated? I know I have. I have done it to others, as well. That is being a Grrrrr.

Instead of rejecting someone's well-meant compliments with a casual shrug or an excuse like, "Oh, that's nothing," I learned to reflect on the intent and respond more graciously. It became easier to say, "I appreciate your sharing that with me. I value your opinion. It is very helpful."

I cannot help thinking how hard it is to be a gracious giver when we are not working with a G.R., a willing receiver. My latest run-in with a Grrrr left me with a hurting heart. After making overtures of kindness—giving personal time, special gifts, even professional assistance—my efforts were seemingly set aside. I felt unwelcome, unappreciated, and rejected, big time. Perhaps I was simply trying too hard to share love and acceptance. Perhaps not.

Consider these words from Acts 20:35: "… *It is more blessed to give than to receive.*" Somehow, we have twisted that phrase into meaning that it is a sin to receive, when it is not.

Maybe it is the gift of friendship, and we let it walk away because we do not see it. We may misinterpret the gesture; we do not recognize the gift. It becomes a lost opportunity. It is a possible cause for future regret. Would we knowingly refuse blessings? Not likely! Yet, we refuse the blessings of the everyday gifts that are sent our way. We need to open ourselves to receiving.

I cannot begin to tell you how many times a life that was drifting has been given direction from an unexpected (and perhaps unrecognized) gift. I have experienced this personally, on many levels.

Someone once suggested that when we are faced with choices, "Always make a right turn." I tried that, but after a few right turns, I just found myself spinning in circles. We must watch for our blessings and be open to redirection.

Now, let us take this a step further. Those of us wrapped up in worries are being ungracious receivers. We are being Grrrs. When we let worry and troubles win, we may be shutting out one of the greatest blessings ever—the gift of "peace." In the words of my friend Jackie: "Peace—we sing about it; we pray for it. We talk about peace for the world. Yet, we hesitate to receive it for ourselves." When we hold on to worry and do not let go, we are not setting good examples in this life. We may be cheating ourselves out of blessings, and we are not graciously receiving the gift promised: *"Peace I leave with you, My peace I give to you ..."* (John 14:27).

Are you a gracious receiver? Have you become an accomplished G.R.? I will leave you with a final verse from the Word. John 1:16 (NIV) tells us: *"From the fullness of His grace we have all received one blessing after another."* Savor them. Thank Him for them.

Please understand this. Being a Gracious Receiver is as important as being a gracious giver, for we have far more to receive than we can ever give. One of my favorite choruses is "Something Beautiful." The lyrics are: (I sing this part.)

> Something beautiful, something good;
> All my confusion he understood.
> All I had to offer him was brokenness and strife,
> But he made something beautiful of my life.

Help us to believe the truth about ourselves, no matter how beautiful it is! Help us to be gracious receivers of those gifts and to shine with the light. Let us reflect the peace within us and contribute to this beautiful life.

Tractor Trauma

And there I was, the summer of 2002, working for my son, The Heir. Working for family? It is what it is ... or is it what we make it? Returning to farm and ranch life after a fifteen-year absence creates interesting wrinkles in the tapestry of life. Volunteering to "help out" during busy seasons or times of crisis adds vibrant color. Yet, it seems for a job that does not pay anything, it surely costs me a lot.

This year's main entry on my medical rap sheet reads "tractor trauma." That simplistic phrase describes an instant of mental laxness that led to my missing many weeks of lazy lake swimming, missing months of dancing, and being dropped from the vintage baseball team's starting lineup until fall tournament time. Count these as costly consequences to a careless catapult from a little ol' 530 John Deere tractor. This is my story:

I spend the morning busily spraying the edges of his cornfields for grasshoppers. I pull into the yard. It is time to refill the spray barrel with water and insecticide. I decide to jump off the tractor on the side closest to the water hose, since the other side of the tractor is coated with insecticide mist.

Misstep One: Unexpectedly catching my shoestring loop on a small, stubby lever as I hoist myself up and over the uncovered clutch housing on the newly renovated (but not quite finished) 530 JD, so I can complete a quick dismount from the offside.

Misstep Two: Grabbing onto the nearest handhold to catch myself and realizing it is the hand clutch, which puts the tractor into forward motion.

Misstep Three: Visualizing that big black tractor tire crushing me, and desperately flinging my hand backwards while still in midair, effectively braking the tractor's forward progress.

Misstep Four: Letting go and pitching face forward onto the graveled driveway, catching my "trailing leg" on that spinning clutch assembly, and gashing my ankle on the spinning cotter keys.

Misstep Five: Gingerly crawling across the gravel driveway to the yard fence, sitting up on the grassy bank, and weakly murmuring "owwww" as The Heir saunters over, having missed the main event.

Misstep Six: Not going to the doctor immediately!

Closer examination reveals a deeply gashed and bashed ankle gushing red blood. It fills the offending running shoe. We quickly decide work is over for this day, at least for me. We carefully clean, soak, and pamper that traumatized limb. We even dig out some pre-owned crutches (left behind by Our Hero, an equally adventurous son). I learn to maneuver them up and down steps and staircases. This situation severely limits my dance moves and dalliances. It is definitely detrimental to fielding fly balls.

For a job that does not pay anything, it certainly costs me a lot. The lesson: Never do business with neighbors or family and expect to come out ahead.

Yard Fire (The Heir's Tale)

And there I was, keeping a close eye on the two piles of trees and rubbish we lit on fire three days before. We had razed the old garage, pushed out some dead trees in the shelterbelt around the ranch buildings, and had them bulldozed into two huge piles, one west and one north of the Quonset, well away from the buildings. The tree trunks were still slowly burning, and the wind was supposed to come up and blow sixty mph. I was worried.

My banker called. He wanted me to drive into town and sign a legal document. I told him, "No, a storm front is coming through any minute now, and I need to be here to watch these burning trees." He insisted, "It will only take ten minutes." Yeah, ten minutes to drive in, ten minutes to sign papers, and ten minutes to get back home. I raced to town, dashed off my signatures, and raced back home.

By the time I got back, the entire yard was on fire. The grass around the granary was on fire. The scraps of hay in front of the barn holding a haymow full of dry straw were on fire. The grass in the shelterbelt was on fire. The spilled ensilage was afire, and that fire was headed down the hill toward the feedlot, in line with a stack yard about a half-mile away. There were over a thousand tons of big round hay bales belonging to our tenant in that stack yard.

I ran into the house and called 911. The operator asked, "Is the fire under control?" I hastily answered, "What do you think I am calling you for? No, the entire yard is one fire. One fire is next to the barn and another is heading toward the stack yard. I don't have time for this." I hung up the phone and ran back outside.

Within ten minutes nine fire trucks and three ambulances were in the yard. It only took three fire trucks to put out the fires. Everyone else just watched.

Miracle Catcher

And here we are, welcoming our long-time member back to our local toastmaster group.

It has been so long since I have shared with you that I believe a reintroduction would be beneficial. For added clarity, I plan to separate my life into three segments: dream catcher, dream weaver, and finally, miracle catcher. Perhaps this will help increase your understanding of my life's progression. It has been a joyous ride, filled with ups and downs, twists and turns, beginnings and endings.

I started out small, as a dream catcher. I listened carefully to those around me and tried to fulfill their dreams for me. My dreams "caught" and reflected their wishes. That is primarily why I became a schoolteacher, a wife, and a parent. I was expected to. While these served their purpose and were rewarding, they did not necessarily reflect the longings of my heart and soul.

When I expanded my experiences to becoming a dream weaver, life became more interesting. I dared to dream, for myself. This was a step-by-step process, requiring courage and major lifestyle changes. I had to ask and answer three major questions:

1) What fear is stopping me today?
2) What lie is giving that fear so much power over me?
3) The next time I face this fear, what shall I do?

The answers actually surprised me, as I did not believe I was afraid of anything!

This became a pivotal moment. I realized I had to stop the aimless wandering, conquer my fears, and decide on some definitive goals. At Our Hero's urging, I created a checklist, so I could recognize the small steps of success and focus on the actual journey.

It became clear to me that there are no mistakes, only lessons, repeated until they are learned. This was a challenging task. Joy entered my life when I discovered that positive life changes take place when we change how we think. It became all about creating an opportunity for victory, and learning to celebrate the small successes.

The best quote to describe this part of my life is one by David Lloyd George: "Don't be afraid to take a big step. You can't cross a chasm in two small jumps."

Becoming a dream weaver required some huge leaps of faith, a strong dependence on the fellowship of friends, and letting go of many ideas, habits, and unhealthy relationships I had been clinging to. It was indeed life changing.

With a renewed sense of purpose and a newly discovered inner peace, the dream weaver in me began reaching for the ultimate goal, to become a miracle catcher. I began constantly asking my "angels" for specific blessings, and constantly received them. The rewards of asking for and acknowledging the daily blessings opened me to the possibilities of receiving "miracles." How do we catch a miracle? Can we do it?

Let us review the four easy steps to Catching a Miracle:

1) Decide which miracle we wish to catch. (Review our list of goals for this.)
2) Get ourselves a really strong net.
   a. Think about our prioritized goal.
   b. Expect it. Visualize it. Recognize it.
3) Notice when our particular Miracle flutters by and ... SWISH! Capture it! Be listening when opportunity knocks, and OPEN THE DOOR!!!
4) Add it to our list of blessings. Tell someone about it that day! Share the good news. Imagine ourselves wearing a nifty "I caught a Miracle" button, or see ourselves stuffing our Miracle and mounting it over the fireplace. Acknowledge and Savor the Success. Wear the joy of the moment on our face!

The world is a looking-glass and gives back to every man the reflection of his own face.

—William M. Thackeray

Becoming a Miracle Catcher is something to be proud of. It measures a landmark on the journey through life. It lets us celebrate the joy of living. Becoming a Miracle Catcher is enlightening and illuminating. My life reflects this change and gives me renewed purpose and energy.

Mentally reviewing these progressive steps of growth—from dream catcher to dream maker to miracle catcher—and being able to share them with you is a small miracle in itself. There was a time when this would have been an impossible and highly distasteful task for me.

Today, it is a joy to introduce myself to you and acknowledge your help on this journey. I will close with this thought from William M. Thackeray: "The world is a looking-glass and gives back to every man the reflection of his own face." Today, I enjoy what I see. For that, I thank you.

How is That Again?

And here we are, awaiting enlightenment. Welcome to our current seminar for budding writers. We are going to get a chance to "Get a Life – Learn to Write." We will be exploring effective ways to play with words and develop our target audiences by gauging reactions to word ploys. We will layer it, lead them on, leave 'em laughin'.

One of my favorite movies, *Aladdin*, appeals because it is written as a children's movie with phrase selections that delight the romantic in the adults. Are you familiar with it? It is layered with meanings.

Shrek, my favorite "once upon a time" story, uses delightful examples of word play. The donkey, with the voice of Eddie Murphy, introduces himself this way: "You have seen a housefly, a horsefly, but have you ever seen a donkey fly?" The stage is set … the chuckling begins. We then meet the gingerbread man who has been brutalized and is missing legs below the knees, yet is unafraid, defiantly shouting, "Eat me!" Some snickers are heard.

Later, when Shrek first sees the Lord's mammoth castle, he comments, "So that is his castle. Do you think he is compensating for something?" The adults laugh out loud. The children wonder why, but the laughs keep building. The suggestive writing adds to the simplistic plot.

Word play that uses layered descriptive references also works well. When the Princess asks about the man she is to marry, they begin by saying, "Men of Lord Farquad's stature are in 'short' supply. There are those who think 'little' of him. You can take his 'measure' when you see him tomorrow." Since they know of his lack of height, and she does not, it becomes a private joke between the ogre and the donkey, one the audience is in on … delightfully descriptive, yet, foreshadowing.

When the audience already has a certain mindset, it is fun to play with their minds. To demonstrate the effectiveness of these techniques, I will share an adapted version of the internet story, "A dark and stormy night."

They were together in the house. Just the two of them. It was an unexpectedly cool, unsettled, stormy night. The storm had come quickly, and each time the thunder boomed he watched her jump. She looked across the room and admired his strong appearance, and wished that he would take her in his arms, comfort her, and protect her from the storm. She wanted that, more than anything. Suddenly, with a pop, the power went out. She screamed. He raced to the sofa where she was cowering. He didn't hesitate to pull her into his arms. He knew this was a forbidden thing and expected her to resist. He was surprised when she didn't. Instead, she clung to him. The storm raged on, as did their growing passion. There came a moment when each knew that they had to be together. They knew it was wrong. Their families would never understand.

They were so consumed in their passion that they did not hear the opening of doors, just the faint click of a camera …

(The camera shot shows a cat and a dog huddled together on a sofa.)

Wasn't this what you expected? What were you thinking? Simple conversations are often understood on many levels. So layer it, lead them on, and leave 'em laughin'.

Since our audience usually suspects the basics of what is going to happen, it is up to us to make the getting there, as well as the action itself, more interesting. I personally enjoy the challenge of creating caring, sensitive characters within this generally suggestive genre. I view it as an exciting mental exercise. I write what I know. I surely cannot beat this for pure fun. It is all in the power of words and in the minds of our audience.

Think about it. How hard is it to imagine your cleverest conversation or your wildest fantasy, embellish it a little, or a lot, write it down, and get paid for it? You might even be ready to join us for our next session, Porn 101. Come again?

Now you are thinking!!! See you at our next seminar for budding writers.

Toastmasters Anonymous

Hi, my name is Kelsey ... (Hi, Kelsey.) I am a Toastmaster-aholic. This is my story, partially stolen from another toastmaster (grasping the lectern tightly and visibly shaking):

Once upon a time, I made a major lifetime change. I attended a Toastmasters Anonymous Conference. Yes, I found myself driving 110 miles for a free speech! This novel experience led to an epiphany.

Are you ready? (pause) Am I ready? (consternation) Where are my note cards? (police pat down) Missing? They appear to be missing. *I wish I were joking!!!* All right then, from the top! (Off the top of my head?)

Thankfully, I find Toastmasters Anonymous to be an encouraging, helpful ten-step program suitable for dealing with almost any affliction. We learn to deal, with a large dose of humor. If we are stressed out, we take it "one speech at a time." We use a sponsor and a mentor to help us cope.

In Toastmasters Anonymous we find a bunch of over-comers, some over-achievers, and those who face chronic "lack of preparation" problems. With one another's help, we adjust. On days I just cannot get out of bed, I now realize I am *not* being lazy. God just does not seem to have anything scheduled for me that day. I do not like to go up against the Big Guy!

Our humor stems from frustration, something I find plentiful. As a financial advisor, I have become adept at taking a sixty-thousand dollar deficit and doubling it in six months' time. I am known to advertise zero interest loans. Please let me clarify. I have *zero interest* in making loans!

I would not be here today if it were not for my special friends. They gave me the directions. From there it all went downhill ... because ... "A mind once stretched by a new idea never regains its original dimensions" —Oliver Wendell Holmes.

I must admit to being initially confused, though. Our special guest was to give an icebreaker. My thoughts immediately leaped to a mental image of a big strong ship running through the ice floes of cold Alaskan waters. All I heard was someone talking about where they lived and what they did there. Things like: I was in the fourth grade so long I got tenure. Nothing but *me, me, me, me, me.* The evaluator seemed to like it, though.

Then we were asked to welcome the table topless mistress. Wait … a … moment! Yep. I misheard. Slow down, my racing heart. It was the tabletopics master.

At TA meetings, there is never judging, *unless there's a contest to which any and all are welcome.* Works for me! I prefer not to be judged. I was always different. As a youngster, I did not want to play doctor and nurse. I just wanted to evaluate them.

We learn to accept the unchangeable things, like being born with a club foot. You understand. One foot is straight. The other likes to go out dancing. We try to replace stuttering, or an abundance of ums and ahs with – a – pregnant – pause!

To incorporate animated facial expressions and gestures, we take members to the beach or a lakeshore. We watch the facial expressions of people as they get into *cold* water … (simulate a demonstration) … and learn animation.

Before we know it, we are giving two speeches a *month*! I remember the first time I got paid for it. I felt so *cheap*! (blushing)

If our problem is that we are excited or anxious, we are counseled to start with a small group. Pick a lounge with six people. (Three of them are probably already drunk. Three of them are making out.)

Our audience usually has one-third listening to the speech and one-third preparing their own remarks. The other one-third is fantasizing. I would like to *thank* that one-third …

We are told, "Don't just stand there like a statue. Please do something with your hands … (tongue in cheek) … so sometimes I just touch myself."

At this Toastmasters Anonymous Conference, I found myself surrounded by notables, often known as PDGs, most notable for being a group of "has beens." They shared some experiences:

• Their tea parties were apt to resemble little Toastmaster parties, including having a sergeant-at-arms.

• A common confession was being caught with a copy of a C & L Manual.

• One mentioned being asked to give a toast, and then going on and on and on. There was no timer!

• Another received a speaking ticket from the VP of Education. When given a breath-a-master, he blew a 4.0.

• I was charged with STI—Speaking To Influence. That GI Joe character (called the sergeant-at-arms) confiscated my notes. I immediately became speechless. The animated gestures I used (demonstrate) irritated the officer, and I ended up in jail. I had to call my sponsor. (Please do not ask me what I called him!)

We are going to make mistakes, but as long as our heart is in the right place (searching), here is mine (pinned to my outfit ahead of time)!

We can always use a disclaimer if we run into difficulties. My favorite disclaimer is: *Overuse may cause mild sexual problems. What???* As far as I know, there *are* no mild sexual problems.

Well, I see we are having too much fun, but we are running out of material (which explains the skimpy outfits).

If I die on my way home from this meeting, I have already accomplished more than most people, and that makes me happy. Consider this. If we make it up to the stage without stumbling on the steps or killing someone, we are already standing taller!

A FINAL THOUGHT: When we stop getting better, we stop being good. Judge for yourself the hard hold that Toastmasters Anonymous Conferences has on me. Why? It is a complete "mystery" to me ...

How do I quit? Go to more meetings??? *I wish I were joking.* Would anyone like a talkative TA sponsor? Sign up right here. Today. (luckee_one@hotmail.com)

Next time, we will be driving 165 miles for that free speech. Join me in Omaha on April 25th and 26th for the Spring Mystery Showcase held at the Holiday Inn Central, 72nd and Grover. Bring yachting attire. Boarding begins at 6:00 PM. Do not miss the "Gilded Vessel" Departure with Captain Archibald Bemmington Frath at 7:00 PM.

Silly Sizzling Snag

And here I am, back at the ranch during the summer of 2003. A second session of inattentive oversight catches me watching my life rapidly flashing before my eyes. One blink, and it is over. It is a shockingly close call. It is one that should not have happened at all.

This time, I am using a loader with a grapple fork on my trusty 4230 John Deere tractor. We have been best buddies since its "born on" date in 1972. We recently tore down an old garage that was hampering our path to the corn storage and drying bins. I am salvaging a twenty-foot-long heavy plank workbench from the rubble. To move it, I suspend it with chains from the loader bucket. The long unwieldy monstrosity still manages to swivel and tip down on one end.

My primary concern is to keep the workbench from swinging back and gouging the tractor or bumping into the tracks for the overhead doors on the Quonset. I gently and carefully thread it between the row of grain bins and the Quonset. I neglect to notice the electrical line immediately overhead. An errant grapple fork tine snags it. The line stretches, screams, and then snaps, leaving the live wire draped over the tractor. I stop the tractor because I hear this very loud crash. Before the electrical line actually snaps, the tension on it cracks the power pole, which topples toward the tractor, narrowly missing my tractor cab as it crashes to the ground. Gasp!

I begin to see the seriousness of the developing situation. I shut off the tractor and cautiously inch the cab door open. Detecting nothing sizzling or frying, I carefully step off the tractor, thread my way through the chaos and cut the current.

I previously shared that this job does not pay anything. It still costs me. This particular stunt is potentially fatal; I do not jump away from the tractor. I hear about that later.

The costly consequences begin immediately. The livestock require electricity for water. The house tenants need electricity just to finish showering and cleaning up for the evening. The shop lights remain unlit as dusk rapidly descends.

Several telephone calls later, the power is temporarily restored, with the downed lines disconnected. Permanent restoration requires trenching to bury the electrical lines; rewiring hookups to the shop, the grain bins, and the submersible well. Electricians do not come cheap. Guess who pays these invoices? Perhaps not happily, but pay them I do. I own the place. Call it "ranch improvement."

Days like this weave an interesting pattern in the tapestry of my life.

The Lesson: We clean up our own messes. We leave the world a better place than we find it.

Figures

And there she was, working alone on the ranch. Yes, she was alone. She felt she needed nothing more than what she had. Yes, she wanted more. She wanted a dancing partner, a traveling companion, a lover. But she knew that desires did not pay the bills. She also knew that some ambitions, when achieved, carry a heavy price. If at times she grew frustrated, impatient, or restless, she only had to remind herself that she was where she needed to be and was doing what she chose. She preferred needing no one and certainly needed nothing she could not provide herself.

She was a petite woman, shapely beneath her denim jeans and baggy shirt. Over her shoulder-length, curly, light hair, she wore a well-worn baseball cap. Beneath the brim, her eyes were the mystical slate green of the sea, infiltrated with a light blue sheen. She stood in the doorway looking out. The light rain dampened her upturned face, the soft curve of cheek and chin, the curving slightly melancholy mouth. Not capriciously, she ignored the shrilly-ringing phone, a practice that was as much policy as habit, particularly when her mind was drifting toward her work. She liked working with figures...

From his trailer house, he listened to the repeated ringing of the phone and swore. He had many projects to complete, new unwanted challenges to meet. Meanwhile, the woman, that sexy, fiercely independent woman from up north, infiltrated his mind. She and her diverse interests occupied too much of his mind. Her figure teased his imagination. Her husky voice subtly beckoned. This new interest called to him, excited him on a different level.

The thrill of discovery was as vital to him as the careful development of an enriching intimate relationship. As with most of his desires, he would not rest until it was accomplished. This woman with the unbridled talent was his newest and most frustrating project.

Just finding the time to develop this new interest required renewed purpose. His instincts reassured him. He was justified in developing this dream, fulfilling the fantasies, initiating the intimacies. He reflected on his most recent friend—the shared good times, the weekends spent together, the companionship, and the fun.

This unrelenting restlessness led him to remember the woman's writing, fired from a passionate mind, fascinating and uncomfortably sensual. It made him wonder what kind of woman could create pieces filled with this skill, power, and depth of feeling. It led him to reach out, to dial her number. The call went unanswered. Mumbling to himself, "It figures." He decided, on impulse, to ...

While she figured he was not interested, he broke down her walls without her even noticing. When he rebuilt them, he put in windows to let the sunshine in.

If Only

And there we were, working round the clock, wishing for more hours in a day. One day—24 hours —which translates to 1440 minutes—86,400 seconds—each one precious "diamonds" to be invested, spent, or squandered. We cannot store time or save it for later. Though renewed each day, it is not limitless. Eventually, our "diamond" supply is depleted.

Knowing and understanding this certainty brings a sense of urgency to my life's work, which is helping others discover how to be their best and to achieve "success," however defined. My greatest frustration centers around those who fail to recognize and utilize their assets. Waste infuriates me, no matter how it is disguised. We often recognize wasted opportunities, time, and assets in the "If Onlys." "If only I had done this!" or "If only I had not done that." I contrast that lamentable "if only" state with a more proactive, positive "can do" approach, one that reflects a more organized, efficient, yet simplistic approach to life and its challenges.

Who trained you to think, to look at the world the way you see it? If this person was your younger self, you did not have the wisdom, the tools, nor the information on hand that we do today. It may have been someone we were taught to respect who did not necessarily deserve that respect. We need to be the one training ourselves how to look at things. We are the ones who have our best interests in mind. We are never as good as we could be; that is a moving target. If we are not aspiring, we stop growing, and then we see limitations and experience "If Onlys."

To illustrate, I share some personal snippets from my life: It seems that as an infant, I was all about order and control. I spent hours in Mom's kitchen cupboards sorting and stacking pans, kettles, and lids. Not messing them up and banging on them, but arranging them just so.

When I reached school age, the issues became more about not being controlled. I defied my teachers, turned in unfinished assignments, and spent my time doing things I valued. My desk was up front by the teacher's desk to encourage me to complete my own assignments. I preferred listening to the upper grades' instructional classes and would answer the questions if they struggled. That really annoyed my teachers.

Teachers tried seating me at the back of the room. I spent my time there drawing or reading books. I only did my assignments if I was learning something from them. When I felt I understood the concept, I quit working on them. How many long division problems does it take to learn how? For me, about one-third of them. It became a lesson in learning just how to motivate me. I am not certain who learned more, my teachers or me.

As a job seeker, I honed interviewing skills. I appeared confident, self-assured, and used a "bring it on" attitude. I usually got what I was after, and more.

During my teaching years I became great at diagnosing problems and helping others discover possible solutions. It was so freeing to realize there is often more than one correct approach or outcome. This same technique helped when I became a financial advisor. My specialty became helping others find some control in their lives. I refer to the process as "stopping the bleeding." That's how I became the "Can Do Kid." I stay organized, operate efficiently, and live simplistically.

To summarize, my advice is to let go of the "If Onlys." Use them to clarify the current situation, then take a page from my friend Anita's book and "do what you need to do" to reach pinpointed goals that define your success. "Success is usually one more step beyond the breaking point." —Rory Vaden

Define, devise, and designate assets. Do not waste another moment. We only have so many of those precious "diamonds." Polish them and let them shine. Your brilliance will lead others to the light. What better way to live!

And the Winner Is ...

And there we were, at "academy awards for toastmasters" night. Aren't the Academy Awards fun to watch? Clips of great films from this year and years past. Songs that touch our hearts. Suspense as the envelope is opened by nervous hands. Beautiful people being grateful to those they love. Let's go to the Oscars in our minds right now ...

It is the big red carpet party. People start to congratulate us on what a wonderful year we had. I find my seat. The tension is amazing. I want to cry just thinking about how lucky I am to be here. I have my acceptance speech in my hand. What will the evening bring? Each of us is up for a different category. My category will be given next.

"And the Winner Is ..." They call my name! The applause begins. The smiles are a blur as I walk down the aisle. I cannot think. I can hardly see the steps. It is all so wonderful. My handsome presenter meets me at the top of the stairs and guides me to the small microphone on the huge stage. I cradle the Oscar. The applause begins to die down as I begin ...

My heart is so full. Being appreciated is one of life's greatest blessings, and being appreciated for enjoying our life's passion is even more wonderful.

Today, I could thank everyone, from Mom and Dad to my sexy chauffeur, and every name would be important. Instead, I have chosen to thank that one special young woman who visited me Sunday night, who personifies joy to me.

When my darling daughter was first placed in my arms, I was frightened. What if I didn't have it in me to be a loving mother to a possibly imperfect child? The moment she opened her eyes and looked up at me, I knew that being her mom was going to be my favorite role. What I had no way of knowing was how this little one would grow up to be my friend, my joy, and the foundation to my happiness.

Through the past twenty-five years of raising her, I have been following a dream of helping others to become even better. It has made for an interesting home life. Daughter and I attended college together before she went to preschool. We traveled to exciting places. We got wet and wild at the water park. We went on vacations together. We were a team.

Some days it seemed that part of her dream was helping me achieve mine. Whether it was helping shampoo my carpets, surprising me with a "kitchen experiment" after a long hard day, or re-decorating my bathroom for Mother's Day, she seemed to love her role.

The things that most Moms do for their little girls, my little girl did for me. I will never forget years ago when we found out we had "inherited" a large debt to pay, and she asked, "Mom, are you going to do what is right for YOU this time? You cannot always take care of others. They must learn for themselves." She taught me this lesson by making decisions and solving problems for herself. She helped me become even better.

Whenever I want to judge myself for not having done more of the traditional things for her over the years, I stop, realizing I must be the best Mom for her. Look who she has become.

While in Colorado renewing ties with valued friends this past week, she found a beautiful tiger's eye necklace and earring set, a symbol of "wellness." She gave me this "thank you" gift with a loving hug and her special smile. A gentle reminder that happiness is not based on possessions, power, or prestige, but on relationships with people we love and respect.

Thank you, Academy, for giving me this opportunity to take this perfect moment to thank her. Thank you, Daughter, from all those who appreciate you, especially me. This one is ours to share.

The music comes up as I turn to walk off the stage. The music in my heart lives on.

To the Hilt

Written as an assignment for the Thesaureans, a writing club in the North Loup Valley of Nebraska, as an exercise in alternate perspective.

And here we are, once again leading separate lives. She loves her life. She loves her horses. She is respected and successful, at least by the standards of her small town. She might once have loved another, but she is not about to abandon a busy and fulfilled life for the uncertainty of an uncommitted relationship.

She is a pragmatist, a self-starter with a strong streak of independence. She has developed a brisk authoritative way of talking that gradually intensifies with her many years of responsibility and success. I admire, even love, her positive energy, but it drains my own. Even if I love her physically, I cannot forever bow to her natural habit of command. Her attitude rankles me.

"The real art of conversation is not only to say the right thing at the right place but also to leave unsaid the wrong thing at the tempting moment" —Lady Dorothy Nevill. Thus, we exist in a perpetual uncontested truce. We would have quarreled endlessly if she had stayed.

> *"The real art of conversation is not only to say the right thing at the right place but also to leave unsaid the wrong thing at the tempting moment."*
>
> —Lady Dorothy Nevill

My inquietude led to her leaving. Perhaps because of the constant chaos in her professional life, she craves peace in her personal life. She quickly collects her belongings and returns to her solitary life. With a thankful feeling, she surrounds herself with her favorite mementos. The glow gradually returns to her eyes. She uncoils and relaxes.

But first she has to dispel the melancholy thoughts left behind. She ponders how much easier it is to do harm, however unintentionally, than to create beauty or to leave a legacy of goodness. As always, the melancholy drifts away, replaced by acceptance. Optimism is a gift discovered at birth. It creates undying hope. It becomes the cornerstone of a successful life.

We continue to meet and mingle our lives. The simple exchange of a trembling hug helps us understand how close we are to being stretched too far. I wish I fully understood all the ways she has learned to hide fear and pain and humiliation.

I keep interpreting her ultra-controlled outer facade to be an absence, or perhaps a deficiency, of emotion. Actually, it is much the opposite. She is afraid to let me see how much she needs me. Maybe I just need to say, "Sweetheart, I adore you."

She pretends to ignore the gift of my love because she is afraid to trust in it. Yet, she gazes over the landscape and yearns for intimacy. She acts like she misses her consort, her steadfast lover. I seem to be someone she desires as a companion.

I apparently steady her. I wish she would let me be with her more often and share more of her life.

The "UnClutter" Party

And here we are … this is our New Year of opportunity. I decide it might be better to look at what needs to be done now to clear out "the stuff" we keep hanging onto, so we can have space for what we really do want.

What "clutter" or "loose ends" are in our lives? Any resentments, fears, confusion, old hurts, inappropriate habits? A lot like dirty dishes piled up on a kitchen counter, they will not clean themselves. We have to scrub them, rinse them, and then put them away. Should we discover anything chipped or damaged, or no longer of use to us, we throw it in the trash, making room for something else. Good practical action for clean up on any level.

Funny thing about clutter, it is totally mindless and happy to stay wherever we put it, whether it is in our thinking, in our home, or in our business. How can we best deal with it? Work one step, one piece at a time. How do we eat an elephant? One bite at a time! If it is physical clutter, we get out large trash bags and designate their titles "trash," "charity," "garage sale," "giveaway." We have an UnClutter Party. What a good excuse to have fun and get "the stuff" cleared out!

How about mental and emotional clutter? It can take up a lot of space in our lives, too, causing us to experience unnecessary grief, emptiness, and feelings of helplessness. Poor mental habits create chaos and disarray in thinking. Too often we close the door to painful memories, but just like physical clutter, it stays right where we put it until we make the choice to recognize its clutter, face it, and then dump it. If we cannot face it alone, we can call a friend or join a support group that will help.

This New Year, why not resolve to take care of being in charge of your life, your space, your priorities that are in front of you now? Cleaning out and straightening up what is needed today will make room and order for the next phase of what we most desire. Possibilities then become realities; the realities we really want begin filling our space, heart, mind, and spirit.

May this year bring you joy, personal power, love, prosperity, and the fulfillment of your heart's dreams. Happy New Year! It can be dynamic and power packed. Enjoy the journey.

CHAPTER SEVEN:
WHIMSIES

Worrying is a misuse of our imaginations!

What Color is the Wind?

And there we were, with crisp leaves skittering across our paths, hurried along by gusts of wind. Leaves once proudly colored with many shades of red, green, and gold. Forlorn leaves now stripped off, leaving bare branches to sway in the autumn squalls. Leaves drained of their life forces being swept into randomly placed piles. Crackly blankets of constantly shifting crunchy brown leaves, teased by blustery blasts.

Brrr! Are we ready for the changes autumn brings? We savor the fragrance of our last rose blossoms. We shiver and bundle up against the brisk winds. Is autumn really here? What a great day to fly a kite!

Fall brings us opportunities to experience the thrills of kite flying. We can share the kite's spontaneous spins while we are doing it. We can see the unpredictability of the wind's gusts as our kite dips and soars. We can feel the uncertainties of life just by hanging onto the end of a kite string. What happens when someone tells us to "go fly a kite"? What color is that wind?

What do the winds of change bring to our lives? Do we see them as chilling, unwanted challenges? Do we treat them as unexpected opportunities? Do we fear the impending changes? What if we took those fears, put them into the form of a kite and let the winds of life lift them into unlimited opportunity? Perspective is an amazing, ever-changing aspect of our lives. We can look at that wind as a wonderful tool. We can use it to learn the skills of life.

Learning to be the kite and to flow with the currents of life is a lasting skill any of us can use. A kite is a beautiful mixture of art and science. Held by a single string, it lifts into the moving currents of air. Once airborne, a kite dances with the wind, performing aerobatic patterns with every upsurge or eddy. We hold the string lightly, watching from our secure spot on the ground. We let the kite and the wind do the dancing while we gently assist. We delight in the moment.

When the wind stops, our kite falls to the ground. We let go of what we cannot control. Be the kite! Learn the lesson. The next time someone tells you, "Go fly a kite!" just smile. Agree that it is a good time to do that. Do not question the color of the wind. Just use it to flow with life's currents of change.

When we understand the gift of a kite, we can discover ourselves. We can learn the true meaning of living in the moment. We can quit worrying about the "color of the wind" and delight in the spontaneity of today. Let's go fly a kite and watch the whimsies of the wind.

Once in a Blue Moon

And there we were, at the Calamus, relaxing after work. Life showed us its frivolity. "Life has taught me that it is not for our faults that we are disliked and even hated, but for our qualities." — Bernard Berenson

That is like saying, "Do not hate me because I am beautiful," or organized, efficient, and difficult to manipulate. What initially attracts people to us is the same thing that ultimately angers them. At times, it just seems to be too much of a good thing!

Life has taught me that it is not for our faults that we are disliked and even hated, but for our qualities.

—Bernard Berenson

I refer to the quip that school teachers make great dates because they keep asking you to do it until you get it right. That can be a two-edged sword. What if "getting it right" only happens once in a blue moon? Oops! Actually, it is our little lapses, our "oops" moments that make us appear to be more lovable. Especially if they happen about once in a blue moon. My friends delight in these moments. They never let me forget these moments.

Last week, I was swimming and tubing with my friend, Maggie May, at the Calamus, fairly close to the Calamus Dam itself. Toward the end of our outing, she spied a school of minnows swimming close to the beach. A novel experience for her, she was trying to catch one in the palm of her hand to closely watch it swim and then let it rejoin its school.

I carefully rinsed the sand off my tube and set it aside, then decided to use it to plop over the school and help her capture a couple of minnows. When she had one in each hand, she nudged the tube aside so she could "swim" them in the water. It was delightful watching her play this way. Did I mention her thirtieth birthday was just yesterday? I was totally engrossed in the experience, and in her joy of discovery.

With a final sigh of satisfaction, she abandoned the activity and started thinking about gathering up things and heading for the pickup. Quietly, yet insistently, she called, "Oh, Kels!" When she had my attention, she pointed toward the water. My tube was out about 100 feet, and heading out toward the center of the lake. Oops!

I grabbed my life jacket, started swimming after it, quickly analyzed the speed it was scooting across the water, and abandoned that plan. I decided to walk up the beach around the cove and look for someone with a boat to retrieve it. As I reached the Point, a boat and water skier went by fairly close to shore. I waved. They waved back. They headed toward Mags. She waved. They gaily returned the wave. We watched them ski along the face of the dam to the other side and up the shoreline. No help there!

173

Returning to our original spot, I noticed the skiers returning along the face of the dam. This time we both waved. They acknowledged our wave and continued around the point and out of sight. What to do now?

While we were gathering up the dog, our swimming things, and the remaining inner tube, they came by again. Despite our jumping up and down and frantic waving, they continued until the skier was down. As the boat cut power and circled back around, we took the opportunity to yell quite loudly, asking them to come over to us with their boat. This actually worked! As they swung by, Mags asked them if they could bring our inner tube back to us. By this time, it was a very tiny speck on the water, three-quarters of the way across the lake. After admitting they had seen it earlier, they sped off after it.

Graciously thanking them for helping, we shared our sense of relief. One fifteen dollar tube is not that big of a deal. It was the sudden outburst of riotous laughter from Mags after the skiers were safely out of earshot that captured my attention. As I gently questioned this display, Mags told me she was reliving the incident in her mind. What caused her to laugh so hard was the look on my face when I first realized I had not kept track of my tube. It had escaped. She had something on me, an "oops" she could really enjoy. I let her laugh.

Actually, I gave up being perfect about fifteen years ago, but not until one of my better friends informed me there had been only one perfect person on earth, and it was not me. He was referring to Jesus. I acknowledged he had me there. It was no competition.

I can handle being disliked for my faults and little "oops" moments. What I am still trying to deal with is being disliked for my qualities. It leaves me disgruntled. I refer you to this sign:

Disgruntled Hour: 5-7
Disillusioned Hour: 7-9
Peeved Hour: 9-12
Happy Hour: When we don't have to listen to you anymore!

Oops, more laughs from my friends. I leave you with this thought shared by Frank and Ernest on July 14th. "From the psychiatrist: Therapy will never cure your perfectionism if you keep insisting that we start over."

Do not play the perfectionist, bail on a situation, and then start over somewhere else. Work through the little imperfections, and learn to appreciate the qualities found in that person. Try not to resent them for those qualities that make them unique. There are no perfect people. Our relationships will never be perfect. We will not be perfect either.

The perfect opportunity to share our appreciation may only come along once in a blue moon. Take that opportunity! The next blue moon is July 31st.

Just WHY Are We Playing?

And there we were, nearly every summer evening after supper, if we were not hauling bales, playing softball as a family.

I was born to play softball. Yes, I was! My parents wanted enough children to field their own team. I was the firstborn of nine siblings. The lessons we learned on the ball diamond crafted our characters. We learned to be versatile players and to respect the rules of the game. We became our own umpires.

In the August 21, 2004, issue of the *Grand Island Independent*, Rev. Dan Safarik poses the question, "Are you an umpire or a player?" After reading his article, I saw myself all too well. There are definite differences between a player and an umpire.

I started out as a player. Everyone in my family did, too. By the time I was ready for college, we had our team. My father or I pitched while the entire family played a creative form of "workup." A batter being called "out" meant a jog out to right field to begin the fielder's rotation. (RF, CF, LF, 3B, SS, 2B, 1B, P (if deemed talented enough), C, and then batter.)

What an absolute thrill if we were not put out! In our games, a batter could run bases and try to score a run for only three consecutive "at bats" before the "mercy rule" kicked in and it became time to jog out to the outfield. This allowed fielders to "work up." After every "out," we had a new person "at bat" and a new lineup in the field.

This proved to be an excellent way for everyone to learn each position and address strengths and weaknesses. We were careful to make it enjoyable for everyone, even if that meant not counting balls, strikes, or outs for the younger players. We learned to be excellent ball players. If there was any umpiring to be done, Dad made the calls.

Moving on to college softball, I was still a player on the field. My specialty was third base, or sometimes second base. Off the field, I was training to be an elementary teacher, with endorsements in physical education. I developed into a fairly competent umpire. Throughout life, I have alternated between the two, in church leagues, even in vintage ball, which I still play and occasionally umpire.

What is the difference between a player and an umpire? Players are caught up in the game, with rules tucked away in their mind somewhere. They may break the rules unintentionally because they are "playing the game."

Umpires keep themselves outside of the game because they are focusing on the rules, the boundary lines, and the actions of the players. They may not even enjoy the game because they are busy evaluating, judging, making the right calls.

As my family members grew older (notice I did not say *more mature*), we each became more skilled and much more competitive. It is a family tradition to play softball during the afternoon of our annual family reunion. This is held on the Fourth of July every year, rain or shine. Many play (or played) legion ball.

Selecting two balanced teams became a political nightmare. Attempting to "call" the game—balls or strikes, fair or foul, safe or OUT—became life threatening. I usually only did this if I was terminally pregnant at the time.

The players decided there were too many umpires and not enough players who had everyone's best interests as a priority. One year, we quit keeping score. Another year, we quit counting balls and strikes and just let people hit the ball. After that, we quit counting "outs" and just had the entire side bat once around before retiring the side. Now, we go through the batting order top to bottom one inning and reverse the order next inning. This last reunion, hitters did not hit the ball and run. Oh, no! They hit until the ball went where they wanted it to go and then ran the bases. Sometimes it took five hits before they would PLAY BALL.

While standing there, hot and sweaty, devouring a slice of chilled watermelon, I found myself asking aloud, "Just *WHY* are we playing?" Still the umpire at heart, uh huh, uh huh! The players always answer, "Because we are here to have fun!" The players do have the most fun. That is so annoying to most umpires. In this family, we keep trying to steal the bases, literally. Or, we invent new rules. We even throw the rule book away.

Ask yourself whether you are a player or an umpire. Then join the game. You do not look good in stripes anyway. Leave the umpiring to someone else. Let them decide who is "in" or "out." When you begin to open your rule book, just remember how much fun it is to be creative, disorganized, and spontaneous. Become a PLAYER! Enjoy life!

The Dance

And there they were, kidding around about leaving on another adventure. "Listen," he said, "I'm leaving home, and there is absolutely nothing you can do to stop me. I want excitement, adventure, beautiful women, money, and fun. I'll never find any of that around here. So I'm leaving. Just don't try to stop me."

As he headed toward the door, his father got up and ran toward him. "Dad," the young man said, "didn't you hear me? Don't try to stop me. I'm going."

His father replied, "Who's trying to stop you? I'm going with you!"

Sometimes we open our own doors. Sometimes doors open for us. God will ultimately work everything out for our good. Always trust God's guidance. All lessons in life are guided by God. The basic temptation, which is always before us, is the temptation to forget our place under God. But look at the circumstances before us. We listen to all the voices around us, and we make our decisions. Many times, we decide to trust our own perceptions and our own way of doing things, when the only decision we ever need to make is to follow God.

A friend noted: When I meditated on the word "guidance" I kept seeing "dance" at the end of the word. I remember reading that doing God's will is a lot like dancing. When two people try to lead, nothing feels right. The movement does not flow with the music. Everything is quite uncomfortable and jerky. When one person relaxes and lets the other one lead, both bodies begin to flow with the music.

One person gives gentle cues, perhaps with a hand lift, a nudge to the back, or by pushing lightly in one direction or the other. It is as if two people become one body, moving beautifully across the floor. Dance takes surrender, willingness, attentiveness from one person and gentle guidance and skill from the other.

"My eyes drew back to the word 'Guidance.' When I saw the letter 'G', I thought of God. That 'G' was followed by the letters 'u' and 'i', which triggered this thought: 'God, you and I dance.'" — Reverend Jim Miller

As I lowered my head in prayer, I became willing to trust that I would receive guidance in my life once I became willing to let God lead.

GUIDANCE

"God, U and I DANCE."

—Reverend Jim Miller

Become willing to let God lead.

Special Labels

And there we were, playing the "label" game. In America, we put labels on everything and everybody. The gamut runs from "What's your sign?" to Bill Engval's "Here's Your Sign." I have learned the best thing about being labeled with a disability is that I can get away with practically anything.

A few years back, I was visiting my uncle in Baltimore, Maryland. He took me to the metro station, so I could visit DC. When I got back from DC, I had this brainstorm. I decided to save my uncle the half-hour trip to come pick me up at the metro station. I walked right past the taxis because I had ridden in one before and paid the outrageous fare. Not again!

Instead, I walked up the long lane leading toward the town, figuring I could ride the bus back and surprise him. Well, I was the person getting the surprise. I could not find a bus stop in the first quarter mile. I was now walking through a very different kind of neighborhood than I was used to, with a camera slung around my neck.

Suddenly, gunfire broke out a block to my left. I could see people running, jumping over fences, scattering in all directions. The sirens were screaming. I kept walking, but I was getting very concerned. There were two people walking behind me, catching up with me very quickly. I was wearing a fanny pack, and was a very different color from the people in the area. I walked faster. When I reached the next corner, an older lady stopped me, saying, "You should not be here." I agreed, explaining I was looking for a bus stop. She pointed to one up the street.

Next she asked me which line I wanted to get on. I gave her a blank stare. She asked me where I was going. Which part of town? When I told her, she explained I would need to get on one bus, ride to another bus route, then change to yet another bus line to get there. I was really bewildered then. That is when she decided I was one of those "special needs" people.

The lady and her granddaughter walked me to the bus stop. Then she spoke to the bus driver and told him where I was going and where I needed to change buses. Seeing someone she knew on the bus, she asked him to see that I did not get lost. He helped me at the first stop, got on the second bus with me, and rode along until he got me onto the third bus. I decided it was not so bad to be taken for a "special needs" person. I actually appreciated the assistance. According to my uncle, being escorted by that helpful stranger may have saved my life. Uncle was more than appalled at my reckless behavior. I thank that helpful lady every time I remember what happened, and what did not happen.

I did learn that when you have a progressive condition, your body does a lot of crazy stuff. My hands do things all by themselves, things I do not even know they are going to do. Not being able to control the shaking can be hazardous. When my little sports coupe was new, I was "flying low" over the hills between Loup City and Ord, Nebraska. I met a state patrolman just as I swept over the crest of a hill. I was traveling more than eighty-five miles per hour. I immediately tromped on the brakes. The cherries came on at the same time. I pulled over. That is when the infernal hand shaking started.

The officer asked for my driver's license and registration. By the time I located them, my face was flushed a bright red, and I was perspiring profusely. By now, the nice officer was not smiling. He was standing back a bit with his hand on his holster and sharply questioning me. "Is this even your car? I have never seen you drive it." I reassured him it was. He checked anyway. He returned from his cruiser with a smile on his face, handed me a ticket for ten over (on a 55 mph highway) and commented that the car must really run nice. I just agreed with him that it did. I silently cursed my shaking hands. But it was my heavy foot that caused problems that particular day.

This summer I have been working with "special needs" people. I really fit in. We play games like "Catch – or Don't Catch!" When I take them to their dances, I can do the "Chicken Dance" with them and not worry about doing it exactly right. No matter what happens, the rest of my life will be better for having met and worked with my "special needs" people. I remember that labels may be limiting. The opportunities to learn kindness and empathy are limitless.

Calamitee

And here we are, watching her strike out on her own. It is her turn to call her own shots in a world gone mad with economic woes, tinged with terrorism, instability, and unlimited uncertainties. Yet, she is unafraid.

She has something her uninspired parents can never give her—an adventurous spirit. After her journeys into the Appalachian Mountains with the Outward Bound teams, she finds she is truly awake for the first time in her relatively young life. It is the kind of wakefulness that insists she leave the corporate world. It calls her to climb mountains, conquer raging rivers, and hike through towering forests and desolate deserts. She develops a quiet, deliberate, and relaxed manner, seeing clearly and moving steadily through her own reality.

Because of this growing awareness of presence, negative people and forces are not really repelled. They just pass through her. She remains focused on keeping

"If adventure has a final and
all-embracing motive. it is surely this:

We go out

because it is our nature to go out.

to climb mountains.

to paddle rivers.

to fly to the planets. and

plunge into the depths of the oceans ...

When man ceases to do these things.

he is no longer man."

—Wilfrid Noyce

her independence and doing her own thing. This process of "reaching her own peace" calls for her to jettison the corporate world that has caused her so much concern. It teaches her to work through life on her own terms. She refuses to return to the daily nine-to-five drill. No way is she going back to that way of living. As she relinquishes her management position, she informs her family, "It's killing my soul to work there. I can't do it anymore. I have to be free."

She credits her shift in priorities to meditation and Eastern influences. It elevates her to a higher frequency of sensing. She resists returning to dulled drudgery or open-ended questioning. She attempts to rise above the world of hurt she traverses after the tragic deaths of her two best friends the weekend before their high school graduation.

Of today's adventures, she writes: Mountaineering leads me from peak to peak. I know I will soon see another place, another valley even more appealing to my restless soul. I want to be everywhere, to see as many places as I can. This sense of constant adventure seems to embellish every journey I take. It constantly renews my spirit.

"If adventure has a final and all-embracing motive, it is surely this: We go out because it is our nature to go out, to climb mountains, and to paddle rivers, to fly to the planets and plunge into the depths of the oceans... When man ceases to do these things, he is no longer man." —Wilfrid Noyce

What is Next?

And here she is, alone on the mountaintop, miles from anyone she knows. She is here. She has done it. "What is next?" Taking a moment to gather her thoughts, she smiles serenely and then steps into her new life.

She messages: "Well, I have packed up all my belongings (again). I am for the first time in my life homeless, single, and unemployed. It is a weird feeling. So much weight to lose so quickly! I leave tomorrow for Washington, where my beloved brother is to house me temporarily. Then off to California for Wilderness EMT Training. My goals for this trip are to lose ten more pounds, stop chewing my nails to the quick, to not get eaten by a bear, and to truly begin a life expedition that will bring me closer to some type of enlightenment. Just in case I need rescued: I do not have an itinerary, I do not know where I am going yet, and I do not know how I am going to get there. I hope this helps. ;o)"

Yes, she is deviating from the road she has been so carefully coached to follow. Perhaps she has disappointed those who have so diligently steered her toward stolid security. She refuses to feel guilty.

Every step she has taken on that planned path has been a strain. Each intersection has taken her farther away from where she believes she needs to be. She has tried, again and again, to explain why she has been unable to continue. Now it is time to forge her particular pathway though life.

She is alone, completely alone. It is what she wants, what she needs, and well worth the effort it has taken. So freeing! She has pushed herself for months to accomplish this. She is filled with a sense of relief followed by fissions of fear. "What is next?"

Glancing into the rear-view mirror, she sees a slip of a gal, and creamy skin tinted with a hint of rose. She carefully climbs out of the car, sun-kissed tresses gently curving toward her chin, framing her pixie face. Those hazel eyes hold a hint of tiredness, but a closer look reveals a glint of purpose.

She has made specific plans, designed her own private itinerary for this trip to a new life. She is fleeing from home, from career, from family. She is carefully but deliberately removing herself from that love that was smothering her as surely as hands clamped over her nose and mouth.

Now, she promises herself, she will find her opportunity to breathe, to think, to explore, to decide. Maybe she can finally understand what it is that keeps her being what everyone else seems to want her to be. She will take these few months for herself. She is here. She has done it. "What is next?"

She opens her tired eyes and lets herself look. Her cramped muscles slowly relax. It is so beautiful here. She notices the grand majesty of evergreens. They shoot upwards toward the sky as the wind whistles past. The silver flash of sun glints off the small stream that snakes down the side of the mountain. A touch of white peeks from clouds surrounding the summit. It is time to truly begin a life expedition bringing her closer to some type of enlightenment.

"Oh, will you look at this!" A smile lights her face. Her heart lifts. She cannot wait to discover the surprises waiting for her. She eagerly inquires, "What is next?"

She adds, "For the first time in my life, I am completely casting off my past, not looking at the future—just the here and now. I have never been more frightened of anything. My security blanket has been roughly removed. I feel I am left exposed. I carry only the best wishes and deep love from my family, plus their hope they will someday understand me and the decisions I make. What is next?"

A Thanksgiving Message to Mom (Daughter's Tale)

And there we were, stretching out after a massive meal of wild goose and honeyed ham. Daughter got in touch :

Looks like the holidays are finally here, and denial gets me nowhere. I will have to bulk up on my CDs and iPOD music in order to avoid the holiday music as much as possible. How do the holidays find you? Hope you spent the day enjoying yourself with the outlaws.

I spent Thanksgiving at home with Our Hero. We made a feast. Neither of us was in the mood for a loud, drunken family party, so we had a quiet drunken one. Just kidding! It was nice. We plan on going to see the movie *"Australia"* tonight, since there is only one college football game on television, and it is not that interesting. No good movies on television tonight, either.

As for what I have been up to—absolutely nothing! I have been taking a couple of classes, Outdoor Survival and Conservation, but other than that and Search and Rescue work, my life has been pretty slow. The first week of December, I am taking a tax course to see if that is how I want to make my wad in the New Year. It will work out perfectly because tax season and Search and Rescue training end at exactly the same time. It is a tiny bit frustrating for me to be out of work here, but I cannot get my EMT switched to Washington without making a trip back to California. So, first I will work, then that will open up some possibilities for me.

The thing I have done is expand my waistline and my library, not all instructional or classics, either. I spent a week and a half reading the entire Stephanie Meyer saga. I loved it. I bought myself a basketball, though, to encourage me to be more active. It does a great job of holding some of my papers down. Someday, it might see a hoop.

If anything works well for me during this next month, I may get a chance to come home briefly, visit people, and pick up some dearly missed items. I wish you the best. I am hoping this message finds you well. Additionally, no matter how a person lives, someone will be disappointed. Live your truth and be sure you are not the one who is disappointed.

"If the world were merely seductive, that would be easy. If it were merely challenging, that would be no problem. But I arise in the morning torn between a desire to improve (or save) the world and a desire to enjoy (or savor) the world. This makes it hard to plan the day." — E. B. White

Seismic Activity in Washington (Our Hero's Tale)

So there I was, working in the garage on the six banger in my hot rod.

Rule #78: Make a plan and stick to it. Of course, I never followed that rule very often. So, I was upgrading my engine after I had assembled it, which required enlarging some holes in the engine block with a grinder. I plugged every hole I could and kept it super clean, but there was always that niggling whisper. You know? The one speaking to me about the evils of metal shavings inside an engine so custom and expensive most of the part numbers were "Rick Cone"? I finally finished drilling, so I wiped and vacuumed and scrubbed and rubbed magnets and wiped and vacuumed again. Still, the whispers continued. So I removed the oil pan drain plug and decided to flush the inside of the engine.

Kerosene would have been the liquid of choice here, but I did not have any. I looked around the shop. My sister had left a gallon of Coleman camp fuel. That is basically just white kerosene, right? I poured the whole gallon through the engine. That would quiet the voices down! Unfortunately, nearly the entire gallon missed the oil drain pan I had placed beneath the engine. Well, that was no big deal. The garage door was open, and the camp fuel would evaporate quickly. Onward and upward!

A few hours later, the bracketry for the clutch was completed, and it was time to start fabricating exhaust pipes. I cut the mandrel bends, got all my pipe lengths approximated and prepared to start tacking the pieces together on the engine. I could finish welding them more conveniently off the engine. I hit the trigger and that first piece of slag fell onto the concrete garage floor. Concrete that, if you recall, had been covered in a gallon of camp fuel a few hours earlier.

Well, at this point, there are a few salient facts you should know. Coleman camp fuel is actually like extra volatile kerosene, which means extra vapory. Concrete is porous, and easily absorbs petroleum products. The oil pan of my engine came off an old ranch truck, so it was rather dented in on the bottom and therefore would not drain completely. Why are these facts relevant?

The red-hot slag hit the concrete and ignited the vapors from the camp fuel. I watched it burn for a minute, figuring it would go out soon. It is not like things in my garage had not been on fire before. And, how many times in Junior High did we pour lighter fluid on our hands and watch it burn off? It did not even get that hot! Well, there is a difference between a few drops, and an entire gallon. After a couple of minutes, I started wondering where the fire extinguisher was located that my sister forced me to buy before she left for California. About that time, WWHHUUMMPP! Cataclysm! Catastrophe! Calamity! Other C-words!

I dug the fire extinguisher out from beneath all the tools, parts, and other debris knocked off walls and shelves and put the fire out. My boys came running from the house. The concussion of the blast had rattled the dishes and made the DVD player skip. They thought I was dead. The neighbors across the road also came running out. They had heard the explosion and felt the thump through their chairs. After the neighbors determined everyone was okay, they told me that I probably should not do whatever I had done ever again. There was definitely some arm-crossing and eye-narrowing from all parties present.

Postmortem revealed that the remnants of camp fuel in the oil pan had been heated up to percolation by the fire underneath it. The fire crawled into the oil drain plug, and a miniature fuel-air bomb occurred. It was unilaterally decided that I was no longer allowed to weld in the garage without someone watching with a fire extinguisher (the genesis of **Rule #311**). Also, my sister got to crow "I told you so" over and over about making me buy a fire extinguisher in the first place. Certain restrictions were put into effect regarding the use of flammable chemicals in the garage.

The good news? The dents in the oil pan were all popped back out without so much as a wrinkle, and it looked brand new and perfect. So I guess that made it all worth it.

The Vegas Visit (The Heir's Tale)

And there I was, helping Our Hero move his family to South Carolina. It was only days before Christmas. I helped Dad brand, vaccinate, and dehorn 600 head of yearlings in the morning, then drove 1,170 miles that day on my way to Washington. It was a very long day. I asked Our Hero to give me a 7 AM wake-up call, forgetting the time change.

The call came at 8 AM. I was already an hour late. I had to drive another 540 miles. Instead of giving me directions to the house, they gave me directions to a karaoke bar. They were having a send-off party for the Princess. It lasted until the bar closed.

Our Hero rode with me from the bar to show me the way to his house. The Princess drove her car but was picked up by the cops for driving drunk. We were trying to decide which one of us was the more sober, so we could go get her or her car. As we drove up, the cops got a distress call. Another officer was in trouble. They told the Princess this was her lucky day. They let her go; told her to drive straight home. Another crisis averted … but another very short night.

The next day, we packed up the Princess and her stuff and headed for Las

Vegas. We were spending Christmas with her folks before going to South Carolina. We had to be there by 4 PM for dinner. We arrived at 3:40 PM.

I was exhausted from lack of sleep, begged off dinner, and went to sleep in the guest bedroom. Less than an hour later, the Princess' cousins came over and decided to go to the strip. A quick change of clothes and off to the bar we went. Several rounds of Yeager bombs later, we went to the Strip. At 1 AM we were headed to the car to go home. The Princess' cousin was so wasted she fell and hit her head. It left a huge knot on the right side of her head. We took her to the ER. It was Christmas Eve. The ER was packed. It was 4 AM before she was released and we were finally headed back. It was another extremely short night.

Everyone was up by 7 AM for their family Christmas. We repacked the truck and headed east after lunch. I was never so tired, and we still had thousands of miles ahead of us.

"Love's Kindling"

And there we were, the man I love and cherish, and me…

> Take my hand and dance with me,
> Time flies by, with precious time for "we."
> Quietly sit beside me; simply enjoy
> Making memories as "he" and "she."
>
> The night is still, filled with our thoughts
> And our dreams as we climb this hill.
> Start the fire with twigs of caring,
> Forget the troubles we may be sharing.
>
> Feel the warmth of our newfound love,
> See the stars as they shimmer above.
> Notice the glow the kindness brings,
> And when we are together, how the world sings.
>
> Come dance with me, be with me tonight,
> Knowing that you are my heart's sheer delight.
> Through calming winds or the harsh weather,
> Stay with me, promise to leave never.

When we enter that special place,
Just you and me in our private space,
It lights the fire of our inner soul,
A true bonding that keeps us whole.

We notice the beauty around us,
With the campfire an added plus.
Living in peace, we chance to discover
Our two souls dancing together.

That'll Never Happen (Our Hero's Tale)

So here I am, spending some quality time in the garage with my middle son, Christian … Actually, he is standing next to me with a fire extinguisher because I have recently attempted to blow up the garage, but you already read that story.

We join Our Hero as he is attempting to install an engine that never came in a car, that is set up to run on an experimental fuel, that is running an experimental induction system, with experimental internal parts. This means anything he wants done has to be created, developed, and manufactured by him as well. Today is bracket fabrication day. Few activities are as challenging as trying to put together a three-dimensional jigsaw puzzle with a welder, when all the pieces are the same color, and there is no picture on the box. I am pretty sure Christian's vocabulary is expanding at a record pace.

Now, just because you are a hero, does not mean you should not be frugal. After all, I am my mother's son. I am wearing a pair of blue jeans that are in excellent shape, very durable, with just one flaw. The zipper is broken. No problem! They shall be repurposed as garage jeans! While this may seem an inspired choice in wardrobe recycling, it does leave a very large chink in the armor, if you will.

After getting all the pieces and parts in the right place on the bench, it is time to stitch it all together with the welder. My son, who has experienced a few "adventures" with me by this time, has refined his skills at identifying potential hazards and seeing points at which they may occur. He points out that welding on the bench with a permanently open fly is risky at best and downright dangerous at worst. After all, what if some molten slag fell down there?

"That'll never happen," I proclaim as I lower my welding shield. I pull the trigger. Zippp, goes the welder. "AAYYEEEEE!" shrieks Our Hero as molten slag springs off the bracket, straight down the open fly, and all the way down inside his work boots. In addition to the expanded vocabulary, Christian now gets to witness dance moves that, if filmed, surely would have been studied and adopted by the professional dancers on *Dancing with the Stars*. I give him extra credit for keeping a straight face until out of sight.

Is That a Violin?

And here we are, at the Sunday night dance. During intermission, we hear my cell phone ring. We wonder what the emergency might be ...

The Heir is now well into living life as an independent-thinking young man. This has a lasting impact upon my life. He has called for the "Ollie and Ollie" moving service numerous times, four times just this past year. He managed to change jobs, legal residences, voting precincts, girlfriends, and banks. Most of these changes proved to be quite beneficial.

Although he has learned to eat a better diet and pick up after himself, he still calls us for "advice" on occasion. Word is he is doing pretty well for himself. His new apartment is clean, spacious, and quite enviable. He attends Jaycee events as a state officer. His friends claim he is irresistible but not irreplaceable. His gal thinks he may be "all that"!

For the last few years, his family has suspected he may have a few too many luxuries in life. He spends his free time watching movies he records on his DVR. He is in the process of upgrading his race car from 940 HP to 1000+. Some Friday nights, he complains of having to choose among several options for social activities, yet, on occasion, falls asleep and misses all of them.

A kid who lives near the action and buys everyone a round is not exactly what we had in mind when we were pinching pennies to help him go to college and get started ranching. When we look back on our "start-up" days, we reminisce about monthly grocery shopping trips, one tank of gas every other week, and one "good" pair of boots. Certainly not several closets full of clothing, bi-weekly trips to the store for fresh fruits and veggies, and nights spent closing down the bar. He refuses to do his laundry unless he has time to wash, dry, and fold his clothing. It is entirely possible he still has a few wrinkles to iron out ...

As an interested parent, I anticipate little time left after work for a consuming social life and a bit of bar time. Yet, when he shows up, well after one in the morning, he is ready to share stories of his adventures. Worse yet, he is usually wearing polo shirts and khakis, or a shirt and tie. Not really ranching duds.

Just as we are beginning to wonder what kind of kid turns the post-college years into a ten-year stint of changing everything as often as we might change our socks, the call comes. "Oh, no!" my partner moans, recognizing the ringtone.

It is not the sort of call that a mother cherishes, or the family is really happy to hear, but it is certainly a sign of a right turn on the road to reality.

He phones on a Sunday night, sounding nearly distraught. We promptly put him on speaker phone and turn on our listening ears. "I have had a really rough couple of days," The Heir announces. I cannot help but wonder if that is a hint of panic I hear in his voice.

"What is going on?" we chorus with faux concern. We are standing on the edge of the dance floor watching the other couples dancing and wondering just how long this conversation is going to take. If Son has picked up on the fact that we are somewhat pleased that he is finally enduring a rough patch, he does not let on.

"I got a letter from FDIC this week. Since the Bank closed, they purchased the loans and are giving me sixty days to pay off the total loan or to refinance it." We remind him that the accountant has informed us this exact situation is a strong possibility. "But it is going to take all of my tax refund (and more) to fix this. I have already earmarked those funds for something else."

"What is that?" I inquire softly.

"I am planning to use that money to finish putting parts on the engine for my race car to get it up and running for this summer's car shows," he declares with a hint of a whine in his strained voice. I think I detect a snort from my partner, who is pointing to the other dancers doing our favorite waltz tune.

"I am already working sixty-five to eighty hours a week and just cannot seem to get ahead. What am I supposed to do?" he asks. I hesitate too long.

"I could cash my Certificates of Deposit, but I would lose this quarter's interest. Besides I am saving them for my future. What is wrong with that? I suppose I should call my other bank tomorrow and have them cancel the CD they were automatically scheduled to do for me this month." I am thankful this is a phone conversation and not face-to-face. Otherwise, he could detect the eye-rolling and shoulder shrugs.

He really catches our attention when he heaves a deep sigh and adds with a hoarse voice, "And that is not the worst part." You may sense the pain I feel as a mother when my dear son delivers his next line. Go ahead, grab yourself a Kleenex, lean on a loved one and prepare for a good cry.

As we listen with anticipation, forgetting all about the dancers on the floor spinning and twirling with grace and delight, he pauses for effect. "What is it, Son?" I finally ask. "This past week was so rough," he continued. I am quite certain he is choking back a sob. "I didn't even get my nap in."

Please, pass me a hankie. I am positive if you listen closely you can hear the violin music.

"Only Yesterday"

It seems like only yesterday
    You came to give a look,
Unsure, restrained, and modest,
    Your smile was all it took.

It seems like only yesterday
    The friendship seed was sown,
Tranquil, subtly persistent,
    You made your presence known.

It seems like only yesterday
    We spent time in the sun.
Warm water, brisk winds, sharp waves,
    And a boat for added fun.

It seems like only yesterday
    We drove all through the hills.
Allowed life to just unfold,
    With experiences and thrills.

It seems like only yesterday
    I asked you to stop by
To shower off, spend some time ...
    The meal and movie, sigh!

It seems like only yesterday
    I asked, "What shall I do?"
You answered, "Anything you want ..."
    My dilemma only grew.

It seems like only yesterday
    You held me in your arms,
Caressing those taut muscles,
    Relaxing with your charms.

It seems like only yesterday
    We snuggled all night through.
That tightly leashed passion
    Promised us experiences—all new.

It seems like only yesterday
    You took me out to dance.
We had so much fun that night
    I said, "Yes …" and took a chance.

It seems like only yesterday
    Lust led us, set the pace.
We reached out, seduced, surrendered,
    Lost in the closeness of an embrace.

It seems like only yesterday
    That trust replaced the tears.
Pervasive, sincere, encompassing,
    Negating all the fears.

It seems like only yesterday
    We captured our day, so neat!
Now we can always remember
    Tidbits of fun—some hot, some sweet!

Learning from Romans 12

"Love must be sincere. Hate what is evil; cling to what is good. Be devoted to one another in brotherly love. Honor one another above yourselves. Never be lacking in zeal, but keep your spiritual fervor, serving the Lord. Be joyful in hope, patient in affliction, faithful in prayer. Share with God's people who are in need. Practice hospitality." (Romans 12:9-13 NIV)

And here we are, studying the Good Book together. These words from Romans 12 are vibrantly alive, a rather obvious list of directions on how to treat other people.

191

Upon hearing them, he says nothing. Instead, he settles back against the couch and returns his attention to her. But this time—in a way that sooths the painful cracks in her heart—he reaches out and quietly takes her hand in his.

She savors the feel of his fingers against hers. His touch feels so good she wants to cry. Even when no one else understands, she feels that he does. As for the changes in her own heart, she recognizes they are partially due to his love. By letting her talk, and listening without judging, he has removed a splinter from her soul. In its absence, the place that has festered, has bled, has constantly pained her is actually beginning to heal. She is learning to live again, learning to love, and learning to live in peace. Every day, she feels less afraid of her past, more confident that she is loved.

Caught up in this rare moment of quiet, she watches the sky turn from deep blue to mauve and turquoise, inserted with streaks of purple.

What to Give Loved Ones

And here we are, wondering what to give that special someone for their special day. If we are on a budget, or pressed for time, or do not remember if they liked what we gave them last year, we wonder what would be best. An even harder task is to know what to ask for in return. We do not enjoy telling people what to get us. We need to come up with the perfect plan, the perfect gift for someone who has everything and really needs nothing else to dust.

This plan works for any size, any age, any budget, and we do not need to gift-wrap it. It is easy. We just take a nice piece of paper or stationary and write five or more things we would like to tell someone. For this month's birthday boy, we could call it:

"Five Things I Know and Love about You"

1. **A memory**: I will always remember how you casually picked up stakes and moved with me to North Carolina, so we could fix up this beast of a house and the other outbuildings, without complaining about any of it.

2. **Something you do that I greatly admire**: You give selflessly to the Senior Center, to the Veterans, to the residents in care homes with no families, and anyone else who could use a leg up. You do this despite having fewer resources than nearly anyone I know.

3. **Something you do that drives me crazy**: You laugh at the most inappropriate things, in the most inappropriate ways, at the most inappropriate times,

and manage to entertain everyone while you are doing it. Most unfair.

4. **Why I like being with you and miss you when we are apart**: You listen to what I say, even if I have said it before. You know things about me that no one else knows and like me anyway. You say what I need to hear, even if I do not want to hear it. You make me laugh every day.

5. **What I would give you if I could give you anything**: A magic mirror to see yourself the way I see you, so you would not need to worry about the color of your hair or the way your clothes fit. Frequent trips to Wyoming to see your family. A brand new pickup for road trips, and a motorcycle to haul around in it for side trips.

That is the list I will give my guy for his birthday. Maybe someone will give it to me, too. Feel free to use it, if you like, or ask someone to give it to you. May all your wishes come true.

So Little Time

And there we were, wondering how the time slipped away. How the years passed by. There were so many things I wanted to teach Daughter.

I remember trying to teach her to sleep through the night. I remember working on teaching her the first word, the name I wanted her to call out in the night whenever she needed attention: "Dad." She learned it well, used it to great effect. The only name she called out in the night, or any time when she needed anything important, was "Mom."

That was fine with me. I liked being the most important person in her world. I still do. I would have liked it even more if I had known how quickly it would pass. There really was not much I needed to teach her. She was so smart, so quick, so eager to learn, that she was always there before I found the time to teach her. She taught herself to tie her shoes. I just bought her Velcro shoes, so we did not have to mess with it. She taught herself to ride a bike, drive a pickup, pick out her outfits, and do the laundry, though each time she let us think we were helping her to learn.

Surely, I taught her something of substance? How to brush her teeth, make her bed, put fresh flowers on the table. How to know when to talk and when to listen. How to wrestle and put the fear of God into her brothers. How to laugh in a leaky tent in the pouring rain (drive to Grandma's and spend the rest of the night!). How to survive the death of someone you love by becoming more alive. I like to think I taught her all those things and more.

But there was so much more that slipped through my fingers when I was busy doing ... stuff. When we were sewing a Christmas gift for Our Hero, I realized I never taught Daughter how to sew, use the sewing machine to make a straight seam, or even do something simple like sew on a button.

I never taught her how to be a master painter, how to work with wood, how to apply lacquer. I never really taught her how to cook, though she learned it anyway. I tried to teach her how to drive a tractor, and rake hay. She tried to learn but found it to be "not her thing." Despite being a pianist and a music teacher, I never taught Daughter how to play the piano, though she asked me to teach her. I never took the time. I wish I could have taught her how to drive a five-speed.

Someday, I will teach her that unlike daughters, mothers are not required to follow orders, or obey rules, or practice manners in their own home. She will pretend to be shocked.

Trampolines

And there we were, discussing the ups and downs of life. John Maxwell writes in his book, *Developing The Leader Within You,* "The first victory that successful people achieve is the victory over themselves." How, we ask? First, we start with ourselves.

The comedian, Jack Paar, advises: "Looking back, my life seems to be one long obstacle course, with me as the chief obstacle." We start with ourselves. We start small. The sooner we learn the lessons of responsibility, accountability, and integrity the better everything will be. It is like a savings account. The earlier we start, the more we will have.

We start with ourselves. We start early. We start small. What we are going to be tomorrow, we are becoming today. It is a process. We do more than stand on the platform waiting for the Fame Train to arrive. It does not stop for us just because we wave our arms. To reach our goals, we have to work at them. We have to get our hands dirty. It is okay if those hands develop a few callouses.

The road to success is never a straight line. Great dreams almost always come packaged with great challenges. At the end of the day, we are left with a question I have never really answered, "Why?" Why is great achievement filled with frustrations? Why is persistence and patience a common trait of the successful among us? Why would the Supreme Source of Love and Light give us challenges?

Yesterday when I awoke, I heard a completely different answer. Einstein's theory of relativity is, "What we expect to have happen will happen; we influence the physical world by our thoughts and expectations. Therefore, we can imagine awful, or we can imagine wonderful, and what we think about we shall bring about." "Imagination is more important than knowledge." – Albert Einstein

Going back to the "Why the challenges?" question, I see that I am asking the wrong question. Rather than, "Why are there often great challenges before a triumph," I need to ask, "Why is there often great triumph after challenges?" When adversity hits the hardest, it brings about a reaction of imagining the opposite. If we forget something important, we immediately ask/imagine our life to be more organized. If we are overdrawn, we immediately wish for abundance and wealth. My friend's husband was released from prison after spending his entire adult life within the walls. This was during an economic depression; he spent several months looking for work. The day his parole officer notified him that he had to have a forty hour a week job or else, things got "real." He used his social media contacts and had a job within the week. It is in response to challenges that we attract the great miracles that this world calls "achievement." That is because we "ask" in a stronger way.

Sports are a perfect example. America watched Super Bowl XLIX Sunday night. The New England Patriots came from ten points behind to win over the defending champions, the Seattle Seahawks. How many times have we heard this about a winning team or individual: "They wanted it more." What if our being behind and the heightened desire to win rather than lose elevates our clarity of desire and is the very reason we win? What if the darkest depths in our lives are not "rock bottom" so much as they are our trampolines? The lower we push down on the trampoline, the higher we jump … if we are willing to.

Without our lows, it is more difficult to experience our longing for the highs. It is that longing that marks every great achiever. Why is it always darkest before the dawn? Or we could ask why does the dawn come after the darkest night? Is it because, in the middle of the night, we long for a new day?

"How far you go in life
depends on your being tender with the young,
compassionate with the aged,
sympathetic with the striving,
and tolerant of both the weak and the strong,
because someday you will have been
one or all of these."

—George Washington Carver

The Seven "Significants"

And here we are, gathered in the auditorium for graduation, the members of the class of 2016, faculty, family, and friends. I share this message:

Today marks a milestone of magnitude, that special moment when you are unleashed upon the world as a new graduate. Congratulations. In your honor, I am here to share seven "significants." These are concepts I wish I could have learned more easily and sooner in life. This is your chance to sift through my ideas and keep those that seem significant to you.

First of all, always be authentic. Be true to who you actually are. I knew I had not mastered this when I sauntered into Mom's house and her comment was, "Who are you going to be today?" There is no need to try to impress others. Let your acts reflect your true self. My sixth grade teacher reminded me that Shakespeare advised, "To thine own self be true."

A close cousin to that thought is to live with integrity. Integrity is as simple and as complicated as keeping your word. It is objectively telling the truth and not living a lie. Integrity is doing the right thing even when no one else is around to notice. Do not make promises you cannot possibly keep. Living with integrity keeps you humble and honest. It means accepting the blame when you make a mistake. It is also realizing, "There is nothing final about a mistake, except it being taken as final," a quote from Phyllis Bottome.

Integrity helps make you someone even you would enjoy being around. That is important because you have to see that same face in the mirror every morning and every night. (SMILE) A well-developed sense of humor can ease many situations and help you through a host of others. If you can laugh at yourself and your own special quirks, you will never run out of material. Laughter releases tension and alleviates stress. Laugh often.

A word of warning: Some people may not be as twisted and warped as you are or share your particular brand of humor. Make sure you do not hurt their feelings if they cannot see the humor in their situations. If that happens, let them laugh first, and then join in. Your life will become more enjoyable. You will be a joy to be around.

Be careful with authority. Power is so easy to misuse. People who need to be in control usually lose it. It is more beneficial to treat others with dignity, to respect their boundaries, and to seek justice for those who need it.

Be ready for responsibility. Those willing to handle responsibility usually get it. As graduates, you have shown you have a great sense of responsibility. Never

SIGNIFICANTS

1. Be Authentic

2. Live with Integrity

3. Laugh at Yourself

4. Be Careful with Authority

5. Be Ready for Responsibility

6. Cultivate your Interests

7. Develop a Positive Attitude

lose it. Whenever you have an opportunity, work for the good of all, especially for those near and dear.

John Stewart Mill tells us, "One person with a belief is equal to a force of ninety-nine who have only interests." Cultivate your interests, but live your beliefs. They become your ideals.

Paraphrasing Carl Schurz, "Ideals are like stars; you will not succeed in touching them with your hands. You choose them as your guides, and following them you will reach your destiny."

A spool of thread, a wrench, a book, a small stone—each of these items may be held in your hand. Each one has a special and unique purpose. Our hands may hold different things. For me, it may be the pen I used to write this commencement address. For you, it may be a shovel, a spatula, or a stethoscope. We are not asked to do the impossible. If we use what is in our hands, we receive innumerable blessings. Our efforts can accomplish small miracles. What we do with what we have is our responsibility. May you use your talents wisely.

Money is not the answer to everything. I repeat: money is not the answer to everything. Learn to manage what money you do have instead of striving for even more money. Remember to share your money. Give some of it away. Do not keep it all for yourself. Never spend it all either, but keep some in savings. An emergency fund is a first priority. Wealth is built day by day. If you take care of the little things, the big things will take care of themselves. Eventually, your investments will take care of you.

Last of all, develop and maintain a positive attitude. Greet others warmly, and treat them kindly. Maybe it is only a few words or a small smile. Any little encouragement can bring sunshine to a gloomy day. Every small effort helps. That one little smile can create a ripple of happiness. Whenever we encourage others, we are showing caring and concern. Encouragement is easy to share but difficult to give away because it keeps coming back.

This is your chance to start your own life anew. Use these seven "significants" to shape your destiny.

Become the person you were meant to be, doing the things you were meant to do, in a way that leaves the world a better place just because you were in it. That is my wish for you.

May all your tomorrows inspire you to keep reaching for your dreams.

Warm wishes as you move toward your destiny. We look forward to joining you on this journey of life.

America's destiny is in your hands!

CHAPTER EIGHT:
LIKE A MOTH TO A FLAME

Attitude

"The longer I live, the more I realize the impact of attitude on life. Attitude, to me, is more important than facts. It is more important than the past, than education, than money, than circumstances, than failures, than successes, than what other people think or say or do. It is more important than appearance, giftedness, or skill. It will make or break a company ... a church ... a home. The remarkable thing is we have a choice every day regarding the attitude we will embrace for that day. We cannot change the inevitable. The only thing we can do is play on the one string we have, and that is our attitude ... I am convinced that life is ten percent what happens to me, and ninety percent how I react to it. And so it is with you ... we are in charge of our attitudes."

— Charles Swindoll

Autobiography in Five Short Chapters

1) I walk down the street.
   There is a deep hole in the sidewalk.
   I fall in.
   I am lost ... I am hopeless.
   It isn't my fault.
   It takes forever to find a way out.

2) I walk down the same street.
   There is a deep hole in the sidewalk.
   I pretend I don't see it.
   I fall in again.
   I can't believe I am in the same place.
   But, it isn't my fault.
   It still takes a long time to get out.

3) I walk down the same street.
   There is a deep hole in the sidewalk.
   I see it is there.
   I still fall in ... it's a habit.
   My eyes are open.
   I know where I am.
   It is my fault.
   I get out immediately.

4) I walk down the same street.
   There is a deep hole in the sidewalk.
   I walk around it.

5) I walk down another street.

— Portia Nelson, "Child Within"

"This Just Can't Be"

It's an overwhelming air of loneliness
That encompasses those of us who
Stop to look toward the horizon
At dusk, thinking, "This isn't me …"
Hurrying to finish the fencing
In the harried half-light
Of evening. That must be

Someone else with a pail of staples
Gripped tightly in her hand
Trudging along the line fence
Of the pasture, thinking,
"This can't be me …" solely responsible
For revamping this ramshackle piece
Of boundary fenceline. At the deepest
Moment of the day, wishing

That I were someplace else, wishing
I were anywhere else; but I'm a rancher,
Looking out at herself from afar,
Hopping into the old ranch pickup,
Starting it up and climbing the steep hill,
Listening to the tires grabbing
For real estate, the engine laboring

Disrupting the endless silence,
Which seems ominously empty
And strange; then suddenly thinking
With a new wave of aloneness
"This really shouldn't be me …" sitting in this
Pickup feeling as if I were miles from civilization,
In the center of God's Country. This must be

Someone else driving around in these hills
Surrounded by miles of grassy knolls
With only wildlife to share the deepening
Dusk, searching to find the trail while
Steering herself home and trying
Not to fret

In the last moments of nightfall
As the red lights on the tower wink
Knowingly, farmsteads light up in the
Valley, and the sky fills with stars.
This just can't be ... me.
Alone yet not alone, seeking the light.

Morphine or Whiskey?

And there we were, surrounded by ugly green curtains in the ER. Why?

Time passes. They no longer retain their 33-year-old physiques. There are days when his body feels wretched, filled with aching stiffness.

She solicitously asks, "What can I get for you?" He solemnly intones, "Morphine." They exchange subtle smiles.

For the times she is not doing so well and is hacking up lugees from her congested lungs, he invariably intones, "Whisky, you need whisky." It is part of their private dance.

The first Sunday of each month, they travel to a special hidden-away diner and order the featured entrée, a catfish fillet dinner. Usually, they drop in at the family ranch, too. This Sunday, she is reading the newspaper during the drive. Pointing to the obits she calmly announces, "Mine might be there tomorrow."

He asks, "Why?"

She replies, "I am not feeling so good," expecting him to say, "Whisky." He does not. He is not amused. Instead, they go inside and order the special. She fights off waves of pain, experiences beads of sweat, nausea, and a deepening concern. Fearing the worst, she telephones her doctor. No answer. She dials the clinic. No emergency contact number is provided. She calls her mom, asks about the symptoms of a heart attack. They seem to coincide with her situation. They leave the diner and quickly drive across the hills to the family ranch. They dash inside. Mom administers some nitro pills and aspirin. No visible lessening of the symptoms occurs.

EMT Sis happens to be visiting and takes her pulse while the little white pill is dissolving. Her breathing is steady. That is good. Her pulse is strong. That is good. The pain is not diminishing, and she is still not feeling well. Sis asks, "What are we waiting for?" She strongly suggests we drive forty miles to the ER. He asks himself, "Why me? Why now? Not this again."

He rapidly delivers her to the same ER he has visited many times before, but never with her. While he is decompressing from the mad dash, she is monitored, x-rayed, poked for the IV, and bled. The pain is building, for both of them. Now he is not doing so well, either, but there is no one sitting with him to ease his discomfort. He is reliving the terrors of those other visits that ended in the loss of his wife.

Finally, he is invited into that familiar little room with the pale green curtains. The nurse brings her a shot of morphine. "Morphine," she exclaims. They exchange subtle smiles. The steroid shots quiet the pleurisy pains. She has coughed too long and too hard. She should have been taking the honey and whisky shots …

Later, when the monstrous bill arrives, they grin at one another and wisely chorus, "Whisky, we need whisky."

Where Does It End?

And there we were, faced with dealing with an addiction. Any addiction begins and ends in pain. When we are in the company of the addicted, we are assaulted by waves of negative energy. We must not believe it is our own fear. It is theirs. Let them own it. We must appear to be having a good time and just be ourselves. We are responsible for dismissing all fear and making a better space for all. We do not need alcohol or drugs or endless "work" to get us through this life. There are many moments when we can be still, when we can notice what really delights, what gives us a natural high …

I can get high on life when I catch a glimpse of a red cardinal flitting from snow-tipped branches or catch the musical notes of his lilting song.

I can get high when I happen on a pair of grouse "booming."

I can get high watching the murmurization of starlings as they travel though and congregate in our trees each spring.

I can get high when I flush a covey of quail or a lone pheasant.

I can get high when I discover a field of wildflowers.

I can get high when I find myself threading my way through the inky darkness of the dripping rain forest after midnight.

I can get high joining my family as we play "Guitar Hero."

I can get high hiking on Hurricane Ridge, Baker's Mountain, South Mountain, climbing the buttes in the Wildcats or the interminable steps at Chimney Rock Park, or just strolling through any quiet area, enjoying nature in all of its moods.

I can get high walking in the gentle rain with uplifted face, letting every care dissipate.

I can get high standing on the northern shores of the Pacific, watching the hard-breaking waves, listening to the pounding surf, experiencing the unrestrained power of wind and water.

I can get high riding a lift to the mountaintop and pausing to savor the view of the valleys below before skillfully skiing down the snowy slopes.

I can get high driving through the mountains with a snowstorm chasing after me.

I can get high bobbing in the gentle warm waves of the Gulf, then sunning on the sand.

I can get high watching the salmon swirling in the cold Alaskan rivers.

I can get high just glimpsing a bear, or a moose, or a caribou, or a Dahl sheep at Denali.

I can get high watching an ice-blue glacier calve into a fiord.

I can get high unexpectedly spying a whale swim by next to our ship while dining.

I can get high circling the floor in the arms of an excellent dancer, following the intricate moves of a country waltz.

Life provides endless opportunities to get high naturally. There is no limit to the opportunities for joy.

Which Way to Go?

And there we were at an important crossroad in life. What to do? I wish I knew. Most likely, I did know, but did not really wish to follow through. Once again, the issue is disrespect, combined with distrust. The relationship has become unbalanced, untenable.

When we are not tolerant of others, frustrations build. Once again, it becomes decision time. To know how much we really love someone, we have to let ourselves feel how much it hurts to lose them. Then we must weigh the costs of any lasting decisions.

When we respect ourselves and others equally, then we have a shot at loving unconditionally. If we let our love dictate our actions, we balance our intents with respectful responses and observe boundaries. We cannot accept disrespectful behavior, especially from our life partner. Each has a responsibility to honor the relationship and one another. This requires carefully constructing boundaries that are respectfully observed.

Unconditional love requires respect, honor, and trust. Respect, honor, and trust are built upon behaviors that are regular and sincere. They are learned by the daily behaviors we show one another. Discernment is a key to building trust. Trust is built using honesty and practicing accountability with clear transparency. It is unloving behavior to continue a relationship in spite of disrespect, dishonor, or untrustworthy behavior. This leads to abuse and an unbalanced relationship.

We can love unconditionally when there is equal respect, honor, and trust in the relationship. When we accept the present reality and relate to it with unconditional love, we are able to confront disrespect, dishonor, and untrustworthy behavior with loving kindness. We are truly being unconditional in loving someone and ourselves when we care enough to stand up for respect, honor, and trust as being important for the relationship to survive.

Building honor, trust, and respect is the goal of every good relationship. By being honest, respectful, and honorable—not only by behaving in these ways in our relationships, but by insisting on others behaving these ways, too—we build a balanced and lasting relationship of value. We do this by honoring the spirit, the self that resides in ourselves and in others. Real discernment develops when we realize we are all one.

Under no circumstances should we team with a person who continually resents and opposes our way of doing things. If we have not learned our lesson, we can expect restraints on our efforts once again. The limitations in relationships eventually reveal themselves. They dictate the steps of the dance.

Smoke and Mirrors

And there we were, witnessing the end of it all. It was a dark and stormy night. Suddenly a shot rang out ... "How did it come to this?" I gasped, lying there with a large gaping hole.

At the dance that long ago evening, it seemed as if we hit it off instantly. I liked his black hat, his black shirt, his black jeans, his black boots and his big white smile. He liked the way I danced. It was as though a connection existed on an alternate plane, as though some primal awareness existed between us. At least one of us could feel the ancient weaving begin, the silken bonds that swiftly formed and shimmered with a primitive urge to become friends and partners, to reform a necessary whole from the shattered parts.

Then I stuck him on top of a white horse, dressed him in shiny armor, and called him my knight. Unfortunately, that simply did not make it true. Perhaps I should have noticed his usual garb: faded blue jeans, a blue chambray shirt, work boots, and a seed corn cap.

In hindsight, taking his self-proclaimed honesty and promises of faithful commitment as truths and not just an easy means to an end could have been my greatest error in judgment.

As the story unfolded, he asked himself, "Why? Why do I have to hurt you again? Why can't you see me for what I am? I am just a man who likes to drink beer. Any other woman would have seen me for what I am and stayed away from me."

For some reason, hidden even from myself, I desperately needed to believe in him, to suit him up as my white knight. Unfortunately, unlike me, he did not even like horses. He preferred his ATVs and tractors.

I tried telling him he did not need to let his fears dominate his actions, that he was a better person than that. He did not need to drink so much. I insisted the defensiveness was merely an unneeded defense mechanism. He clearly stated, "You have just managed to steal every bit of humor and joy from this situation. That is not who I am. I am just a man who likes to relax in the evening and drink beer."

Gazing at him with an expression that let him know I truly believed what I was saying, I reminded him that underneath it all, I believed him to be kind and considerate, warm and generous. He just stared at me wordlessly and then turned away.

It seems he understood that calling him a knight would not make it so, and imbuing him with these characteristics in my mind would not accomplish anything positive, either. He needed me to see him as he was and to be happy with that man, not the mythical man I had created from quixotic wishes and long lost dreams.

He claimed to respect me. When did that respect disappear? Despite the change in his feelings for me, changes that clearly distressed me, I remained constant. In fact there was little that changed in my demeanor toward him. I was still as strong-willed as I was generous and trusting, just as willing to fight for the fast-fading relationship. Finally, he decided, if it was the last thing he did, he would end the foolishness. He sent me away with a large gaping hole in my heart.

Our world changed that night. He turned my fantasies into a bloody reality of revealed false hopes, unfulfilled promises, and personal betrayals. With one shot, it was all over. He must have found the bullets ...

> "Don't sacrifice your peace
> trying to point out someone's true colors.
> Lack of character always reveals itself
> in the end."
> — Mandy Hale

People do these things because they are messed up, not because you are. Choose wisely! "Don't sacrifice your peace trying to point out someone's true colors. Lack of character always reveals itself in the end." — Mandy Hale

Black and Blue ... and Color, Too

And here we are, on the journey of life. Life's journeys can be stupendous. I reflect on how much my friendships have meant to me. Some friendships are special; I can open up and let my whole self out. All those miniscule mosaics of self that, half the time, feel barely held together with the plaster of personality. Splinters of the soul, it seems, that when shared are no longer secret.

Healing arrives with the realization that we were created to be loved. For us to live as if we are unloved is a self-inflicted limitation. Even when we do not feel particularly loved, we are. We do need an object or a person to love, someone to share a relationship.

If, for some reason, we do not have this sense of relationship with ourselves, or within ourselves, we risk not being able to love at all. We might only be able to love as a limitation of our personal nature. That kind of person could possibly act without love, and that would lead to disaster.

I think of myself as an independent woman living in relationship with a unique and loving man. That can present some difficulties. When we choose independence over relationship, we become a danger to one another. Others may become objects to be manipulated or managed for self-interest or personal happiness. Authority, as we usually think of it, is merely the excuse the strong use to make others conform to what they want. If used in a selfish way, power can inflict great harm, which only leads to fear. It can turn us black and blue.

Why do we have so much fear in our lives? We are afraid because we do not believe. We do not believe in the power of love. We do not believe that we are loved. The person who lives by their fears will not find freedom in being loved. I am referring to imagined fears, experienced by those who project those fears into the future. If those fears have a secure place in our hearts, we may neither believe in the goodness of others nor know deep in our hearts that we are loved. We hear the words, have the conversations, but do not know it to be true.

As we become wiser in the ways of love, we more fully understand that it is not only love that grows, as felt with our ever-expanding heart, it is the knowing that grows. Love simply expands to contain the knowledge. Love fits around what we know and understand. It is fairly difficult to understand what we have not actually experienced.

We begin by learning to love our children. We know them well. We develop a wonderful and real love while forming our relationship with them. They become our source of joy and of hope. Hope introduces a myriad of colors into our life.

On the flip side of any relationship, we experience the pain of growth and change. Have you noticed that in our pain, we may think the worst of others? We need to stop and reflect on the love we hold for others. We may talk, we may share, but we do not always hear the messages being given. Not that those times are a waste. They resemble little cracks in a wall. One at a time, they prepare us. The colors filter in.

I used to insist that I was not angry. My friends would say, "Oh, yes, you are! We can see it in what you do. We can hear it in what you say. You are angry, through and through." We hear, we feel, we believe, after we have prepared our hearts to listen. The ripples from our hearts bounce off others, weaving a magnificent tapestry. Our new image of love is not one of heaven and its pearly gates, but rather a cleansing of the universe, seeded with pearls.

Pearls are the only precious stones created from pain, suffering, and in the end, death. They represent life. Life is all about relationships. Simply sharing life, as we are doing right now, builds those relationships. Being open and available to those around us, being real, just sharing life, is really what we are here to do.

Marriage is a relationship based on sharing life together in a meaningful and fulfilling manner. It thrives in an environment of divine goodness and unconditional love. It is not a system to create a sense of certainty or security. It is a process, much like an oyster creating a priceless pearl. Mostly, it is the freedom to live with and love that special partner without an agenda. When we become afraid of uncertainty, afraid of the future, and resistant to change, we may choose unwisely, and slip off the path. We may even discover more of that black and blue hue.

Some roads traverse a landscape of loss. In actuality, most roads don't lead anywhere. Yet, when we truly love someone, we will travel any road to find them. If we can free ourselves to overcome our fears and just concentrate on believing in the goodness of love, we learn to trust. It is not our job to convince others or to try to change anyone. We become free to love without an agenda.

What we cannot do is lie, to ourselves or to others. Some of us try to hide inside of lies. That is how we have learned to survive. Lies are easy places for survivors to run. They give us a sense of safety, but we find ourselves in a very dark place, in a fortress built with walls of justifications. We do this to keep from feeling pain, to protect ourselves from hurt.

We get lost in our personal perceptions of reality. We become sure of our own judgments. It becomes difficult to even begin to perceive, let alone imagine, what real love and goodness are. True love never forces. It does not abuse. It does not control.

The consequences of our selfish deeds are part of the learning process that brings us to the end of our delusions. It is not love's way to force a relationship. It is the nature of love to open the way. Love allows emotions to surface. Emotions are the colors of our soul. They are not to be feared. They are spectacular and incredible. When we damp them down and keep ourselves from feeling, the world becomes a panorama of monotones, flat grays, and blacks. So many of us are scared of our emotions. We can then live in a prison of our own making.

True relationships do not actually follow rules. Rituals and rules never give us answers to the deep questions of the heart. Rules will never love us. Sharing life in relationship with another is far more illuminating, a way of coming to be. Living in love gives life meaning. We can quit worrying that something bad is going to happen. We just remember that we are surrounded by goodness and trust in the love we have inside us.

Many of us have a world of love inside us. Too much love, maybe. When we have that much love, it scares us. Without trust, we may become frightened into thinking that something will come along to steal that love away. There is no limit to love. The hard part of loving is feeling safe enough to give it away, safe enough to quit running from it, safe enough to fully feel the love and be unafraid to reciprocate.

Our writings are simple accountings of the walk we have shared with those we have loved. Something we can look back on every now and then as a way of charting how far we have come. A way of remembering what is important. We must believe in love.

We can already feel the place we are heading. We can see the signs. It is a place so amazing, so full of love and goodness and beauty that even if we need to face a long goodbye, we are assured we will be together again. Not just in this lifetime but for always.

The Wedding Toast I Will Never Give

Many wedding toasts begin with these positive declarations: "I will always be your best friend." "I will never let you down." "This love of ours will last forever." More realistically, a wedding toast, mine anyway, will read, "I will always be authentic. What you see is what you get. You have been warned."

Authenticity is frightening. It makes us vulnerable. It is also freeing. We can be just who we are. Trying to be something we are not is exhausting. Authenticity is exciting.

Two people living together in a relationship, be it marriage or other arrangement, will face adversity. Occasionally, they will suffer disappointments, which may trigger not only sitcom-worthy squabbles but possibly even dark-night-of-the-soul despair. It is highly unlikely they will be each other's best friend every single moment forever after. It is much more probable that one or the other may slip into snippets of fantasy that involve planning the perfect murder or plotting the best place to hide the body. Twenty-four/seven relationships can be taxing, trying, yet tremendously rewarding. They may be any or all of these at the same time.

Yes, it is admirable to have lofty goals. It is much more realistic to realize we will let one another down occasionally in ways both petty and profound. This is despite our best efforts to be supportive and attentive. Profound failure looms on the horizon. It is what we do as we live through these maddening moments together that lets us return to our shared love and its haven of happiness.

I promise there will be days when we look at this person sharing our life and feel only rage and frustration. We may slip back into the fantasy of a quick and easy removal. For those carefree individuals who thrive on spontaneity, we smile gently and recite, "Focus." Our favorite phrase to insert levity into dramatic moments is, "You were warned." This intentional reminder opens the door to acceptance and paves the passage to happiness.

The best part of any relationship is waking up to a new day, still friends, still loving, and yet knowing there will be more opportunities to deepen and strengthen that love. The wedding toast I will never give is "You were warned!"

CHAPTER NINE:
RAINBOWS AND ROSES

Stretch

Born: August 27, 1863

Stretch was "born on a horse" and by age four started training horses to ride and drive on a pony cart. She rode horseback to school every day (nearly 3 miles - one way) through blizzards and rain. She graduated to riding rodeo rough stock and training roping horses. Each morning she single-handedly harnessed a team of Belgians and fed the cattle. Striking out on her own (still does sometimes), Stretch taught school for 20 years, beginning in a one-room schoolhouse in Loup County. Stretch umpires Tiger games and occasionally takes the field as a base tender.

Batter Up!

And there we were, back at the ball field, at least theoretically.

Hey, Lucky, here you are up to bat in the big baseball game! Life is the pitcher. Nature is the umpire.

I step up to the plate. Up comes a curve ball. I swing weakly. "Strike one!" the umpire calls. "But why? I don't understand this at all!" I whine. The umpire does not care.

Next, it is a fast pitch. I swing wildly. "Strike two!" the umpire cries. "I'm doing the best that I can," I protest. The umpire still does not care.

Up comes a blooper ball, an apple on a string, a "gimme" pitch. I just stare at it and indignantly refuse to swing. "Strike three!" the umpire bawls.

"This is not fair," I decide. "I am just not getting this. I cannot win. But if you say I am out, at least I can go sit down."

"Batter up!" the umpire yells at you. "Lucky, you are still up to bat!"

~~~~~~~~~~

Is there a situation in life making you sick and tired? Do you find yourself getting discouraged? Why not just quit? Perhaps it is the negative self-talk that is weighing you down. I sometimes have issues with this. We worry about what others think. Like cockroaches in the dark, words of negativity scurry around, creeping us out. Thoughts like: This is not my game. Why did I start this? I will never finish. Who do I think I am? Why do I even bother trying? I am just going to disappoint myself or others. There's nothing in it for me, so I am out of here. I am gone. It is over! I quit!

If only it were so simple. Maybe this is our lucky day. Maybe not! Perhaps we did not win the big prize. We are still in the game. We are still up to bat.

What do we do when faced with challenging situations? Do we just quit? Do we look for different situations, better solutions, or other perspectives? Life gives us three main options:

1) We can choose to continue as we are.
2) We can decide to change the situation.
3) We can work at changing ourselves.

Different situations dictate different solutions. Sometimes we do just quit. That certainly changes the situation. It does not prepare us for the next curve ball life tosses us. Sometimes we continue just as we are. More than likely that fast ball may just blow right by us. We strike out again. That leaves us eyeball to eyeball with life, trying to learn how to hit those pitches, run those bases, avoid the tags, and successfully cross home plate, scoring the big run.

I have been told there are not always definitive answers in life, just excellent questions. I am going to pose a few of those questions and invite you to think about how you might answer.

Since we live in a less-than-perfect world, my first question is: "How do we adapt to less than perfect situations?" My first response is "Not well." It gets better with practice.

My second question is: "As a parent, how do we keep an open mind for fair solutions while maintaining firm principles?" This is tricky. It may feel like we are trying to maintain our balance while walking a tightrope that is swaying with the wind. Again, it gets easier with time.

My third question is: "As a leader, how do we direct these free-thinking, non-conformist spirits, yet not stifle creativity?" This question applies to anyone working with other people.

I have gone to bat over a few of these questions. Sometimes I have struck out; soetimes I have hit a long fly ball. I will even cop to hitting into a big double play. When that happens, things really take on a different perspective. All at once, life seems desperately serious. It does not have to be. We can savor the beauty, believe in the magic, and be aware of the awesome.

If we celebrate the base hits, the successful steals, the RBIs from our sacrifice flies, we discover the joy of the game. We cherish that stand-up triple and continue to seek that elusive home run. We smile and step up. Positive energy brings positive outcomes.

Throughout life and its many "at-bats," I have found a key element of success to be respectful listening and empathetic understanding. Mutual respect creates bonding experiences. Developing this respect is something we cannot give up, for ourselves or for others.

My secret to surviving difficult times with serenity, to achieving success without losing heart, is to simply live through the tragic sides of life and focus on the positive outcomes. I do this by limiting any negative self-talk and holding on to respect. I look for the small successes, the minor miracles, the blessings in life. I build on them.

Yes, I continue to step up to the plate, to face those pitches, to swing away, and to hope for that extra base, that home run. We cannot just stand here, indignantly refusing to swing, and watch the ball go by. Life is not like that! It is not "Three strikes and we're out." We are still up to bat! "Batter up!" the umpire cries.

Midnight Massacre

And there we were, in the middle of the pasture, at midnight, watching flames lick up the boles of live ash trees, catching the smaller branches on fire. The wind was coming up. The flames were flying out of the canyon. Something had to be done, and fast. Otherwise, the sparks were going to set the prairie afire.

The plan, quickly devised to avert certain disaster, was to cut off the parts of the burning trees that were above the canyon walls and drop them into the ravine. That would contain the fire. I watched The Heir disappear into the darkness, a chainsaw in his hands. He was headed up and around the head of the ravine to the burning trees on the other side.

213

After waiting and watching, I finally heard the chainsaw start. I knew he was ready to cut off the sparking tree branches. He asked me to shine the lantern in that direction. Suddenly, he disappeared. He slid down the steep bank about ten to fifteen feet, with the chainsaw still running. He was able to snag a tree to break his fall. After a short break to regroup, he cut down more of the tree than just the part sticking up above the canyon walls. Disaster was averted.

Originally, it was a day perfect for burning. The local fire department issued the burn permit. We started the fire early in the day and watched it carefully. We had things well in hand.

We were cleaning up an illegal dump site created by the previous tenant. There were at least twenty years' worth of old fence posts and wire, shop and household garbage, empty feed sacks, five gallon oil pails, couches, chairs, and who knows what else. The thirty-five-foot-deep ravine was filled nearly to the top.

The fire burned fast and hot. Flames shot fifty feet into the air. A big black cloud spiraled up. It was awesome. It was frightening. It burned for hours and hours. It had nearly burned out. Only embers remained. We were confident it would be safe to go home.

Then a storm front moved through the area. The wind came up. The fire grew. The flames spread. The live trees caught on fire. It was midnight. We were miles from home in the middle of a very hilly pasture.

Eventually, the wind brought the rain, and the rain extinguished the coals. The excitement was over. The danger was past. Yes, The Heir could have been killed during that fall. He could have severed a limb. It could have been a real midnight massacre.

The lesson: Always have someone with you to call 911 if you are going to do something foolhardy. Even simple projects can get complicated under the right conditions.

Instant Aging (Our Hero's Tale)

So there I was, cruising down the highway on my Honda Hawk GT with my mom on the back, going to her vintage baseball game at Fort Hartsuff. I met some initial resistance to the idea of owning and riding a motorcycle, and here was my chance to show my parent I was a safe, responsible rider. Riding the bike to the game was her idea, really. The first six miles were a cinch, with straight flat highway and a big easy turn onto the Fort Hartsuff road.

We then came to some square corners where the road follows the section lines. They are marked 15 mph or 25 mph; I can't remember precisely. Mom assured me she had ridden tandem on a cycle before, but I was skeptical. While the Hawk GT is an extremely capable motorcycle engineered for ultra-light v-twin racing in Europe, I decided to take her inexperience into consideration and took the first corner at an "easy" 65 mph.

As I laid the bike over into the turn, Mom made the first mistake of a novice passenger on a sport bike; she looked down at the pavement. It seemed like it was only a couple inches from her ankle, mainly because it *was* only a couple inches from her ankle! She shrieked and started yanking on me, trying "to stop us from falling over." By the end of that square corner we were on the wrong side of the white line, with only an inch of pavement left between us and almost certain death. Too close, even by my standards.

The next corner, equally aggressive, approached rapidly. A little wiser this time, I grabbed Mom's arms, wrapped them tightly around me so she would move with me, kicked the bike up a notch and sailed around the corner. I hit this corner pretty hard. She let out this "horror-movie worthy" unending scream that continued until we were once again upright and cruising down the highway.

There were several more turns before we reached the Fort, although much tamer and less adrenaline inducing. We arrived safely, and I parked the bike. Mom crawled off, straightened herself, and with dignified poise, very quietly stated, "Well, that took ten years off my life."

Stitch Leaves Us in Stitches

And there we were, at the team meeting after the big ballgame. I report in: I had a really great game Sunday and want to remember vintage baseball that way … with Son there to cheer me on. He "got" what we were trying to do and insists I try harder to be a vintage player. I have borrowed a vintage dress from our friend Ruth, bought some leather lace-up boots and an "undershirt" to preserve modesty, plus Dolly is lending me a bowler with a feather in it to wear next Sunday. Should be all decked out and ready to play, even if playing on the 1890s Ord Tiger's team is a S-T-R-E-T-C-H for me. Really, I only want to play for fun. I would rather be the umpire.

Team manager, Stitch, replies: All right, Chippie, unsaddle that self-pity high horse you seem to have crawled on and get your butt back in the dugout. This is why women will never get the right to vote; they are too dadblamed emotional! For one thing, since it seems to have escaped your feminine sensibilities, you are not the absolute cause of this little mix-up, nor do you need to apologize for those who had the misfortune to be born without a funny bone. And while I am at it, Madam (cigar smoke exhaled approximately two inches from recipient's nose), I will be hornswoggled if I will allow myself to be swayed by those who think they know who I should play where and when.

As to the aforementioned gentleman, one Crip by name, he thinks Duck should play in the outfield because that is where Duck has always played, despite being our best behind (catcher). Enough said on that subject. Duck and I will resolve the problem with Mr. Sikes, perhaps not to his personal liking, but it will be resolved. As for yourself, you have done an absolutely splendid job of managing the team finances and promotions, possibly as well as a man might be expected to do in the same situation. But don't let that go to your head, Missy; we will be keeping an eye on you. This little bit of sugar don't mean you can slack off, you know ...

Somewhat sincerely,
Stitch

Crossville

And there we were, traveling to the East Coast to gather up Our Hero's family and furnishings: three boys, their mother, their two dogs, and all their personal possessions. School was out for the summer. We were moving them to Washington State, where Our Hero was currently deployed.

For this trip, Our Hero was driving a huge International truck outfitted with a flatbed. Again, he was towing his thirty-three foot enclosed trailer, empty heading east. I jumped in at the ranch and was riding shotgun. Because it was fitted with a governor, this rig would travel no faster than 62 mph, even with a brick on the accelerator. It was a long, slow trip, but we were on schedule to be at Jimmy's in North Carolina for supper that evening.

We were about midway through the state of Tennessee when Our Hero casually commented, "This is the one state I don't have a ticket in." No chance for a speeding ticket, so we were pretty relaxed. Not five minutes later a patrolman started dogging us. He did not turn on the cherries until we were just past the exit ramp for Crossville, Tennessee.

What caught his attention was the custom lettering on the cab. Our Hero bought it used. Then the TSP officer noted the truck had Nebraska farm plates, but the trailer was licensed in South Carolina. The officer asked for driver's license and registrations, ran them, came back, and asked Our Hero to step out of the vehicle. He quickly handed me his wallet before getting out. This turned out to be very important. He kept his phone.

Despite several trips to the DMV in Washington, and then receiving a letter

216

that informed him his license was reinstated, it came up listed as suspended in five states. I thought they were just talking about why things were licensed in different states. The officer slapped the cuffs on Our Hero and put him in the back of his patrol car.

He then came to the passenger side window and asked to see my driver's license. I wondered why, as I definitely was not driving the vehicle. It was acceptable to him, as it matched up nicely with the truck registration and license. He asked if I knew how to drive the rig. I assured him I could and had been. He told me to get it off the interstate, or he would call a towing company to move it.

By now, I was confused. Where was Our Hero? He told me he was taking him to the county jail in Centerville, thirty miles south of there. He had him in his cruiser. I could not believe this was happening and said, "This I have got to see; can I?" He took me back there. Yep, Our Hero was cuffed and sitting in the back of the cruiser. When I muttered, "Where is my camera when I need it," he did not even crack a smile. He told me I would need to come to Centerville if I wanted to try to bail him out of jail. That is when he told me the next exit was seventeen miles ahead. I would need to get off there, come back to this exit, and go to Centerville. He turned his cruiser across the median and headed for the county jail.

I spent the best part of that long afternoon driving to Centerville, meeting with the warrant officer to find out how much bail money I needed, finding a bank that would give me a cash advance on my credit card (a bank with a parking spot big enough for a full-sized International truck pulling a thirty-three foot trailer), and turning in the cash I managed to scrounge from Our Hero's wallet, my purse, and the maximum cash advance the bank would give me.

The warrant officer spent quite a while counting the crumpled ones, fives, tens and twenties. Bail came to two thousand dollars. Before Our Hero was released, he was informed if he was caught behind the wheel it would be an automatic ninety-day jail sentence, so make sure I was the one driving. We were very late for supper at Jimmy's that night.

Our first stop in South Carolina was at the DMV office. That letter's fine print read, "There may be a reinstatement fee." There was: a one hundred dollar cash fee, which would not be processed for seven to ten business days. That ensured Our Hero would be riding in the passenger seat all the way across country from South Carolina to Washington State.

I had to call my boss and tell her I would not be able to work my 64-hour shift that coming weekend. I had planned to help pack and load, clean the apartment, and ride back to Nebraska. I would then collect my car at my house as they drove through. My boss was less than pleased with the change of plans. She could find no one available for those kinds of hours and had to fill them herself.

After we got to Silverdale, I had to get a ride to the Seattle airport, fly back to Omaha, and get someone else to give me a ride back to my house and car. Our Hero's court date corresponded with my birthday. How ironic. Our Hero would be underway in the Pacific Ocean by then. He asked for a continuance, so he could appear. I did not get my bail money back until his case was settled, nearly a year later. We now carry more than three hundred dollars cash when we travel, just in case we need bail money!

Hey, Aunt Linda

And here we are, relaxing for the weekend. Whoosh, the outside door flies open. In burst several bundles of energy. I detect whispering, giggling, and quick footsteps scampering up the stairs. There they are, smiling faces radiating excited enthusiasm. They eagerly inquire, "Hey, Aunt Linda. Do you want to jump on the trampoline or go for a bike ride?"

Just between you and me, I am plumb content sitting in the La-Z-boy reading a book, working my Sudoku, or watching my favorite TV shows. But, no, chair time is obviously not an option right this minute.

They gently persuade me to join them. They get out their big sis's bike for me, pump up the tires, and have their dad adjust the seat. After my short test run, he even selects a gear for me.

Bicycles are not exactly my thing. I am a ranch gal. I can sit a good cutting horse, bust broncs, and have even ridden rough stock. I find bikes to be unsteady and extremely wobbly. Nothing like a good horse!

Off we go, their dad demonstrating to all how to signal right turns and left turns. Like I am going to let go of the handlebars for even a second? Pedaling leisurely, we make a lazy turn onto a quiet street. Suddenly, the five-year-old shoots by me on his little bike, his legs churning. "Hey, Aunt Linda, can't you keep up with me?" The pace picks up.

There are mini-races between riders. The pace picks up. Suddenly, we are flying down "Suicide Hill." Only our fearless leader is ready for this adventure. We arrive at the bottom, not entirely unscathed. Seeking an easier return route, we bike over to Fifth Avenue and pedal up the gradual incline to the cemetery. I discover forgotten muscles. Stiffly, I climb off that bike and park it back in the garage. I walk funny for a while.

Next week, the same question is posed. I choose not to go biking. I timorously climb up and join them on the trampoline. I have a nice high rhythmic bounce going. "Hey, Aunt Linda, aren't you going to jump?" I think I am jumping. I am really going up and down. I quickly realize I am way out of my league with this bunch. I keep the bounce going while they do their flips, turns, and somersaults.

"Hey, Aunt Linda, will you come watch us play ball?" I am honored to be asked. Sitting in the bleachers cheering is something I can do. The five-year-old plays T-Ball. The eight-year-old plays coach-pitch. The twelve-year-old plays in the Junior League with her mother as assistant coach. The fifteen-year-old plays on the Senior League team. Before I know it, I am at the ball field several nights a week and, come tournament time, weekends from 9:30 in the morning until well after dark. I dine on sloppy nachos, traveling tacos, and even try dill pickle sno-cones. I get sun burnt, wind burnt, mosquito-bit, soaked to the skin, and nearly freeze to death. There is no "quit" in this family. As long as someone is on the field playing, the rest of us are in the bleachers. As Daughter puts it, "That's two months of your life you will never get back."

With the start of the school year and the change of seasons, the queries change. "Hey, Aunt Linda, will you read with me?" "Hey, Aunt Linda, can you help me bake these cookies?" "Hey, Aunt Linda, which jigsaw puzzle shall we put together?" "Hey, Aunt Linda, let's play Go Fish." "Hey, Aunt Linda, can you get those big clips from your office and help us build a blanket tent in the living room?" "Hey, Aunt Linda, would you help me put this fire engine together? Where do the tabs go?"

Whenever I hear the phrase "Hey, Aunt Linda," I realize that 'chair time' is not happening. We are too busy making memories and living life. How lucky can I get?

Victory!

It was a looong weekend, our first family outing after the Great Motorcycle Trip. Our Hero and his brood of four left early, pulling the venerable travel trailer on yet another family adventure. The trip was already exciting before we even left. The poor, neglected trailer had to be pulled from the Swamps of Dagobah and made habitable before we could actually start the trip. For some, this was their first experience with filth, fungus, or rat nests. When Pink saw the condition of the trailer and heard Our Hero's plan to use it, she gave him the look. But, we got it shipshape and shortly were on the road.

The first mini-adventure was a short stop to add oil to Big Red, the dually pickup transporting us to our destination. The truck had been working hard to get over the passes, and everything was quite hot under the hood. One careless tilt of the oil bottle, and the exhaust manifold instantly ignited the spillage. Our Hero calmly requested a bottle of water and doused the flames. The trip recommenced, passengers none the wiser.

The crew with the venerable travel trailer arrived late in the day, to park in the very last available spot, in between the drunken guitar players and the insomniac tweakers. Everything got set up just in time for Pink and Mom to show up and have dinner. We settled in for the night, tuning out the loud neighbors, eager to pit ourselves against the mighty Yakima River the following morning.

Bright and early the next day, slathered in sunscreen, we trekked 23 miles to the drop off point. We pumped up the tubes and then tied them together to form a raft. At this point, we realized we forgot the paddles. Several bad puns about creeks and paddles later, we embarked on our first trip down the river. YIKES! The Yakima River is formed by snowmelt from the Cascade Mountain Range. The temperature of the water at the point we were at was approximately 32.1°F! We perched on top of the tubes until hypothermia set in, and we no longer felt the cold.

Without the paddles, the entourage traveled the river at the whim of wind and current. The frequent encounters with the banks, trees, rocks, other tubers, and deadfalls created a sizeable amount of both perceived and actual drama. One particularly malevolent tree branch grabbed Mom by the leg and slowly tipped her over backwards. We watched her helplessly balance upside down on the edge of tube, and cackled gleefully as she slowly tipped backwards into the water, doing a perfect flip. She quickly swam after and retrieved her shoe, righted her ball cap, tipped up her sunglasses and started swimming after the rapidly disappearing raft. Our Hero jumped down and anchored the flotilla until she caught up, picked her up by the scruff of the neck, and tossed her back on her tube.

Crisis averted, we wiled our way downstream. By this point, Christian, the part-time conspiracy theorist and full-time comedian, had taken to proclaiming, "That's it. We're done. It's over!" every time we floated within ten yards of any perceived obstacle. Smooth sailing occurred until after we passed the Big Pines landing area. Our Hero spotted a cooler bobbing along upside down in an eddy and immediately decided to jump out, grab the cooler, and climb back into the raft. Executing said fool-proof plan without vocalizing his intentions, he retrieved the cooler and started running back across the slick river rocks while the current rapidly picked up speed. He tripped, slamming into an even bigger and slicker rock, dislocating his shoulder, and dashing any hopes of catching the tubes, which were now flying along in the grips of the strong current.

Meanwhile, the rest of the team were feverishly attempting to pilot the raft, without any steering mechanism, in order to retrieve the lost crewmember. Chance was wailing, "I've lost my only Dad!" Others were simply wailing. Christian, no stranger to our adventures, was laughing uproariously, drawing the ire of others less acclimated to this sort of thing. Paddling with cupped hands, they managed to get the raft parked on the opposite-side bank.

Pink scrambled up the bank through the prolific stand of POISON IVY to scout for Our Hero. Unseen, he was a mile upstream, steadily hiking his way along a deer trail back to the campsite. Christian quit chanting doom and gloom, wondering whether or not it really was over. Dylan offered to walk back to search for Our Hero. Sarah was attempting to console Chance. Our Hero appeared on the opposite bank, wondering why the crew was waiting for him on the far side of the river. He ran ahead, waded into the center of the river and waited for the crew to pick him up. Everyone expressed concern about his physical condition; he expressed regret that after all that, he had not managed to retain possession of the refugee cooler.

At long last, the campsite appeared on the horizon! We wearily slogged up to the venerable travel trailer, definitely ready for some evening relaxation. What is the first step to an excellent evening of relaxation? A fire, of course! The boys set to work digging a fire pit. Our Hero started his own fire in the grill. Pink worriedly expressed reservations about the fire's ability to remain contained in the fire pit. Our Hero scoffed at her concerns and built an enormous fire. Pink rolled her eyes and went to get the shovel. She returned just as the fire escaped the fire pit, heading for the trees and the river. Pushing Our Hero aside, she beat out the wildfire, and gave Our Hero the look. He meekly replied, "Thanks, honey."

After the fire burned down to coals, we extinguished it and headed to bed. We snuggled down in the venerable travel trailer and closed our eyes, only to listen to our drunken neighbors murder songs on the guitar. And our tweaker neighbors rapidly discourse nonstop on random subjects at the top of their lungs. All night.

We blearily attacked the next day in defiance of our lack of sleep. Our salvation appeared that morning in the guise of a pair of park rangers. They were making the rounds to collect the site fees and check for problems at the campsites. That cleared out our neighbors but quick. Slathered with even more sunscreen, especially on the areas we realized we missed the day before, we trekked upriver once again, determined to have a much more successful float down the river. This time, we made certain the paddles were onboard. We also made sure the snacks were not in Chance's raft, as they all managed to disappear last trip before anyone even asked for any. We embarked once again, eager to experience what the day had in store for us.

Fortunately for the more conservative members of the group, but unfortunately for Our Hero, the thrill seeker, having the paddles available made it all too easy to stay in the center of the river, well away from any potential dangers. We did enjoy lots of scenery. People were cliff diving off Pac Man Rock. A small herd of mountain goats were grazing on a ledge. We soaked up the sunshine, munched on chips and sandwiches, and reveled in the tranquility. The only minor speed bump was when Our Hero flicked a spider off one of the tubes, NEAR, not ONTO, just NEAR a fellow crewmember, who may have also been his wife. Abandoning the look, she went straight for the paddle. Quoth she, "I almost died!" The raft meandered onward.

Our Hero, attempting not to succumb to boredom, spied a small island in the middle of the river. On one side, the river flowed wide, slow, and shallow. On the other, it rushed by, narrow, deep, and fast. He immediately began paddling for "The Narrows." The others figured out his plan, but by then, they were far too late.

Everyone started laughing, crying, or screaming. The raft flew spinning into the narrows, flying by the island. It rammed itself straight into a sunken log, rupturing the lead tube piloted by Our Hero and his lovely assistant, Pink! Instantly, Our Hero jumped into crisis mode. He assessed the situation, determined that the tube was unrecoverable, stopped the raft, ordered Pink to the neighboring tube, rolled the damaged tube into the corner of Chance's little zodiac, and jumped across to the opposing tube. Pink, however, was not a member of the military and had not jumped when he started barking out orders. He went back and got both her and the clothing she was attempting to rescue and tossed them all onto the neighboring raft.

At this point, some members of the excursion were no longer having any fun at all. Others, however, were ready to declare the entire weekend a smashing success. The debate was raging as the battered-but-not-beaten raft continued downstream. Then it appeared in front of them—the cooler! Our Hero immediately changed his name to Ahab, christened the raft "the Pequod," and started paddling for it. The rest of the party—poopers; the rest of the party poopers, I should say, immediately relieved him of his command and his paddle. The remainder of the trip occurred without incident. Our Hero managed to have the last laugh, though. On his trip upriver to retrieve his pickup, he spotted the cooler on the near-side bank! He stopped and used a tree limb to extricate the cooler from the water. "I shall name it Victory," he proclaimed.

Identity Crisis

And there we were, back seeking assistance from the Geek Squad. I could not be found? I did not remember who I was.

Who am I? Once again, I fail my social network's identity test, the one that questions me about my life. I fail to identify my favorite teacher, my former address, and my paternal grandfather's middle name. I am sure the person overseeing the site thinks I am an identity thief or completely demented. During my recent move, I misplaced my cheat sheet with all my passwords and cryptic clues. I am sure I put it in a safe place.

I have no clue how to add someone to my LinkedIn network because I cannot get logged in. I do not even remember my user name. I set it up when I was trying to be clever. Since then my computer crashed, my external drive that was supposed to save that data does not seem to be operating correctly, and the cryptic clues are not clear-cut. I simply do not use that site anymore. I am no longer LinkedIn.

Recently, I went into Staples to use their reward program. With the tech's help, we attempted to print off the necessary documents. They had an incorrect address listed on that account. After we got by that roadblock and found my user name (which I do not remember today), the security questions popped up. Who was my first boyfriend? Define boyfriend. Was it my first crush? That tall, lanky eighth grader I absolutely worshipped when I was a kindergartener? That special guy I never got to wish goodbye and good luck because I came down with the measles the last week of school and missed the school picnic? His name escapes me at the moment. Perhaps it was my junior high boyfriend. I typed in his first name. Nope. The tech warned me that if I got three strikes I would be locked out of the account. I could call the help line on Monday for more hints and possible answers. It was Saturday. The rewards expired on Sunday. What to do? I went back to my office and typed in that boyfriend's nickname. Voilà. Success. They were surprised when I walked back in with the document. I got my reward money cashed in for more printer ink.

Just who am I? Facebook has a category—"It's complicated." That fits my situation. In high school, there were five "Lindas" in my class. I went by my initials: LC. Some wits called me Elsie. I just smiled. My last name was Charron, C–H–A–R–R–O–N. To this day, many of my classmates think it is my first name and call me "Sharon." I gave up correcting them. I understand they are talking to me. My friends make me smile.

I married a Cone, so my initials remained LC. We moved to our ranch. I became known to our new community as Rick's Mom. That was because Rick was so active socially and participated in many church, school, and 4-H programs. I am still known in Ord as Rick's Mom. Small towns make me smile. (I am shaking my head side to side).

When I decided to start a Facebook profile, I was extremely cautious. I used my anonymous email address, luckee_one@hotmail.com. I chose Lyn Con (a play on the town Lincoln) as my profile name. I could find friends, but no one could find me. Eventually, I added an 'e' to my last name. That helped family find me. My Facebook friends call me Lyn. My close friends call me Lucky. I just smile and answer, knowing they are referring to me.

After my midlife crisis, I started writing and publishing books. To protect the innocent and the guilty, I developed a pen name. My readers know me as Kelsey Lynn. I wrote *I Hope You Dance* from Kelsey Lynn's perspective. The details of our lives became entwined. Her story is not necessarily my story. That confused my family. I just smiled.

To eliminate further confusion, I got in the habit of introducing myself as Linda, without any last name. When I was living in Grand Island, I self-published and distributed my best-selling book, *Panic and Panache*. It was basically a collection of essays, speeches, and presentations I had given over the past ten years. I published it under my real name. One of my small-group friends from church then admitted that she had always feared I was a felon or someone in the witness protection program because I would never share my last name. When she shared that story, I did more than smile. I laughed out loud.

Last year, I discovered the Toastmaster Clubs in Scottsbluff and Gering. When I rejoined, Toastmasters International did not readily locate me in their files. They thought I was a brand new Toastmaster. Once again, I had an identity crisis. I had to prove I was Linda S. Cone, Distinguished Toastmaster (Twice Over) and a District 24 Past District Governor with twenty years of Toastmaster history. Because I now had two separate profiles and two separate identification numbers, I was unable to log in. The Toastmasters International website did not recognize me. Even after they merged the two profiles, I have difficulty logging in to the TMI site. I usually cannot remember my user name or the password. I finally caved and just use the same password for every toastmaster website. No, it's not IPB47-8.

Because of the real threat of identity theft, I need a better approach than that for my online banking accounts, my social networking sites, and my business accounts. I need to find my cheat sheets. I may need to invest in a memory improvement seminar, so I can remember who I am today. I can always become a different person tomorrow. Now, who am I? IPB47-8?

The Wizened Ones

And there she was, returning to her home after the monthly visit with her parents. Instead of meditating, she is lost in a reverie of that last visit to the "old ones." What a pathetic sight they are today. Two defeated and weary souls caught in a cold union of non-intimacy. The "over-eightys" continue to live in the unkempt ranch house because it is what they know. With its water-stained ceiling tiles and peeling paint hanging from cracked plaster walls, the place appears ready to be pushed into a hole and burned. The miserly old man refuses to sink another souk into its upkeep. So it declines daily, as do they.

Despite their declining health and lessening physical capabilities, they carry on the daily rituals. She walks and works with the help of a "cart." Her spine seems slightly angled to the right, a lasting souvenir of last summer's ATV accident. Constant and severe leg pain radiating from bulging discs and pinched nerves keep her confined to the house most of the time. She sits in her favorite chair when he lets her.

Most of the time, she is consumed with tasks designed to appease his unrelenting selfish demands. He believes he requires constant attendance and instant obedience. Today, his vanity requires a comb-over to hide his increasingly bare pate. He has taught himself to live on little but his energy and his manipulative charm. Both are becoming tired, and old; they are trapped in the shadows of age.

Today is enlivened by the visit of three daughters, each vastly different from the others. One lives nearby and is there to help with chores. She downplays the importance of appearances, yet entertains by aping with exaggeration the actions of the old ones. Hilarious! Another drives for hours and arrives late at night to be there just for the day. She spends time visiting with each of them and lets them know they are important to her. The other daughter drops in for lunch as scheduled, dressed quite inappropriately for ranch work. No one really knows why she makes her monthly visits …

"Visits always give pleasure —
if not the arrival, the departure."

— Portuguese Proverb

Vanity Card #379

And there we were, swapping stories. He never let the truth get in the way of a good story:

"More than anything, he craved an intimacy that might transcend the physical. He urged her to reveal herself, to step out from behind the self-protecting wall of fear she had carefully constructed over a lifetime of loneliness. Secrets, he assured her, were the one big thing that stood in the way of their ever finding true happiness.

At first she was reluctant. As the days and weeks passed, she came to trust the relationship. She saw the wisdom of his request. One evening, after a good dinner and some particularly heated love-making, she decided to take the leap.

Lying in the glow of the black light, their naked, spent bodies entwined around each other, she quietly told him all the things of her life she had never told another living soul. When she finished, he kissed her and thanked her for being so honest and open.

She slept peacefully that night knowing that her days of hiding from herself and from him were over. The revelation left her feeling closer to him than she had ever thought possible. He instantly developed insomnia. It is difficult to sleep next to a gal when you are pretty sure she is a psychopath."

— Chuck Lorre

Soon after that, he discovered her handcuffs and long, two-inch wide binding straps. He wondered if a helmet was going to be enough protection ...

Covering the Angles

And here we are, making our first visit to Easy Street. We check out the premises, decide the house might be habitable after some sprucing up, and put in a purchase bid that stipulates a contractor will do some twenty-five thousand dollars' worth of repairs to be taken out of the purchase price. We are the owners of a bona fide fixer-upper.

We fail to note all the angles, convoluted plumbing (which the contractor is supposed to correct when they install the new sewer systems but do not), and downright dangerous electrical wiring schemes. The house is not truly evil, despite the previous owner's demise within the premises. It just is not easy. It is literally crooked.

Any attempts to modify, remodel, or restore reveals its deformities. There are no square angles or straight lines anywhere. Any simple project becomes a carpenter's nightmare. Everything is crooked. There is no geometric symmetry or sanity.

We decide to add kitchen cabinets over the stove and refrigerator. We begin by drawing a "level line" to set them on, so the tops are some six inches from the ceiling, two inches above the refrigerator. When we get the cabinets installed, the one in the corner fits tightly to the wall toward the top and has over a half-inch gap at the bottom. The wall is that crooked. How do we cover that angle? We still have not decided. We note the gap between the cabinets and the ceiling gradually decreases from the original six inches to more like five inches, in less than seven feet of cabinet area. It looks terrible. We have no idea how to make it more aesthetically pleasing. We stack items up there. It does not mask the deformities.

We have a long-haired cat that sheds constantly. We do not like cat hair in the carpeted bedrooms or the guest bathroom. We decide to slap a screen door on one end of the hallway to protect those rooms from said cat. We measure. It appears a standard thirty-four inch door will work perfectly.

Not so fast. First we discover the floor bows upward on one end. We trim the bottom of the door to accommodate that. We attempt to attach the hinges and discover there is nothing but drywall for two inches in. We trim the drywall back to bare wood and modify the face of it so the door will swing open ninety degrees. Yes, progress. When we close the new screen door flush with the wall going down the hallway, we discover a three-inch gap toward the top of the door. The hallway is obviously built for tall people with wide shoulders. We have to make a drywall wedge to square it to the door. It takes days to dry in the high humidity of this drought-ridden summer.

Finally, we get the door to close evenly and put in the door jams. That is when we look up and note the drywall molding over the top of the door slopes hugely from one end to the other. There is an inch and a half gap from one end of the thirty-four inch door to the other. We discuss making another drywall wedge so the top of the door will look level. Grandson is due for his one-month visit the next day. It will take another week for any new drywall to cure. We need the cat door to be operational. We shrug our shoulders, and say, "It will have to stay that way. It keeps the cat out." It creates an interesting angle to complement the angle made by the top of the kitchen cabinets.

We can spend a day measuring, pondering, and plotting before we begin any project. We can focus on keeping the lines straight. We can use levels, squares, measuring tapes, saws, or any tool that carpenters normally employ. It is a huge waste of time. Now we just eyeball it real good, cut everything and hope for the best. We are going to end up with odd angles and uneven lines no matter what we do. We even discover a large walled-in area that must surely cover a former fireplace. We leave that area alone, absolutely. It may be where our resident ghost hangs out.

Blowing Up the Backyard

And there we were, on a windstill winter day, cleaning up the backyard. Envision a giant rick of tree branches, brush, rotted lumber, and brambles piled as high as we could throw them, ten or twelve feet wide and nearly thirty feet long. This monstrosity was strategically placed in an area surrounded by the house, the apartment, the tack shed and the barn. It was no more than thirty feet from any of those buildings.

Since the trees were freshly cut and green, they would not burn. Rambo had this brilliant idea to "sprinkle" (pour) gasoline all over the brush. It was a cold day, so the gas fumes stayed close to the ground and spread out. Whoom! One small spark from the lighter and it sounded like a blast of dynamite. We checked our eyebrows. Still there! Slowly, the darn thing started to burn.

Within a few short minutes a neighbor from two streets over came running through the forest and into the yard. Wild-eyed and panicky, he asked if our furnace had blown up. The explosion had rattled the windows in his house. He rightfully feared that something terrible had happened.

Upon hearing Rambo's nonchalant explanation, this newly introduced neighbor became somewhat agitated. He complained that the noise had awakened his elderly mother from her afternoon nap. What a way to meet the neighbors! **Rule #71** was born that afternoon. No gasoline on bonfires.

From that day forward, Rambo was banned from using any accelerants except stove fuel. In fact, he began using a propane-fueled torch for his fire-bugging stunts. Quiet torching became especially important after we learned these three things:

1) This area's fire chief visited the neighbor across the street on weekends.
2) Burning without a current burn permit was illegal and carried a hefty fine.
3) Only leaves, branches and brush could be burned.

Before those salient details were kindly brought to our attention, we had already torched the debris from the auto shop and some old buildings that had been shoved over the big bank in the backyard. Fuel barrels, car parts, and trash mixed into the morass that "accidently" caught on fire had darkened the skies. Not one of our neighbors reported our burning. Perhaps they were pleased to see the property cleaned up and productive. Apparently, our guardian angels were working overtime to keep us safe and out of legal trouble.

We have many more brush piles to burn. On our last outing, Rambo singed his eyebrows and blistered his face from the heat. He claims the wind changed direction on him. Keep us in your thoughts and prayers.

Refurbishing the Façade

And there we were, this warm, sunny spring day, fixing the face of Pink's barn. Rambo was high up on his twelve-foot, fully-extended extension ladder. He was completely occupied with fitting some replacement lumber onto the right side of the barn face. He did not miss the excitement, though.

I was painting the equally high part on the left front barn façade. It had recently undergone its upgrades and was ready for the finishing touches. I determined that it was time to reposition my twelve-foot, aluminum step ladder, so I could reach another area to paint.

So engrossed in coming back down the ladder with my can of paint and paintbrush, I inadvertently skipped the last rung or two of the ladder. As it happens, I stepped off that ladder while at least three feet from the ground, fell backwards heavily, crashing onto the freshly painted barn door sitting up on buckets and situated directly behind my ladder. That is what attracted Rambo's attention.

The most salient point was this: I saved the can of paint. Not one drop of paint was spilled. My denim jeans carry a green, corner-shaped patch on the right rear pocket, permanently attesting to the collision with the corner of the barn door. I may have complained of a backache and sore muscles the next day, but I climbed right back up that pesky ladder and continued painting.

Rule #88: Do whatever it takes to get the job done.

An Anvil of Adversity

And there we were, putting the finishing touches on the apartment, getting ready for the imminent arrival of Our Hero and his entourage. We even gave Phil, the housewarming philodendron, a shower to freshen him up before placing him on their kitchen counter. We were enjoying a nice, warm, sunny day on Easy Street the last week in April.

Our Hero and his wife were moving cross-country from west of Seattle to

229

Easy Street in North Carolina. They had stopped for a couple of days at the family ranch in Mid-Nebraska to see family, let the dogs run, and give themselves a break from driving. They let us know they were en route and would be here in two or three days.

The phone rang. The Heir brokenly delivered the breaking news: The lead vehicle, the newly restored Crown Victoria bus, was wrecked. Our Hero and his wife were on their way to the ER with injuries; he was trying to deal with the officers on the scene. He had witnessed the accident. He would call when he had more of the story.

Within the hour, the phone rang again. Visibly upset and shaken, The Heir related these details: At Thirteenth and Capital Avenue, one of the busiest and most deadly intersections in Grand Island, Nebraska, a drunken elderly man on his way home from church waited in the oncoming left turn lane until the signal light turned yellow, then turned left across two lanes of oncoming traffic. Our Hero's bus was rolling at 45 mph, loaded with a household of personal possessions and furniture, carrying their two dogs and his wife, his Kawasaki motorcycle strapped on special racks on the back of the bus, and towing the yellow Jeep Unlimited. He reacted instantly, yet was unable to avoid hitting the slow-moving pickup crossing directly in front of him. It was a violent collision. They ended up in the road ditch, with the other pickup pinned between a small concrete structure and the big old bus.

The Heir was driving Big Red, a Chevrolet Silverado dually pickup, and pulling a thirty-three foot enclosed trailer filled with Our Hero's two race cars, shop tools, garage supplies, and racing parts. He was about a half-block back. He pulled over to the side of the highway and parked that rig. He ran to the scene of the accident, watched Our Hero refuse medical care as Pink was transported to the hospital. The officers ordered him to stay away from the scene, not realizing he was family.

The rescue workers had to use the Jaws of Life to release the other driver from his vehicle. First, they had to drag the bus backwards to separate the vehicles. They needed to get the wrecked Jeep out of the way first. Nothing was drivable. Even the Kawasaki on the back of the bus was wrecked.

Daughter had eaten breakfast with them, said her goodbyes, and then headed back to western Nebraska. She turned around as soon as she heard about the accident. She went to the hospital, collected Pink, and took her to St. Paul where Cousin Ashley lived. Together, they helped Pink clean up, get the shards of glass out of her hair, and even found some comfortable clothes for her to wear. That evening, they returned to the ranch, beaten, battered, and bereft.

As soon as The Heir found out Pink could not walk without crutches and needed to keep her leg elevated, he advised us to come back to Nebraska and help pick up the pieces. Within the hour, Rambo and I packed, fed the cats enough for a week, and hit Interstate 40 heading west. By the time Our Hero called us with updates, we were nearly in Tennessee. He was a bit surprised.

The Heir, meanwhile, called Uncle Bruce and asked him to bring the car trailer from the ranch, seventy miles away. The wrecked bus was towed to a locked storage lot somewhere nearby for safekeeping. They loaded the Jeep onto the car trailer and pulled it back to the ranch. They turned Big Red and the trailer around and headed back to the ranch. They cried.

Rambo and I arrived at the ranch early Monday afternoon. That is when the real work began. We rented a large U-Haul truck, pulled the personal possessions and furniture out of the wrecked bus, and loaded them in the U-Haul. We salvaged most of it. Broken jars of home-canned tomatoes made it a very messy job. All of the interior walls were broken and shifted forward from the impact. The boxes were crushed and accordioned. Reloading them was an adventure.

The poor Crown Victoria was totaled. The front end was crushed. The windshield was shattered. The frame was bent. Five months or more of restoration work destroyed, just that quickly. Our Hero was heartbroken.

It took a few days to get everything ready to run down the road. Before we could leave, it snowed on us. It was now May. Pink and I loaded up the Cadillac and gave The Heir a lift to Omaha to pick up his car. Originally, he had planned to drive Big Red and pull the thirty-three foot enclosed trailer to Easy Street, visit for a day or two, and then fly back into Omaha. (He would not make it to Easy Street to visit for another year and a half.)

By the time we dropped him off in Omaha, it was snowing, with rain in the mix. Eventually, it changed to heavy rain. We soldiered on to Kansas City, Missouri, before stopping for the night.

Our Hero, with his two dogs for company, drove Big Red and pulled the enclosed trailer. Rambo was elected to drive the U-Haul, towing the Jeep. Before they could leave the ranch, they had to start a tractor and pull the U-Haul out of the yard. They were tired, muddy, and late before they even started. Also, they had to go through that wretched intersection in Grand Island again. That was not easy, emotionally.

By the time the guys got to Lincoln, Nebraska, they could not even see the road, much less one another. The blowing snow was making traveling downright hazardous. They used cell phones to stay in touch. Eventually, the storm changed to torrential rain. It was past midnight before they reached our motel. We were relieved to see them arrive safely. It was a short night.

The next day, by comparison, was relatively uneventful. We had to stop a time or two to reattach tin that was coming off the side of the trailer and waving in the wind. They tried to get Big Red to run better by adjusting the carburetor. It missed badly and ran out of power on the upgrades. The truly scary part was watching Rambo slam on the brakes of the U-Haul as he was merging onto the interstate after one of those stops. An elderly woman driver two cars ahead of him just stopped in the middle of the "on" ramp, instead of merging into traffic. Pink and I were right there to see it happen. Unsettling, nerve-wise!

Our caravan arrived at Easy Street in North Carolina late in the afternoon on the third day. Pink had to stay in our guest room for a week because she could not maneuver the thirteen steep, slippery steps to their apartment. Our Hero made her a traveling cart by strapping the driver's seat from the bus onto a hand cart.

Life here on Easy Street has been forged on an anvil of adversity.

Rolling Down the Hill

And there we were, killing trees, creating pastureland, reclaiming the back yard from the forest. Rambo had chain sawed about thirty trees. We were piling up the pieces for our next big bonfire. Working on a steep slope, I stepped with one foot onto an untied shoelace from my other shoe. Unable to right myself from forward progress, I slowly toppled over. Rapidly picking up speed down that steep slope, I somersaulted several times, miraculously coming to rest with my back against the only remaining tree, which was on the brink of a sharp six-foot drop into a cold water-filled creek.

Sheepishly looking around to see if anyone noticed, I saw many eyes watching in astonishment. Even the goats were in awe. Pink immediately asked if I was injured in any way. She is a nurse, after all. Being assured that nothing important was damaged, the masses began laughing hysterically, clapping and calling out scores. Ratings were excellent. "Well, that was fun," I muttered as I slowly trudged back up the hill.

Pinto 1, Pink 0 (Pink's Tale)

So there I was, enjoying my day off work, spending quality time with my Pinto. First, we did barn-sour exercises in the round pen. We graduated from the "invisible" lunge line to riding away on a nice easy loose rein. It was going well. First, I rode her out the driveway to the mailbox and back. That went so well, I decided to ride to the stop sign and back, about a quarter-mile. It was such a beautiful day I then decided to go even farther.

For some reason, I did decide to wear my helmet, but I did not have my cell phone, as I was not planning to leave the yard. It was going so well that I ended up riding by the stone mansion on the next highway. I rode along the shelterbelt and up the hill. There was an opening in the tree line. I was looking right; my pinto was looking left. I saw three deer. She did not. I immediately stopped her, so I could flex her head to keep her from bolting. Since I am right-handed, I flexed her head to the right. I should have flexed her to the left.

I flexed her directly into the sight line of the three deer. With her front feet planted, she snorted, and spun around with her hind end. The G forces threw me off the left side. Next thing I knew, I was mid-air. I hit the ground and looked up to see my pinto running toward home. She was looking back over her left shoulder at me as I kept saying, "Whoa, whoa, whoa!" I swear she was laughing at me. She kept running.

I prayed she would stop and eat grass, so I could catch her. When I heard her feet clattering on the pavement, I prayed she would not get hit by a truck. All I could think was, "There goes my $1,500 saddle running down the road." Then I thought about all the time and money I had invested in that pinto. That was a bad day. You do not realize how far you are from home until you have to hoof it.

Thor

And here we are, caught in "The Winter That Will Not End." We consider ourselves lucky to make it to our "favorite" motel in Paducah, Kentucky, before getting stuck in the foot of heavy snow stacked on an inch of ice. For three hours, Rambo and I have been following trucks traveling 25-35 mph with their hazard lights flashing, watching other motorists slide into the ditch or the median of the interstate, seeing trucks wrecked or slid off the side of the road. Thor is shaking his hammer. Records are being broken, first for snowfall amounts, then for falling temperatures.

Meanwhile, back on Easy Street, the daffodils are blooming, and it is seventy balmy degrees. We left ten days earlier, traveled to Nebraska and Wyoming to visit friends and relatives, and helped The Heir relocate from the ranch to his new headquarters in Grand Island. It snowed on us before we could leave for Easy Street. Thor made the return trip more than interesting.

Ewww! (Our Hero's Tale)

I grew up on a cattle ranch. I have been covered in cow manure. Horse manure. Hog manure! I have had to "go in" to put the pulling chains on the stuck calf's hooves. I have cleaned out a chicken coop. I currently am a superintendent for the utility division of a construction company. I work on wastewater treatment plants. I once climbed down in a tank full of raw sewage to install a missing check valve.

But today, I had to clean a cat box. Oh. My. God.

I Missed the Tree

And there we were, making preparations to construct a small shed under the magnificent magnolia tree. Some limbs needed trimming to create a pocket the shed would fit into. Rambo could not quite reach the higher ones, could not get a good grip on the trimmers. I decided to climb up into the tree and push those pesky branches down within his reach.

"Are you sure you want to do that?" Rambo inquired, with a worried look on his face. I scooted along the branch toward the outer tips of the branches. The branches were snipped. No problem!

Going back down the tree was not as easy as going up. I could not see underneath to find the footholds. I stretched my foot downward. Whomp! Suddenly, I am seated on the ground with my spine a half-inch shorter. It was a hard landing. "Oh, dear, I missed the tree."

Life as The Heir (The Heir's Tale)

I began life as an "oops," the lasting legacy of my parents' first real vacation from the ranch. Mom reportedly returned to the ranch with morning sickness. Restless and red-skinned, I was a colicky baby, constantly crying. When I was nine months old, my folks took me to a local doctor known to be an allergy specialist. The skin test showed I had allergies to everything in my usual diet except green beans, rice, and fish. We did not raise a lot of rice and fish on the ranch.

Every few months after that, I had a specially mixed allergy shot. I became a happy, playful, and extremely active toddler. That doctor was killed in an airplane accident when I was four years old. Tragically, he left no written record of his "formula" for my allergy shots. The generic shots I was then offered were not nearly as effective. We modified my diet and my environment.

When that did not work, my parents were instructed to empty the house of all flowering plants (there went Mom's African violet collection), pets, and stuffed animals. I absolutely adored my stuffed family of friends. They sneaked most of them out of the house. I discovered remnants of them in the burn barrel. I was devastated. They had been murdered, burnt to death in the burn barrel. I cried.

As rowdy and rambunctious as I was on the ranch, my behavior in school differed. My mom, who was teaching school at that time, went to my first-grade parent-teacher conference. My teacher was her friend, a neighbor, and a church group buddy. This was their first "professional" encounter.

My teacher began her spiel about how well I was doing, how wonderfully well-mannered I was, how good a student I was, how proud she was of me for trying so hard to do everything I was asked to do. Mom finally interrupted her and said, "I don't think you have the right folder. My son is Ross Cone." My teacher looked at her sharply and stated, "I know who your son is!" Mom quietly nodded and replied, "I don't recognize him from what you are telling me. He is nothing like this at home." They smiled. My teacher then told her I was able to do addition, subtraction, and even multiplication mentally. Numbers were my thing. School itself was not, but I attended anyway.

In 4-H, I entered my horticulture projects at the Valley County Fair. I won the junior horticulture trophy, the youngest recipient to ever receive it. My gardening projects were selected for State Fair. Over the years, I won many ribbons and more trophies, including the senior horticulture award.

In high school, I joined Future Farmers of American. I won the Chapter Greenhand Award as a freshman. I was a Star Farmer my senior year. I had my custom hay-baling operation, rented farm ground, and raised corn, alfalfa, and soybeans. I started my herd of Herefords. I won the award for best Nebraska Diversified Farmer and earned my American Farmer Award. My parents and sister came to the Kansas City, Missouri, presentation celebration. They took me back to my college classes at Beatrice where I attended Southeast Community College. They continued on to Ord, driving first in pouring rain and then met a raging blizzard. It was mid-November, but that snow-on-top-of-ice stayed all winter.

The following spring, I was graduated with honors from Southeast Community College with a degree in Diversified Agriculture. I landed my dream job, managing a feedlot operation near Gretna. My boss was a former State Senator and mentored me like a father. He was tragically killed in a "farm accident" there. I was one of his pallbearers. My girlfriend sat near the front of the church and chatted with this nice, sociable guy seated next to her. We were at the cemetery before she overheard others talking with him and realized it was Bill Gates.

My dream job disappeared with his death. I moved to North Platte and managed a different feedlot. It was just not the same. I returned to the ranch, bought some Red Angus heifers, and started ranching, in addition to managing Mom's ranch. Over the years of my management, I developed a six-pivot irrigation system, built cross fences in the huge, hilly pastures, drilled a new submersible well, ran in miles of underground line, and placed stock tanks, so all the grass would be utilized. I tripled the value of the ranch. During this time, I went to Lincoln's University of Nebraska and got my four-year degree in Diversified Agriculture.

I learned so much about pivot irrigation while I was installing and fixing those pivots at the ranch that I got a side job fixing them for other people. Since I now work out of Grand Island, I recently purchased a house there. I put my old furniture in the downstairs den, built a mudroom, and installed an industrial washer and dryer. I bought new furniture for the rest of the house. I am on the Nebraska State Board for Jaycees. My open house for Jaycees members, neighbors, friends, and family is scheduled for March, on my 39th birthday. My first house-warming gift from family was a stuffed bear. He watches over the house for me while I am away.

Maximized Opportunities

And here we are, trying to find the "easy" in Easy Street. I share my legacy of learning. To achieve our dreams, we avoid self-limiting behaviors. We remove any rose-colored glasses and clearly see and define the obstacles ahead. We address them with open eyes and perceptive minds. We develop the mindset of success: "I have what it takes to navigate through this. If I fail, I will wake up tomorrow having learned something critical. I know exactly who I am. I am okay with that."

We take bold action toward our visions. We crush our ideas into smaller, courageous action steps. We first set a firm foundation. We then build on this until we reach our end goal. I offer this set of principles to maximize our opportunities:

- Advocate and negotiate strongly for yourself and for others. Know how you uniquely contribute. Fully understand what value you bring to the table. Speak and write about these positives openly. Tackle any challenges head on. Don't wait.
- Invest in yourself. Put money, time, and effort into your own growth. It will pay off. Believe. Faith is its own reward.
- Go with the flow. Resist drowning in the changing tides. Embrace the trends.

Be flexible, fluid, and quick to seize open opportunities. Improvise deftly.

- Captain your own ship with a firm hand. Know what matters most to you. Do not honor other people's priorities over your own. This does not mean becoming self-serving. Develop well-defined boundaries. Honor the legacy you wish to leave behind. Know how to use your talents and passions. Commit to living out these visions.

- Trust in your instincts. Do not second-guess yourself. Any "power gaps" or blind spots need acknowledged as areas that could use special skill sets. Forgive yourself for what you do not know and the mistakes you make. Accept yourself. Keep going forward with hope and optimism. These life lessons will serve you well in the future.

- Always treat others equitably. Understand that you deserve that same fair treatment. Do not settle for less. There are no short cuts or easy answers on the road to success. Mostly, there is just hard work and sometimes a bit of luck involved.

I have been fortunate to learn from amazingly successful professionals and entrepreneurs, compassionate caring friends, and students who provided innovative insights. I am defining "success" as achieving what matters most to you as an individual. I have seen how my mentors think, react, work with others, problem solve, and lead.

I share these principles with those I lead, teach, and coach. I believe in leaving others with better life skills than I found them. That is my legacy. Share any of this that may apply to your life or your situation with your loved ones, associates, and peers. May you accomplish your dreams and leave this world a better place for having lived here.

CHAPTER TEN:
IN LOVING MEMORY

There are things that we don't want to happen but have to accept, things we don't want to know but have to learn, and people we can't live without but have to let go.

— Author Unknown

Choice ...

I'd rather be a COULD BE
If I couldn't be an ARE
For a COULD BE is a MAYBE
With a chance of reaching par.

I'd rather be a HAS BEEN
Than a MIGHT HAVE BEEN, by far,
For a MIGHT HAVE BEEN has never been
But a HAS BEEN was once an ARE.

— John Hand

The Reality of Release

Change will always be present in our lives. The most pronounced variable is what we do with those changes. Resisting the inevitable is a definitive cause of pain and stress. The ability to release becomes the gift that keeps on giving. We can learn to:

- Release expectations that people and circumstances will always be a certain way
- Release fear of the new and unknown
- Release regrets that we "didn't see it coming" and somehow avert the "disaster"
- Release resentments of those who changed a step or two before we did on our journey
- Release belief in limitation and lack by replacing it with confidence and caring.

That last point has always been a good friend of mine. I have been able to release experiences and people in love and joy because I knew they would be followed by something just as wonderful. In the words of Herbert Spencer, "Life is distinguished from death by the multiplicity of changes at any moment taking place within it."

How alive we feel at any moment is greatly affected by whether or not we have embraced the moment-to-moment gratitude of a childlike wonder and developed an attitude of acceptance and release. Nothing and no one is the same as they were yesterday.

Grammy Sez

"You feel sad about breaking your remote-controlled car, don't you?" Grammy asked.

"Uh huh. Really, really sad," Grandson replied.

"Well, a minute of sadness does not last any longer than a minute of happiness, so let it go," Grammy ordered.

(Grammy's not big on sympathy.)

Goodbyes

I have needed to say "goodbye" more times than I would have liked. This I have learned: Though we will never forget what we have left behind and what we have given up, we have to move on. We owe it to ourselves to keep moving forward.

What we cannot do is live our lives afraid of the next goodbye because chances are they are not going to stop. With practice we get better at starting over, developing a "new normal." The trick is to recognize when the "goodbye" can be a good thing, when it is our chance to alter our course and begin again.

To begin … again! This trip I am free to return to the ranch, to wrap myself in solitude. Nothing is bothering my quiet mind. I am ready to accept whatever happens on this move. As some doors are closing, other doors open. It is a divine, perfect destiny. Just as my mind is debt-free, this life I have created is one many would envy.

The Mirror Laughs

And here we are, looking at old age in the mirror. Getting old is not something for which we plan or prepare. Seemingly, it slowly creeps up on us, and happens without warning. If we are actually paying attention, there are signs:

Our friends may laugh hysterically when we tell them we are thirty-three years old. We fit in with the other "blondes." We may begin resembling gnomes, walking slightly stooped. We still shave, but more of the time it includes random wild hairs. For the ladies, it may be shaving the face instead of the legs. Suddenly, we do not need a bikini wax before we go swimming.

We lose weight in our extremities and develop "wings" under our upper arms. Our "turkey necks" can become quite animated. For youngsters this is fascinating to watch.

We do strange things as we age. Mismatched socks are not nearly as conversation-worthy as mismatched shoes. We decide to wear our "comfortable" clothes, all the time. We wonder why the neighborhood children do not think we are likeable, much less lovable.

Driving becomes an adventure. We do not hear the clicking of the car's turn signals. Those following us do not know if we are planning to turn or already did but left on the blinker. We order a beer and pizza while at the drive through window of a fast food restaurant. When shopping, we leave the store and attempt to unlock a car that may or may not be our own. We act surprised when the panic button on our key ring does not shut off that annoying loudly honking horn.

We may stop at green lights or stop and then go while the light is still red, just because we are tired of sitting there. We do not immediately know why our passengers start screaming loudly when we slow down and signal our intent to turn the wrong way into a one-way street. Other drivers make weird gestures and take all kinds of evasive action when that happens.

We consistently do random and unpredictable things. Unless we have worked with the elderly, we have not practiced being old. This is the first time we have ever been old. It is a confusing time. No wonder the mirror laughs.

Master Shift

And here we are, in absolute shock. One foggy evening, three days before Christmas, our family college guru is returning from Kansas State University to his family home not all that far away. A drunk driver speeds over the top of the hill, driving on the wrong side of the road. A deadly head-on collision brings sudden death to ours. The drunk walks away.

Master shift: A scholastically superior senior student, gone, five days before his twenty-third birthday.

> "*Some people come into your life as blessings; others come into your life as lessons.*"
>
> — Mother Teresa

Sometimes the bad things that happen in our lives put us directly on the path to the best things that will ever happen. Sometimes we end up in another world. Sometimes we are not sure what just happened. The secret of sacrifice: The person who makes the sacrifice usually gets the gift. His gift was eternal life. Ours was to remember his goodness and try to follow the example of his teachings. To live life with not so much flourish and much more grit. "Some people come into your life as blessings; others come into your life as lessons." — Mother Teresa

My brightest, warmest memory came about midway through the service to celebrate his life. A church member played his favorite hymn. Tears were flowing freely. The church suddenly glowed more brightly. I felt the essence of his presence hovering above us, between the mourners and the piano player, on the left side of the room. A great wave of peace entered my heart as I gazed at this shimmery nebulous presence. He sent a warm message of love to us: "I am wrapped in the arms of Jesus, not suffering, not struggling, but very content." He let us know Heaven is not a place to fear, but is a refuge and a safe haven.

His quiet, yet insistent reassurance, made the trek to the rural cemetery in the midst of that desolate Kansas prairie where we laid him for his eternal rest and his commitment ceremony almost bearable. I might even have heard these words:

> Dear Lord,
>> Thy will be done.
>> For all the joy thy child shall bring,
>> The risk of grief we'll run.
>> We'll shelter him with tenderness,
>> We'll love him while we may.
>> And for the happiness we've known,
>> Will ever grateful stay.
>> But shall the angels call for him
>> Much sooner than we planned,
>> We'll brave the bitter grief that comes,
>> And try to understand.
>>> — All in a Lifetime

That following spring, to keep you with us always, beside your grave we planted a tree. Just now, a sparrow lights on its limb; I wonder if it is a message to me.

In Loving Memory of David Leslie Hill

12-27-73 to 12-22-96

A Final Farewell

And there we were ... feeling bereft at this, an early exit. An unexpected ending. Many unfinished endeavors. Some strings left dangling from the tapestry of life. Yet, our Bob will be remembered as a kind, caring person with a beautiful soul made even better by his choice of a loving life partner.

He shared family traits of individual "toughness," creativity, and competitiveness. Many of life's lessons came at a terrible personal cost. He learned to treasure beautiful moments, precious people, and capsules of calm. Bob served as a reminder that we do not always choose the cards we are dealt, but we must play them anyway. Partnering him in a "friendly" game of cards and laughing delightedly with him at the feints and bluffs he offered, unforgettable!

Conversations sprinkled with acute observations, interspersed with his dry witticisms and sharp humor reflected his keen interest in those around him. He took the time to know his family and friends. I would have benefited by knowing him even better.

January 9, 1950 to September 11, 2004

Just a Sandhills Cowboy

He was getting old and crippled,
    And his hair was thinning fast.
He lunched daily at the Stockman,
    Sharing stories of the past,
Of a life of cows and ranching
    And the deeds that he had done,
In his exploits with his buddies.
    They were heroes, every one.

Though sometimes, to those listening,
    His tales became a joke,
All his cowboy buddies nodded,
    For they knew of what he spoke.
We'll hear his tales no longer, for old
    "Slim" has passed away.
The world's a little poorer,
    For a cowboy died today.

He will be mourned by many—
    Grandkids, children and his wife—
Though he lived an ordinary
    And quite uneventful life.
Held a job, raised his family,
    Gently making his own way,
The world won't note his passing,
    Though a cowboy died today.

If we cannot do him honor
    While he's here to enjoy the praise,
Then at least let's give him homage
    At the ending of his days.
Perhaps just a simple headline
    In the local that would say,
The Sandhills are in mourning
    For a cowboy died today.

Man doesn't choose the moment. The moment chooses the "man."

245

Joan E Z Charron

Last week I stopped by the old ranch house
       To visit Mother and to spend some time.
Her 87+ years of living have used up some energy,
       She no longer turns on a dime.

As she sits in her chair resting,
       I notice her hands still aren't frail.
I remember it was just last spring
       She milked a cow, without spilling the pail.

We found how tender those hands could be
       If we were hurting or sick.
The quiet voice, the concerned look,
       Couldn't beat it with a stick.

I think of all those hectic years
       And how busy she has been,
As she made clothes for our family
       And kept goodies in the cookie bin.

My mom is constantly working
       To meet her family's needs.
Each spring she plants a garden,
       And scavengers it for weeds.

When it comes time to harvest,
       There's no rest, no end to toil.
She picks peas, beans, cucumbers,
       Corn, and tomatoes from the garden soil.

I watch the shelves in the pantry
       Fill up with jars and cans,
All filled with fruits and veggies,
       Placed there with loving hands.

I think there surely was a mountain
    Of potatoes that Mom did peel.
It seems we always had some spuds
    With nearly every meal.

Oh, so many fish, pheasants, and ducks
    She cleaned and plucked and dressed.
All us hunters and fishermen knew
    Our family was truly blessed.

Each of us remembers how
    She'd mix and knead the bread.
She took her job seriously
    And kept the farmhands fed.

If you were a small girl or boy
    Staying an hour or two,
Mom would say, "Find your favorite book,
    And I will read to you."

When I first was away from home
    And living my new life,
My mom would often write to me,
    Teaching me how to be a wife.

As the years kept coming,
    She dreamed of peace and rest.
Of sitting in her rocking chair
    After her children left the nest.

The house is still not empty;
    It's filled with girls and boys.
The grandkids come to see her
    And fill the house with noise.

This fast-paced world we live in
    Gives us money, gold, or land.
But none of these can top the memories
    Of our Mother's gentle hand.

I Am Free

And there we were, after the funeral, mourners gathered under the rustling trees, talking softly like clusters of leaves. Wearing western shirts and denim jeans, boots and hats, trying to cover up the raw hurt. We came this afternoon to say goodbye, but now we keep saying hello, peering into each other's faces, slow to let go of each other's hands.

Two weeks ago, or was it three, or four, or just yesterday,
Or, sweet, please, not at all—
I think I have not accepted that cruel fact yet,
I think it has not fully hit me yet—
It is like I am anticipating, cringing through my days now,
Waiting for that blow to finally fall
To my heart, my gut, my life ...
Ah, maybe if I tell you about it,
Maybe that will help me
To that hurt I do not want to feel ...

Because somehow it feels like he is still here,
Because when he was here it was
Like a song of pride always playing softly
In my heart where there is now
Emptiness and sadness and absence,
This bleeding hole of hurt and sorrow
Aches at the suddenness of loss,
Our sunshine behind the darkest days
Disappears when a dive into the depths
Turns into terrible tragedy and loss ...

But now the sunshine is gone
Now he's gone, at just eighteen, and
That sunlight fades and darkness lurks.
Now that he's gone, I strain
To hear that song of pride we shared.
I awake at night from tear-stained dreams
Into the silence of his absence ...
But I will keep listening to the wind,
Listening for far off strains, of our dear one
Singing of his love for his family.

248

Time does not in any way heal the pain of losing a child. Time allows us to digest the reality of loss. Time allows the pain to become less raw. Time allows us a way to be a bit more in control of our fluctuating emotions. But, time does not heal. The pain of losing a child is always there. Even on our best days, we still have that ache in our heart that reminds us there is an empty hole that will be there forever, a scar that will never go away. Oh, how we miss the blessing of our child, our family member, our loved one.

June 2003 in Loving Memory of Wes Derek Gideon
2-11-85 to 6-17-03

Letting Go

And here we are, two hunting buddies, staring down death, yet unafraid. Told by a mutual friend that my favorite coyote hunting comrade has been re-admitted to our local hospital, I feel called by God to visit immediately. As I walk in, I surmise it is most likely just another bout of pneumonia. I am not really worried. I then discover this is the time of reckoning, the dawn of realization, the day he knows the disease is going to win.

Watching his hope die, grieving with him, acknowledging what his cancer is stealing from him, I want to find a way to pierce the darkness, to share solace for the time and opportunities that are being ripped away.

I remain there with him as he lashes out with hate and anger at the disease. I hold him in my heart as he sobs with frustration. I embrace the person he once was and the person he has become. I feel his hatred of what cancer does, how it strips away the dignity, the very essence of life. I pray for Jesus to wrap His arms around him.

I can see his frail failing body slowly deteriorating in that hospital bed. The situation fills me with compassion and rage. It tears at my heart. My spirits sag, but my faith reassures. I listen for the lesson.

We treasure the time we have together. We reminisce. I see acceptance dawn. I watch as he acknowledges the inevitable. I listen as he outlines his plan of action and defines his ultimate goals. I marvel at how his faith strengthens him and gives him the courage to selflessly do the things he feels are important for his family and friends. I find inspiration in the brave man with the kind heart and the gentle soul. I cherish every moment of our journey together. I feel the love that is his legacy. I cry as I walk away.

When I return, less than a week later, I realize our time together is now a matter of hours, not days. I try to make him comfortable. I sit with him and hold his hand, so he knows he is not alone. This seems to quiet him.

Midafternoon comes. He looks at me searchingly and quietly asks, "What will you think of me if I just give up?" I reply, "You will know when the time is right. Remember, there is someone waiting for you." He nods. I then respond, "I will miss the hell out of you. You have always been a wonderful friend to me. But if it is time to go, it is all right." Again, I pat his hand, and I reassure him, "It will be okay." He rests.

Sometime later, he wakes up and says, "Come hold my hand." I do this. He then confides, "I hate to do this to you. You have been such a good friend. But you are the last person I am going to see on this earth." I remind him that this, too, will be okay. He rests.

Later, around suppertime, he wants to "mobile." He asks the staff to put him in a wheelchair, attach his oxygen, and wheel him outside. It is a perfect autumn day, in the 70-degree range, with no wind and bright sunlight. He is joined out there by some of his closest friends. His first request is for a ball cap. We get him one. He soaks up the sun and the companionship. His soul fills with peace. He feels well-loved, as he is. His dad joins the group and shares this special outing. When he is ready, we wheel him back to his room. Without really realizing it, people say their final goodbyes.

Shortly after 8:00 pm, he announces out of the blue, "It's time for me to go home." I do not fully realize that what he actually is saying is, "It's time for me to go HOME." About 9:00 pm, he opens his eyes, turns to me and asks, "Well, what do you think?" Not really on the same page, I ask, "About what?" He just smiles and asks me to open the shades, to pull them up so he can see the lights outside. I do not know what he sees, but his face changes. There is a softening, as if a deep peace and awareness enters. Once again he rests.

At 9:30 pm he awakens, cheerfully yet decidedly announces, "Home, James." As I look at him questioningly, he clarifies, "It's time to go home." (A short pause.) He removes the oxygen line, then instructs, "Shut off the machines. Shut them all off. I don't need them anymore."

As I turn off the television, and yes, at his request, even the fan, he repeats, "Shut it all off" ... takes a deep breath ... and he goes HOME.

Our destiny cannot be changed, but it can be challenged. Every man is born as many men and dies as a single man. He was a special person and leaves a legacy of unconditional love and unfailing friendship. I miss my friend. I will always miss my friend. He will be waiting to welcome me home.

"DAD"

Is the strength of a man found in his face?
Or is what matters most found by the care he takes of his place?
Things were never done just to finish
But were done with meticulous care, never a blemish.
His children used to struggle and work by his side;
Not always sure what he wanted, but willing to try.
Now like most birds his children mostly have flown;
Time and distance a factor, with dreams of their own.
Off his chosen path he sometimes would stray,
With the silly notion that all things should pay.
Often we see him as a man that travels alone,
No one really tending the seeds he has sown.

Remembered, but in life, memories are all we keep.

As we drive through his pasture, it's easy to see
The pride that he takes in that bull by the tree.
Then picture a big black cow with her calf, grazing on the side of the hill.
Now that's his greatest achievement and still life's biggest thrill.
The only thanks at the end of the day,
Also in life's somber game his only pay.
We see the strength of the man in what he has done
Through the trials of life, the work and the fun.

—By Janet Charron Gideon

Requiem to H W

And there we were, grief-stricken loved ones gathered together to give the goodbye, the long goodbye. Forgiveness was all over the room. We got to hear stories that day that we had always needed to hear. With a due deference to the self-proclaimed patriarch, I am not saying, "He was so wrong!" but I still fail to see the point of his always having to be "right." All differences aside, together we celebrate his life and remember his legacy. We celebrate our lives as they reflect his influence. We will grow stronger from this day as we focus on these positive feelings and healing words.

H W was a complex, complicated, contradictory man. He was not always

251

happy with the man he saw in the mirror. Prone to vanity, as a young man he decided his ears stuck out too much. Every night he wore nylon hose to pin his ears back to his head while sleeping. He prided himself on his youthful good looks. When we moved to Ravenna during my sixth grade year, he was pitching during the softball game at the end-of-year school picnic. My teacher took me aside and asked who that kid was and would not believe he was my father. That made his day!

During the last half of his life, he changed. He began wearing this scraggly beard to hide his effeminate features—his words, not mine. He claimed it was to hide his weak chin. I believe it was just something else to hide behind, so he did not have to face himself.

In later years, as his hair thinned, he developed this unsightly comb-over. He did not face aging in a graceful manner. His greatest fear was death. Through sheer stubbornness, he managed to cheat death a few times. It sneaked up on him in the end.

For him, close personal relationships were not easy. Acceptance of self and others was difficult. He was a master of quick verbal jabs. If you listened carefully, you could pick up the back-handed compliments. One of my life's maxims was to treat unjustified personal attacks and unwarranted criticism with silence. After my adolescence, there were many long silences between us.

To his credit, I will cheerfully acknowledge that my father devoted many hours to my education and upbringing. I accompanied him to machinery auctions, to livestock sales, to the neighbors to cut wood for the winter, to the pasture to fix windmills and to fix fence, to the fields to plant, cultivate, and harvest. I trained his horses and worked his cattle. I did his farming and his haying. As a teenager, I ran his ranch when he was not there or was indisposed. I learned to be responsible and fiscally frugal. I learned to be strong in every way, just to survive each day.

He taught me to appreciate excellence and talent, to diagnose problems, to be a forward-thinking problem solver. He was not always comfortable with the results, especially if they were not his preferred answers. He did teach me to ask the right questions and to keep seeking the best possible outcomes. He taught me to find and appreciate beauty in nature and in my surroundings. He shared the beauty of music, art, and dance. Under his tutelage, I became a rudimentary mechanic, a dangerous electrician, an accomplished gardener, an excellent judge of cattle, and a master teacher of horses, children, and dogs. Yes, he left us quite a legacy.

Now, we are left with the lesson, a lesson that is never completely learned.

Saying goodbye is never easy. With each goodbye, there is a loss. There is also growth. An inner growth we each feel in our own way. Perhaps the most difficult goodbye is the one-sided kind. The kind that is spoken, knowing full well it can never be returned. This is one of those goodbyes. No one planned it that way. It just happened. It became another of life's lessons. Thank you for being there on our journey.

Dad's Final Farewell

And there we were, being comforted by the kind words of Reverend Jeff Zinnel, just a week before Christmas:

I remember the first time I met Harold Charron. I was a boy of about twelve. My dad had arranged to sell his fat cattle through the stockyards in Omaha. He made arrangements for Harold to haul them in his semi-tractor trailer. I stayed home from school to help sort and load the cattle. The plan was I would help load and then clean up and go to school. But between Harold and my dad, plans changed. After we finished loading, they offered to let me accompany them on the trip to Omaha. It was an adventure for me, my first ride in a semi. It was a small cab, so I had to ride sitting backward on the engine cover. Despite the discomfort, it was still an adventure. It was the first time I had been to the stockyards in Omaha. I was twelve years old, but they treated me like a man that day, including me in their conversations as we traveled together.

Harold and Joan shared sixty-six years of married life and raised six daughters and three sons. Harold was not one to spend a lot of time socializing outside the home but was very close to his family. Every time I remember hearing Harold mentioned in conversation, it always included a comment that he was a hard worker. His family worked right alongside him. He played the accordion and the harmonica. Joan reminded us that he would play these musical instruments at home in the evenings, sharing time with his family. He also enjoyed teaching the skills and sharing the knowledge he had acquired. He passed them on to his children, making sure they were raised to think and care for themselves. He was very proud of his family and enjoyed seeing each succeed in their lives.

He was a man dedicated to nature and the land. He loved his cattle, horses, and dogs. Beyond his family, his animals were the focus of his life. Personally, as someone just driving by the ranch, I always thought what a beautiful place he had. In the spring, I would marvel at the beauty of the pastures next to the river, the deer seen on the edges of the wooded areas, the Canadian geese that seemed to return each year and nest in the wetlands. I suspect Harold enjoyed this beauty as well. He enjoyed hunting and fishing. In the winter, he would run a trap line. Joan related how Janet always liked to go along to check the traps when she was young. When she tired of walking through the deep snow, Harold would carry her.

He enjoyed harnessing and working with his Belgians daily. He could be seen hauling hay to the cattle with his team and hayrack in the winter when the snow was deep. It was a testament to the history of agriculture and to a man who never abandoned the past. When tractors had replaced manual labor on the other farms and ranches in the area, he was still harnessing and driving his team. This is a skill that has almost disappeared. Each of you who learned it from Harold should be proud that you share a legacy with him that is unique and special.

Harold was not a man who attended church, but that does not mean that he was not a man of God. He would speak of the blessings of the dear Lord. As scripture relates, even without words, the rock and the hills attest to the power of God. Harold enjoyed the land and the animals; he lived and worked daily in God's creation. People often try to judge based on what they see, but God looks on the heart of a man to know his true value.

In the passage from Isaiah 40 (vss. 28, 29), we see the road to strength for life. To those who lack strength, might, and power, God gives strength. In the 23rd Psalm we see a man who knew God and trusted in Him for strength and life. In nature we see the renewal of life. As the grain and the corn ripen, the plants die, but the life continues in the seed. God designed the natural world to reflect His glorious creation and plan for us. As we age, as we come to the end of this life, we can see that God's design is for life to continue in a new form, in more wonderful power and strength. We were designed to live with Him for eternity; no more death, no end, no suffering or pain. Through the sacrifice of Jesus Christ, we have been offered that gift. It is up to us to accept or reject life with Christ.

We deal with sorrow and grief at the loss of someone dear to us. But God is here with each one of us as we suffer the pain, the grief and the trials of this life. We have numerous memories that were shared with Harold during his eighty-seven years. We have the example of his life to remind us of what is most important: An understanding and close relationship with God, and patient understanding and a close relationship with the people who touch our lives. Amen.

12-18-13

A Life Well-Lived

Writing personal stories can be a bit like "an emotional striptease." Sometimes it leaves us feeling a little naked. As personal as it seems, we are writing not just about our own life, but life in general. You may catch glimpses of yourselves within these pages.

To write about things that happen in life, we just have to stay alive and pay attention. Things will keep happening. We wake up each day curious to see what will happen next.

Sometimes they are things we do not want to happen, but they happen sooner or later to most of us, to some more than others. We cannot always choose what we get, good or bad. We can only choose what we do with it. That is the choice. What we do with what we are given is the difference between being alive and just marking time.

About a year ago, we took several days off to attend a memorial service for our family Marine, one who left us much too soon. It was a time of heartbreak.

Most people are good, and incredibly human. As often as we screw up, we also have a great capacity for caring. On this day, a multitude of Marines dressed in khaki, Navy men in dress blues, friends and family came together to share and to support one another. The Facebook webpage, "Remembering Tyler Cone," is filled with reminisces, photos from family life, photos from a meritorious military career with tours in Afghanistan and Kabul, personal stories of carousing and carrying on, cartoons featuring specific antics. These mementos of his life demontrate how alive, passionate, and deeply caring our Marine was. This webpage helps keep his memory alive and serves to remind us how much he was loved.

He was loved because he loved. Because he was a fearless fighter, a faithful friend. Because he had an uncanny ability to make you believe in yourself.

At his memorial service, we met dozens, if not hundreds, of people who shared their stories of what our Marine meant to them and how he had somehow made them feel important.

Of course, we told them our stories. I met him almost twenty-six years before, as my newest nephew. I watched, mostly from the sidelines, as he grew into a wonderful young man. We shared some family history, some feelings of not really belonging. He referred to himself one Christmas as "the black sheep of the family." I jokingly reminded him that was my rightful role. He smiled in his charming way, told me I was becoming old and tired. He would cheerfully accept the burden and carry the torch. I chuckled and told him to carry on. His last Facebook posting to me began: "My fellow black sheep …" It made me feel loved.

His life reminds us we must always be good to each other. To those who sent us kind wishes and sincere sympathy, please know that we are grateful beyond words. *"Always pray to have eyes that see the best in people, a heart that forgives the worst, a mind that forgets the bad, and a soul that never loses faith in God."* @Godfruits.com

Death casts a dark shadow that cannot linger long in the lovely light of a life well-lived. As you were!

In Loving Memory of Tyler James Cone
2-22-88 to 2-15-14

"Cherry Blossom Time"

It's cherry blossom time: warm days and balmy nights.
Mother Nature freshens Earth's face with spikes of green,
Sprinkles lawns with tiny monkey-faced violets,
Creates riots of colorful daffodils amid beds of dancing tulips.
Trees burst into flame; tiny birds flock to feeders.

Drizzly days, crisp evenings, and then
With a sudden about-face,
It's blackberry winter. Shivery, icy cold. We wonder,
Can the sweet succulent cherry blossoms survive?
With dreams of tart cherry pies, we wait.

A Brand New Spring

And there we were, looking forward to spring. It had been a long, cold winter, accompanied by displacement and visits to the daughters' homes. The groundhog promised us six more weeks of winter. He did not lie.

In Nebraska, wild plums bloom by the roadside, usually before the first of May. With a sweet smell strong enough to freshen the air in the entire house, their lacy white blossoms contrast with the jubilant green of new grass. We enjoy their timeless perfume each spring and cut a bouquet for you.

The meadowlarks and barn swallows come back. Those same two geese return to nest near the backwater. The peonies I gave you several summers ago poke through the sand, red sprouts waiting to turn to green, with showy blooms of red, pink, and white by Memorial Day.

Everything is ready to burst with loving. We look at the world and see life at play in everything. The new house beckons. Its landscaping possibilities excite. We rejoice in a brand new spring. Otherwise, we would have to be lonely forever.

Lost, But Not Gone

Our guiding hand, our gentle soul we seek for solace, our family's unheralded leader, still here but lost in the wilderness. Her husband of sixty-six years has crossed that Rainbow Bridge. She is left with unexplored options foreign to her and not exactly welcomed. She has inherited a new life marked by that undesired sign—Widow. She must now navigate mounds of paperwork, mountains of memories, rivers of regrets, and most of it she must do alone.

There is no question she is somewhat prepared, though his life's end comes quickly and unpredictably. She has excellent coping skills. She has acquired numerous resources to steer her through any crisis. This journey has surprising turns and twists. She sees the road ahead, takes her bearings, prepares as best she can. Nothing makes the long road of bereavement easy to navigate. The trail of tears leading to the unmarked path of being "left behind" has no shortcuts.

No one escapes the utter disorientation of death. There is no way around the haunting loneliness, the unrelenting sorrow, the despicable despair. She is lost in the wilderness of grief. While her home is being demolished, her new ranch headquarters assembled, her new life rebuilt, she is left to wander the wilderness.

Her children and grandchildren serve as her guides. They surround her with companionship, share the comforts of their homes, and take her on long-dreamed-of trips and excursions. She still finds the road exhaustive and unrelenting. There is really no other way but to more forward, or be left to wander in the wilderness.

"Be still in My Presence, inviting Me to control your thoughts. Let My Light soak into your mind and heart until you are aglow with My very Being. This is the most effective way to receive My Peace." —*Jesus Calling*, devotional for May 31

Lost… Remembering… Letting go… Moving on… Celebrating the legacy!

To the Top of the World

And there I was, reliving my recurring fantasy. Or was it a vision? Voila! Was this the top of the world? With a sense of surviving a long trek through high hills and deep treacherous valleys, she haltingly stumbles through the few remaining steps. Welcoming the amazing vista, she sinks into the lush grass. Drawing a deep calming breath, she soaks in the verdant greens and gazes into the distance. She must be sitting on the top of the world.

This arrival has the pervasive feeling of a final destination, the reward after years of endeavors. Perhaps it is her idea of heaven. Maybe it is merely a resting spot on her spiritual journey. She is delighted to be here, where she can see forever, in any direction. She smiles softly and rests.

Eventually, she notices someone else completing the climb. As he approaches, she looks up and extends a welcoming hand. She knows this person well. Querying "What took you so long?" but not waiting for a response, she adds tenderly, "I have been waiting for you."

Unfortunate Son

I thought we would be together forever, sharing a lifetime of smiles, but **here we are ...**

My grandson, Derpy, died tragically today. His main goal in life was to live to be one thousand years old. He fell short. The art of walking is defined as a lifetime of not falling down. One misstep, and it was over ...

Derpy had definitive tendencies. He was highly protective, of his pastries. He instantly switched into Code Red if glazed donuts or chocolate cupcakes were involved. He enjoyed being in stealth mode. He donned sunglasses as he left the international spy museum "so people wouldn't know he was undercover." Brother informed him, "I think they will know."

Derpy accomplished many things in his short life. He was chosen for the All-Star Little League Team and played well, sporting his favorite number TEN on his jersey. He was reluctantly dragged into the Team Chaos mountain trail hiking club and initiated on Baker's Mountain. After an extremely hot several hours of traipsing through constantly changing, uphill and downhills trails, he shouted in relief, "Oh, my gosh! Finally! I can see the car. I thought we were going to die on this mountain." The following year, he earned his stripes on South Mountain but eschewed sliding down the waterfall.

Derpy believed he was born to entertain. His vivid imagination could seemingly conjure up anything, with little encouragement and no audience at all. He was proud of his ability to multitask. He liked breaking the rules and not getting caught. He sincerely believed if he did not take his cancer pills, he would turn into a ninja turtle. That is how the cake ninja was born. He suffered his first broken heart at age nine.

Born on the east coast, educated on the west coast, with family in the Midwest and the South, he became an experienced traveler, making his first unaccompanied cross-country trip at age eleven.

Wanting something to do other than study, he chose to play the viola. Not overly fond of musicals, his talents eventually lead him to rock music. My favorite photo of Derpy was on his album cover for his CCR tribute band, "Unfortunate Son."

Following the footsteps of earlier influences in his life, Derpy aspired to become a Pro-Gamer. Left unsupervised, he would battle night and day. Playing a video game in the Room of Horrors, which Rambo had left undusted, he accidently cut off a couple of digits. The dust infiltrated his system, built up pressure, and caused a massive heart attack. Later in life, he became a dust bunny and was never seen or heard from again.

Left to mourn his memory are his Sire, Our Hero; his "annoying" half-brothers and step-brother; his fascinating step-sister; his terrifying Grandma Luckee; his indulgent Aunt Calamitee, his oohhh-so-tall Uncle, The Heir; and his helicopter parents, whose presence magnified the problem of locating the body.

Last night, the evening breeze smelled damp; the night fell silent. It was the hour when even ghosts whisper. I thought I heard Derpy laughing and talking to himself, as he often did when playing his video games. I peeked into the gaming room. Nothing there but a dust-covered gaming console and a black television screen. I miss my favorite youngest grandson.

Cornelius (Rambo's Tale)

It started with a smell, like rotting wood from a leaky toilet. It was more pungent and lingered as an aftertaste in her mouth. She could not quite put her finger on it. It awakened her suspicions.

Next, she detected a creaking noise that reminded her of the expanding and contracting of rafters and ceiling boards. This old house was certainly spooky!

I heard a muffled snort and clinking as a pile of gold coins began to shift. Cornelius was stirring. I sent the missus to look. Next, I heard a roar followed by a blood-curdling scream. And she thought dragons didn't exist.

Shadows and Stillness (Pink's Tale)

Words that whirl around in my mind, sometimes landing for a bit to reflect orderly thoughts, often take flight again and disappear. If I write them down it helps lessen the sharpness of grief.

So there we were, enjoying a rare visit from The Heir. It was a warm autumn day with gentle breezes flitting around, teasing the fallen leaves. Pink's quiet stroll through the pasture revealed Our Hero's rescue horse, Sarge, in acute distress. Instantly, it became "all hands on deck," with friends and family doing everything possible.

It turned into one of the most difficult twenty-four hour stretches. Our vibrant, quirky, sassy, delightful Sarge suffered an acute bout with colic and was put down to end his misery. It was sudden. It was shocking. It was so very sad. Our little rocky horse ... gone.

His three years with us were his best years. There was no more abuse, no more neglect. He learned to trust and to love. Ever vigilant, he was the best trail horse ever. He liked to lead. He played in the water while crossing mountain streams. He never stopped trying to please. Never.

Sarge had a low pitched "seal with a sore throat" sound at feeding time and a high pitched elk sound when calling to other horses. He never officially whinnied. His bright sparkling eyes are deeply missed. He is at peace now, prancing around, sniffing the fairy houses, and munching on pine bark and acorns in heaven.

Two short days later, calamity claimed our Diesel Dogg. It happened with lightning speed. One second, he was milling around under the horses' feet at feeding time, and the next, he was gone! No suffering. A startling, unbelievable loss.

Diesel was a constant companion during Derpy's entire life. He never missed chore time. He went to the forest for fencing, tree cutting, grass seeding, and squirrel hunting. He greeted everyone every morning and waited patiently for his daily treat from Rambo. He knew the mail lady, the UPS and Fed-Ex men personally. He liked to go on trips in the truck. He traveled cross country more than once. He adored Our Hero.

Now the quiet is deafening. Daughter reflects: Diesel would always wait up for me, no matter how late I worked. I miss his bark at night. It always made me feel safer because I knew nothing would sneak past him. Nothing. Not even a fly. I mean, he literally barked at everything.

The shadows lengthen. The stillness grows.

—October 11, 2016

Mom's Legacy (Daughter's Tale)

I was born into a life of service and volunteerism. My earliest memories were of being "volunteered" to be in the "Adopt a Grandparent" program. I was only eight years old. It was an awkward situation for me. What does an eight-year-old talk about when visiting an octogenarian living in a retirement village or a care home? I practiced empathy, kindness, and selflessness. This experience set a firm foundation for later years when my dad was living in the secure ward with chemotherapy-induced dementia.

Recycling became second nature as I was "volunteered" to help with the monthly sorting and baling of recyclables in our small town. Getting dirty and smelly for a greater cause became a way of life. Mom led by doing! I learned to persevere in the face of adversity.

My worst nightmare begins with the phrase, "You remind me of your mother." We share perfectionist tendencies, though they present themselves differently. Did you realize a procrastinator is a perfectionist in disguise? A procrastinator just needs everything to be thought out before beginning.

Because my mother appeared to be open to alternate solutions, she taught us to think outside the box. By pushing us beyond perceived boundaries, she let us try new things despite a fear of failure.

Together, we learned to travel somewhat spontaneously. We would plan our basic route but stop if something caught our eye or called to our hearts. One time we stopped at a fireworks outlet just over the state line, right at the beginning of a three-week adventure that did not include Independence Day. We filled a corner of the car's trunk with our "must-haves" and enjoyed them (illegally) the next Fourth of July in Nebraska. Side trips and traveling "unknowns" led to us being adventurous and to discover that being lost is not always a bad thing. It may lead us where we never would have gone.

Often, our conversations reveal things I need to hear. That does not exactly endear her to me, or make our conversations restful. Truth is truth. Truth builds integrity. Integrity builds trust. Trust builds endearing relationships. We need to use the "rule of five" to survive harmoniously. *(See page 20.)*

Thoughts on My Passing

And here we are, on a hilltop in the north pasture, ready to release the ashes of the incomparable woman we knew as Linda ...

We are here today to celebrate the life of our dear friend, Linda.

> She left quietly, her thoughts unknown,
>   but she left us memories we are proud to own.
> So treasure her, Lord, in your Garden of Rest,
>   for when on Earth she was one of life's best.

In my lifetime, I have known many people who loved mankind very much and had difficulty getting along with individuals. Linda did have a genuine interest in mankind, but she cherished individuals, especially the children and the wizened ones.

She believed in spending her life on something that would outlive her. For this reason, she spent her life teaching children and young adults, gently guiding them on paths of discovery, encouraging their creativity and individuality, letting them experience freedom and self-knowledge. Nothing gave Linda more fulfillment than spending time with someone, listening carefully, and then trying to share her knowledge, compassion, and understanding with them, so they might be more at peace with themselves and the world.

She never lost her love of dancing, playing volleyball, shuffleboard, or softball. It was never about winning but about doing her best that day, in her own unique way. Wherever she lived immediately became known as "God's Country," for it was obvious that God walked there with her and sent his angels to watch over her. At times, she kept them plenty busy.

Linda had a deep love of beauty, especially nature's beautiful creations. Her gardens always produced enough to feed her family, her relatives, her neighbors, and anyone else unlucky enough to stop by during gathering season. Her farm animals grew sleek and fat and were a joy to the eye. They won top ribbons at the local fairs. She enjoyed her horses and working with the livestock, particularly the baby calves. They were a symbol of renewal.

Yes, she always lived in "God's Country." Flowers bloomed for her continuously, enhancing the beauty of her home. Many plants and flowers were given by friends and family and cherished forever. Her most obvious domestic quality was that she lived in a house, but it was a happy house filled with handcrafted items made by her special friends and family members. To Linda, these were truly beautiful things. They turned her house into a home.

For herself, she asked nothing from life but unqualified acceptance from those around her, from us—her family, her friends, and her loved ones. In this, she died truly blessed.

She leaves these thoughts with you; these memories, written by Rae Turnbull:

> When I look back on raising my children …
>
> The things I did right and the things I did wrong,
> I see it was mostly stumbling along that took me
> where I needed to go.
>
> When I made mistakes, and I did many times,
> my children forgave the errors I made,
> and sometimes I truly wondered why.
>
> One day when I wondered out loud to my youngest child,
> who was then fully-grown, I heard her say,
> "You never gave up or turned away."
>
> I took that thought with me to bed that night.
> To have raised a child who would see things that way,
> I must have done something very right.

In Conclusion

And here I am, writing my life story. I imagine that today I am to die. I ask for time to be alone, to write down for my friends a sort of testament to my life. The points that follow could serve as chapter titles to my life story.

The things I have loved in life must include my first pony, Sandy. She was a half Welsh, half Shetland that liked to buck me off every chance she got. My dad raised her for me. As soon as he knew he was going to be a first-time father, he had his favorite mare, Roxsie, bred. Sandy was that foal. We grew up together. She was about as skittish as I was. The first time Dad sat me on her back, she bucked me off. She never quit trying to surprise me. We loved one another.

I took Sandy with me to the Sandhills when I got my first teaching job. She went with me to the ranch after I got married. We raised many foals from her, which I broke to ride and then sell. I left one of her offspring for my siblings to use on the home place, as he was especially talented. Dusty could jump over four-wire fences. I could ride him bareback and steer him by looping my belt around his neck. He never bucked! Sandy lived with me for thirty-eight years. Her sorrel hair turned gray. She died from a strike of lightning that traveled down the fence she was standing beside. It was her time to go. Much better than the glue factory, which we had been sadly considering. We buried her on the ranch.

Favorite things I have tasted include succulent cherries from an orchard I planted, tended, and watched grow. I must include the honeydew, cantaloupe, and watermelon from our garden. Best of all were the tender roasting ears from a sweet corn patch hidden in a cornfield to keep the raccoons from eating them first.

Beautiful scenes from my memory include watching the big snowflakes drifting straight down, while sitting in front of a fireplace at a Keystone, Colorado, condo. These are rivaled by memories of traveling through Yellowstone National Park with Daughter, standing at the precipice, and admiring the colorful canyon wall while fearing for my life. The deep drop left me breathless. A more vivid scene developed while fishing at Marion Lake in Minnesota, watching the water change from a smooth glassy blue surface to a raging, churning fury of whitecaps and wondering if that fourteen-foot johnboat was going to make it back to shore or capsize. My most awesome experience was visiting Denali and touring Alaska.

The most acrid smell I ever encountered was when I was four years old. The neighbor's hog shed ignited from faulty wiring and burned, with most of the livestock inside. I will never forget watching it burn, seeing the flashing lights of the fire trucks, witnessing the tired defeated faces of those who had tried in vain to save the hogs, and smelling the stench of the burned carcasses.

Another persistent and unforgettable smell was the one Daughter and I encountered while driving through Montana on Interstate 90 with fierce forest fires burning on both sides. Trees were exploding into fireballs of flame, lighting up the night. The smoke was heavy. The air was hard to breathe. It was unbelievably awesome and somewhat frightening. Absolutely unforgettable.

The times my children sang in choirs, or played in their bands—especially the pep band performances—were some of the proudest moments of my life. My favorite sounds I created were while playing the piano. "The Entertainer" and "Winter Wonderland" were my favorite party pieces to perform on the piano. I love music, whether I'm playing it, listening to it, or dancing to it.

Satin sheets and pillowcases, silky lingerie, velveteen and velour delight my fingertips. Running my hands through my lover's hair is delightful. Giving and receiving massages can relax me. Touch is important to me.

These experiences are among my most cherished: Learning to square dance in grade school, again in college, and yet again while first married. Then teaching those skills to my fourth grade students and letting them entertain at area hospitals and care homes. Delightful. I also cherish my ballroom dancing experiences at singles dances with some very special partners who make dancing a dream. I remember spiking the volleyball (I'm 5'1" stretched out!) and making a "kill" when I was over fifty years old while playing against high school boys and "A team" men and women. Astonishing, even to me!

These experiences are the most historically significant events that occurred during my lifetime: November 22, 1963 will be forever etched in my mind. During my freshman year in high school, the teachers interrupted classes shortly after lunch to share the stunning news of President John F. Kennedy's assassination in Dallas, Texas. The nation mourned. Conspiracy rumors flourished.

On January 28, 1986, I was the teacher, with a classroom of fourth graders. Due to our interest in watching Christa McAuliffe become the first teacher in space, we were watching the launch of the space shuttle Challenger live on television. It became a very "teachable moment" when the Challenger broke apart 73 seconds after launch, and the seven astronauts aboard lost their lives.

Twenty years ago on April 19, the Oklahoma City bombing, a terrorist attack on American soil by one of our own citizens, ushered in a new era. It was a saddening and somber occasion when I later visited the memorial, saw the rows of chairs arranged in testament to those who sacrificed their lives, and the ravaged walls left standing where the Alfred P Murrah Federal Building used to be.

Thirteen years and some months ago I turned on my television to tape that week's shows. As I was scheduling them, I saw what I believed to be a film clip of an upcoming movie. It turned out to be live coverage of events as they were developing. At 9:02 AM on September 11, 2001, disaster visited America, not from nuclear bombs but from hijacked American airplanes. The 9/11 terrorist attacks caused the single greatest loss of life from a foreign attack on American soil. Ground Zero was gruesome. The cost of freedom became astronomical.

These ideas bring me liberation: I can love someone fully and appreciate them for who they are, even if they are unwilling or unable to return that love. I speak here of my parents, who most likely did love me the best they could, yet, left me wanting more. I can fully love myself and appreciate my own abilities without expecting perfection. I can forgive myself and others for the occasional lapses of judgment that are bound to occur. I believe I deserve to be treated with kindness and respect. I can and should define boundaries for myself and others. I deserve that consideration and may expect to experience the consequences. I am responsible for my own happiness. If I am doing things that create unhappiness in my life, I can change what I am doing so that a different outcome is possible.

These beliefs I have outgrown: Parents have to love their children equally. These are convictions I have lived by: It is not okay to observe injustices and do nothing. We are responsible for our actions. There is *some* good in most people and *some* evil in others.

These are the things I have lived for: To make the world a better place by teaching and showing others how to be caring, considerate, and self-sufficient. To demonstrate life's skills. To share my knowledge with those who request it. To learn how to love unconditionally. So much of who I am and what I have done has been centered on trying to prove I belong, which I sometimes doubt.

These insights I have gained in the school of life: As to the existence of God, I say: The spiritual side of life has been revealed to me during quiet times and moments of crisis. I have been shown a gentle caring presence that resides within me, surrounds me, calls me to walk in the ways of the faithful, and deters me through wise counsel from straying completely off the road to salvation. I do not always listen or observe, but the presence is always there.

The world is so fast-paced today that it requires a major commitment to self just to find time for "listening," for centering, and for rebalancing. I have simplified my life enough to let that happen, even if I have to make an appointment with myself to do it. I call it "Me Time."

Human nature is fickle, greedy, selfish, fear-driven, self-centered, and self-absorbed. It takes a monumental effort to recognize and compensate for these tendencies. Sometimes I am better at it than at other times.

Love, like life, is about making choices. Love is life's most powerful force. It

266

causes unbelievable highs and lows. The pursuit of love can consume us, but it comes unbidden, to a receptive heart, and grows through nurture. Love carries us through the abyss, if we remember its existence and honor its needs and responsibilities. Unconditional love creates peace for the soul and liberates the spirit.

Prayer is a form of love, actively seeking what is right, even when we have no idea what that may be. It is a channel of connection that lets us ask and receive answers. I believe in the benefit of prayer.

These are risks I took: Every time I opened my heart to someone, I risked being hurt. Every time I trusted someone, I risked being abused. Every time I offered help or advice, I risked being rejected. Every time I tried something new, I risked failure. Every time I obtained something, I risked losing it. Each day is one risk followed by another. Some risks scare me more than others, but to quit taking risks ensures an inner death right here on earth.

Definite dangers I have faced and lived to relate include the time the South Loup River flooded unexpectedly and very rapidly raised after a twenty-inch downpour someplace upstream. Our herd of twenty-seven horses was pastured in the timberland along the south side of the river. My dad, three of my younger sisters, and I got out our fiberglass fishing boat and unloaded it on the road we had made across the backwater. We used cut trees, a culvert, and built a six foot deep fill. It was now completely underwater from the floodwaters. The fence alongside it showed us where it was.

We motored through the trees, poling around bushes, searching for the horses. We hoped they had not been swept downstream. At last, we found them cramped together on top of a sandy knoll, surrounded by the flood waters, a quarter mile from where we had launched the boat.

I bridled one, jumped on, and led the herd through the water, toward that filled road across the backwater. The waters were still rising rapidly and threatened to sweep the entire herd, including me, downstream. I targeted a spot upstream but eventually was forced too far downstream, against that barbed wire fence just below the filled road. The horses were thrashing against the fence, and got caught in the trees and logs we had used to pile the dirt on. Worst of all, the horse I was riding went completely under the water. Fearing for the life of the horse, I slid off, on the upstream side, with the idea of swimming and leading it to safety. The bank was about fifty feet ahead of us. The flood waters carried me underneath my horse. I found myself struck by thrashing hooves, unable to get free, and then was pinned against the barbed wire fence with the horses against me. I thought I was going to die.

The people in the boat got the herd moving toward the high bank in front of us. I pulled myself along the fence and made it ashore, gasping for breath, throwing up muddy water. I was bleeding from the wire cuts and heavily bruised. No one noticed or seemed to care. I carry the scars from that scary experience to this day. The important thing was we got the horses out of harm's way. The end justifies the means, right? I ask why a father would put his daughter at risk like that. Afterwards, he treated it like "no big deal!" I still wonder why he did not lead the horses from the boat, with the bridle reins. The brush was probably too thick where they needed to go.

I have experienced an eventful life seasoned with suffering. In the beginning, I daily witnessed my father abusing my mother—physically, emotionally, mentally, and spiritually. He said he was trying to break her. From my earliest memories, I was trying to distract him, and directed his energies and abuses toward me, in a misguided attempt to protect my mother.

During my school years, I was beaten daily, sometimes several times. He used straps, sticks, ropes, whatever was handy. The most horrific beating was when he used the bullwhip on me. That really stung. The leather on the tip cut my skin wherever it landed. My father once told me it made him feel better to beat on me. It relieved the rage inside him. Where was the justice in that?

One night after supper, when I was sixteen, my father realized the day was disappearing, and I had escaped the daily ritual. He made a big deal out of circling the date on the calendar with a red marker, celebrating the occasion, and calling the entire family as witnesses. Like it was my fault I got whipped every day. Actually, he failed to notice me at all that day. That realization on my part compounded the hurt. I used to think negative attention was better than no attention. I no longer believe that.

I left that "delightful" life on my twenty-first birthday. I was not allowed to leave until then. That was the family law, if not the letter of the law. I moved to the Sandhills, to a job teaching in a one-room school. I met and married the area's "most eligible bachelor" (oldest unmarried son of the school board president) after a five-month chaperoned courtship. I was living with the grandparents of some of my students.

I came to Easter dinner that year with my new fiancé, sporting my brand new diamond ring. (Oops, I forgot, the ring was back on the bathroom sink. I had taken it off and polished it up, so it would really sparkle!) My mother's parting words to that future husband as we were leaving: "I don't know whether to congratulate you or offer you my condolences." My father advised him to beat me if I got out of line. I had no idea that, as my husband, he would do just that.

I found myself in a marriage that featured escalating abuse and violence.

After nineteen years of this, I showed up at school with a black eye one day. No one noticed, not the students, the other teachers, or the principal. (I was teaching a room of fourth graders.) I did not report it. After that, my life was in danger because my abuser felt safe. Eventually, I had to secretly tape record some episodes and use them as leverage for a restraining order and eventual divorce. It took me twenty years to leave.

During that last year, my health deteriorated, probably tied to the stress, the virus circulating the school, and my unperceived allergies to the germicide used to combat the virus. I lost my tenured position as a side effect.

When I returned home, three weeks before the end of the school term, and told my husband I was unable to continue teaching, his response was, "What good are you if you can't even keep a job?" I went to the hospital for thirty days and came home with an altered perspective. My choices became clearer.

My resolve to do the right thing for me and my children deepened. The irrevocable decision to dissolve the union was made the day my husband broke his arm while striking my seventeen-year-old son in the forehead because he could not get the tractor started. He did not even hide the truth from the doctor. He bragged about it. It was not reported, as he was the "injured" party. How ironic!

I moved into town, rented a house, got an unlisted telephone number, and started a different life. I tried to raise my three children in a safe, supportive atmosphere. They wished I had done it ten years before that. I told them I did not believe in divorce. Now I do.

I thought I learned how to better shield myself from the toxic people of this life and the dangerous situations of this world. Yet, I found myself involved with a man who chose to willfully dismantle our car, threatening to break the window out with a sledge hammer if I did not unlock it so he could continue to take it apart. I have photographs of the car, blocked up, with no battery, with flat tires or no wheels, the emission system messed up, and the trunk unable to be closed.

A week after this happened, my mother, who rarely, if ever, came to see me, dropped by with my baby sister to give me a birthday present. The crippled car was still there, a testament to my poor judgment in men. Mom told me I had better do some thinking about my future. Sis reminded me that others treat us like we teach them to treat us and wished me well.

When I was given an ultimatum a couple of days later, to give him the spare keys, sign the car title over to him, and get out of "his" house, I made some decisions. I "couldn't locate" the spare keys. I reminded him the car title had been "lost" since we moved, and it was "our" house. We went to the courthouse, got a duplicate title, which he signed over to me, with the stipulation I get myself and my things out of "his" house.

I found an apartment in three days' time, packed things when he was at work, got someone to help me move, and left. This did not keep him from insisting that he "got took." I am now to understand that if I really loved him, I would have refused his offer, declined to accept the gift of the Cadillac, and signed it back to him. It is an ironic situation because I never wanted or needed the car. I only accepted it because it was his mother's pride and joy. She entrusted me to take care of it. I always thought of it as "R" car, something we could share and take on our outings together. It was a symbol of our love. In a fit of pique, he dismantled it anyway. Unreal! I remind myself: "Never wrestle with a pig. You both get dirty. The pig likes it."

I have learned how to take care of myself and fulfill my responsibilities. I have learned how to listen to others and empathize. I have learned how to receive gifts from others appreciatively. I have learned how to understand heartache, to consider the perspectives of others, and to forgive, whether it is "deserved" or not. I have learned it is best to always try to be the right person, to always do the right thing, and to strive to appreciate all the good things in life—the beautiful moments, the unbelievable events, and the special people.

These influences have shaped my life: When I was a tot, my father's parents, Grandpa and Grandma Charron, lived less than a quarter mile east, just at the far end of the cornfield. I liked being with them and ran off a time or two to be there. I even rode my pony Sandy over there whenever I thought I would not be missed. Grandpa Charron taught me to watch baseball and to be a Yankee fan. Grandma Charron took me to Vacation Bible School at the Fairview Methodist Church, introducing me to religion. She started a 4-H club in the area, so I had one to attend. As my project leader, she encouraged me to do my best.

I won the prize for most purple and blue ribbons in the club, served as club secretary, and wrote news articles for the local paper. My road to achievement, social recognition, service, and ideas about the value of religion were instilled.

My father, of course, opposed all this. He claimed to be an atheist. Actually, he was just jealous, as he apparently wanted to be viewed as the Supreme Being. Yes, he was a control freak. An abusive control freak. He took me with him everywhere he went. He taught me problem-solving skills every time he asked me what he should do. He taught me responsibility every time he made me do his chores and do his work. He taught me co-dependency because he could never be alone. When he left the family farm and moved to a ranch east of Ravenna, he isolated the family and ended the influence from his parents.

After the move, I landed in a rural one-room school with twenty-six students, not one of them in my grade, the sixth grade. Mrs. Wilke was a master teacher, instilled a pride of excellent work and a love of learning. She set the scale. When my school records finally came (my father dragged his feet at signing the request to have them forwarded), Mrs. Wilke had a "cow." She insisted they could not be the correct records because they showed Cs, Ds, and Fs. I was a B+ and A student. I became an A student to prove her faith in me was accurate. She used to tell me I could not see the forest for the trees. It took me many years to understand that comment. I never forgot her lessons. I wrote to her over the years to reaffirm my appreciation. The last time I wrote was two weeks before her death. I miss her.

In addition to my grandparents, my parents, my teachers, and my children, I have to thank my friends for helping me find my way through life's events. They support me, their "hostess with the mostest," and tell me to "chill" or "take a deep breath" if I need to. They know me well and like me anyway. We used to have monthly card parties, go dancing, go deer and coyote hunting, play volleyball year-round, and go swimming, canoeing, or tanking in the summer. They are in Ord. I sold my five-bedroom house and moved to Grand Island to build a life there. Eventually, I moved to North Carolina to build a new life. I miss my old friends and the things we used to do together. I have new friends here that are just as special.

I joined Toastmasters after my divorce in 1990. Gradually, I reclaimed my confidence and shored up my shaky self-esteem. I started participating and became a leader, a mentor, a consultant. I was elected the District 24 Governor after holding nearly all offices at the club, area, division, and district level. I was something to see! I did it with the help of my fellow toastmasters.

Agriculture and finance have been the most significant influences in my life. From my time on a farm in the Platte River Valley near Central City, to my life on the ranch east of Ravenna, to my time spent in the Sandhills, and culminating in the purchase of my own farm-ranch northeast of Ord, I have been involved in agriculture. As soon as I was able to keep ranch accounts, I have provided that service to others. I dabble in estate planning, writing wills, creating trusts, and providing financial advice.

My favorite books include Homer's *The Iliad and The Odyssey*, Ayn Rand's *Atlas Shrugged*, the *Harry Potter* series, *Christy, Shane,* and *Jonathan Seagull*. I read voraciously and write sporadically.

I based my first book, *Color Life Beautiful*, on the verses of Ecclesiastes— "For every time there is a season"—but my favorite Scripture is still the Twenty-

Third Psalm. Mrs. Wilke had me memorize it, something that would not be allowed in today's schools. She taught it as an example of excellent literature. My favorite gospel is Luke.

One episode I most regret in my life happened "that" summer after I had attended college for two years. I lost a lot that day, some of my self-respect, any respect I had for my father, and any rapport I had with my siblings. Some things are irreversible and carry lasting scars.

My life's achievements must include raising three wonderful, loving children and being blessed with five grandchildren. I am rewarded with every contact, every conversation with my children. They are so open and honest. That is a precious gift!

Other achievements include scholastic honors for Top Eighth Grade Student (Mrs. Wilke's influence), Salutatorian of my high school graduating class, graduating Magna Cum Laude from KSC, being voted the town of Ord's Ms. Volunteer, being selected Valley County's "Homemaker of the Year" in 1984, earning my five-year pin as 4-H Leader, taking the MYF group to Colorado skiing and learning to ski with them, at the age of forty. I have numerous scholastic ribbons and medals, many track ribbons and medals, multitudes of speech contest trophies, and have held many elected offices in various organizations. I have self-published six books of my writings and twenty chapbooks for the Thesaureans, as a member of that mid-Nebraska writer's group. My nickname is "the lucky one."

These persons are enshrined within my heart:

• My "children," each one a miracle, someone who has taught me much.

• My grandson, Chance, who is indeed a "no-chance" miracle. I hold him in my prayers.

• My grandmother Valasek, who let me visit her, spoil her, and love her unconditionally. Her last words to me were, "Linda, promise me you will take care of yourself." She saw more than she ever said. I look forward to "seeing her" again. We share that gift.

• My Grandma Charron, who helped me find a wedding dress and plan my first wedding.

• My Grandpa Charron, who taught me to rest when I need to and to have some "Me Time" every day. He never quit loving those around him, no matter how they treated him.

• My departed cousin, Rick, whom we lost in an automobile accident when he was fourteen. I adored him, recognized him as another kindred spirit and soul mate. I cherished the times we got to play together when I was a child. His death left me lonely.

• My adopted mother, Grace, who was a gentle and kind mother to me. She saw my talents and shortcomings and accepted me anyway. I miss her smiles every single day.

My unfulfilled desires include white water rafting on the Colorado River and exploring the Grand Canyon. Also, I would like to visit Hawaii. I may still have time to check these off my bucket list … I suspect my greatest desire involves peace, and living forever in harmony with kindred spirits.

I have never lost faith, despite losing my "dream" job, struggling to pay bills because the bank went under (who expected that?), and being betrayed and abused by those who claimed to love me. I focus on learning how to live a full life every day, through developing my connections with people. Life's challenges in no way diminish the simple joys found in relationships and intimacies. Ironically, I am shy, reserved, quiet, and self-conscious. I often stutter. Yet, life has called me to be a leader, a teacher, a counselor of sorts. I spend time listening to others, eliciting their stories, discovering their perspectives, seeing their good sides, and gently laughing at life with them.

Coincidentally, I seem to be most entertaining when I am not trying to be amusing. The dry witticisms just slip out unexpectedly. It seems I am most helpful when I am not trying to "help." Others value me for my tenacity, for my unflagging problem-solving techniques, for my "can do" attitude.

Anyone who really knows me finds me "amazing" at times, excitable or overly passionate at times, but always focused on creating something workable out of whatever I am given. I continually assume I am going to discover the "answers" while learning how to live. A wise man can learn more from a foolish question than a foolish man can learn from a wise answer. I believe the journey of life brings happiness as long as we are looking for it and recognize our blessings. To me, what matters most are the people in my life and the quality of my connections with them.

"Life has dark moments, and it is out of our darkness that we often find our greatest beauties and strengths."

– Bryant McGill

"Trails We Leave"

Dreams are fragile
Seem to shatter at will.
Visions condemn
Lest held safely in our heart.

Projects can tire,
Yet give direction to life.
Trails we leave,
'Til it's time to start "forever."

One Pair of Hands

One pair of hands for the mountains;
    one pair of hands for the sea.
One pair of hands made the sun and the moon,
    every bird, every flower, every tree.

One pair of hands formed the valleys,
    the ocean, the rivers, and the sand
Those hands are so strong, so when life goes wrong,
    put your faith into one pair of hands.

One pair of hands healed the sick;
    one pair of hands raised the dead.
One pair of hands calmed the raging storm,
    and thousands of people were fed.

One pair of hands said, "I love you,"
    and those hands were nailed to a tree.
Those hands are so strong, so when life goes wrong,
    put your faith into one pair of hands.

— Written by Carroll Roberson and Sung by Elvis Presley

This song helps us to realize that one person can do many things, intentionally or unintentionally. Never underestimate the power in a pair of hands, or in the power of words. I still may not have a best-selling novel, but I do have a plan, friends, and memories to take with me wherever my literary journey continues to lead. What is your plan?

... And that's just what happened

... as far as you know.

Meet the Author

Linda S. Cone

As a retiree living in the Appalachian foothills of North Carolina, Linda Cone has many strands woven into her tapestry of life. She grew up on a working cattle ranch near Ravenna, Nebraska, and continues to be involved in agriculture. She trained horses to ride and dogs to hunt; served as accountant, marketing specialist, and financial manager for farms, ranches, and corporations; was graduated from college and pursued a teaching career. She has been married, is the mother of three children, and has five grandchildren.

Linda has a Bachelor of Arts Degree in Elementary Education but is retired from her teaching career. She is a Distinguished Toastmaster and a Past District Governor for Toastmasters International. Her hobbies include dancing, woodworking, and coaching others in life skills. She encourages us to make the most of our connections and attachments and to live in relationship with others.

This book is a metaphor for the whole of our existence. It speaks to the relationships of one being to another and how they relate to the whole. Each strand in our life's tapestry is connected to everything else. This book explores those connections: those we have from birth, attachments we develop through living and learning, and events that prevent the bonds of relationships from occurring.

No one is really willing to admit they are related to her, so she has occasionally used aliases to protect the innocent. Everybody has a chapter they do not publish.

You may contact this author by emailing: author@thelauruscompany.com

Please include author name in Subject line.

Photography by Brenda Barnes and Linda Cone